D1521545

American
Worlds
Since
Emerson

American Worlds Since Emerson

★ ★ ★

DAVID MARR

The University of Massachusetts Press

Amherst

1988

Copyright © 1988 by The University of Massachusetts Press

All rights reserved

Printed in the United States of America

LC 87–5989

ISBN 0–87023–588–5   88- 3054

Set in Linotron Bembo at Rainsford Type

Library of Congress Cataloging-in-Publication Data

Marr, David, 1943–

   American worlds since Emerson.

   Bibliography: p.

   Includes index.

     1. Emerson, Ralph Waldo, 1803–1882—Influence.

2. American literature—History and criticism.

3. United States—Intellectual life.   4. Philosophy,

American.   I. Title.

PS1638.M29   1988   814'.3   87–5989

ISBN 0–87023–588–5 (alk. paper)

British Library Cataloguing in Publication Data are available

Acknowledgments for permission to reprint selections under
copyright are made on page 235.

For Susan

CONTENTS

ACKNOWLEDGMENTS

This book is about some of the intellectual origins of a politically dangerous time—our own. Given my topic—the political danger that comes from the continuing eclipse of the political—it is with great pleasure that I gratefully acknowledge the many benefits of citizenship I have enjoyed in one of the American worlds that fall outside the scope of these studies. I refer to the academic community of colleagues and students at The Evergreen State College. For their contributions to this experiment in learning, I am deeply indebted to the following: William Arney, Priscilla Bowerman, John Burbank, Stephanie Coontz, Beryl Crowe, Leo Daugherty, Ken Dolbeare, Judith Espinola, Dale Favier, Donald Finkel, Jeanne Hahn, Steven G. Herman, David Hitchens, Norman Jacobson, Richard Jones, Hiro Kawasaki, Mark Levensky, S. R. Martin, Jr., Gail Martin, Charles McCann, Donna McMaster, Alan Nasser, Rita Pougiales, David Powell, Thomas Rainey, Sandra Simon, Leon Sinclair, Robert Sluss, Barbara Smith, Susan Strasser, Nancy Taylor, Charles Teske, Kirk Thompson, and York Wong.

Mary G. Land, whose intellectual vigor and courage have been inspiring during all the twenty years I have known her, helped me clarify the original idea for this book.

I am grateful to Patrick Hill, Evergreen's Provost, for his encouragement and kindness. To John McDermott, who read an earlier version of this book, I owe a huge debt; I thank him for his sympathetic understanding of my aims as a student of the American philosophical past. Two anonymous readers for the University of Massachusetts Press gave the manuscript detailed criticism which I wish to acknowledge here with sincere appreciation. Two editors at the Press have been especially helpful to me. For his expert guidance and wise advice, without which I could not have completed this book, I gladly thank Richard Martin. For her many suggestions for stylistic improvement, I am grateful to Pam Wilkinson.

Susan, my wife, and Amy, Erinn, and Sara, our daughters, were not long-suffering as I wrote; had they been, I would have received the clearest signal that my efforts were the wrong ones.

These persons make up a large part of the background from which this book emerges. Each of them contributed indirectly to whatever merit there may be in it. Sole responsibility for the rest, of course, remains my own.

American
Worlds
Since
Emerson

Emerson and After

... and strut about so many walking monsters,—a good finger, a
neck, a stomach, an elbow, but never a man.

RALPH WALDO EMERSON, "The American Scholar" (1837)

NEW NAMES FOR OLD WAYS OF THINKING

Emerson said he had but one idea. He was preoccupied throughout his
life with what he called "the infinitude of the private man" (*Journals*
7:342). Though cast in a distinctively American dialect of philosophical idealism, Emerson's notion of idealized privatism was grounded in
a keen consciousness of both the terrors and the promises inherent
in American society. At bottom an anti-political stance, Emersonian
privatism recurs in various guises throughout American literary-
philosophical history. It influences the development of the American
novel since Melville, American poetry since Whitman, American criticism after Poe, and American philosophy from William James and
George Santayana to John Dewey and Nelson Goodman, not to men-
tion the moral tone, hence indirectly the political life, of much of the
nation in the nineteenth and twentieth centuries. In this book I illustrate the history of the discursive formation constituted as the legacy
of "the infinitude of the private man" in studies of: Emerson's ideas of

nature, culture, and politics; Walt Whitman's fantasy of the autocrat of letters; William James's critique of "vicious intellectualism"; contrasting outgrowths of radical interiority in the poetry of Robinson Jeffers and the criticism of R. P. Blackmur; and two contemporary pictures of public discourse as displayed in Joseph Heller's *Catch-22* and the essays of Ralph Ellison.

Emersonian privatism, moralism, and anti-politicism are major elements in American social character. They belong, therefore, to the history of American politics and the eclipse of the political in the modern age. "The bourgeois defense of privacy," Christopher Lasch has written, "culminates—not just in Sade's thought but in the history to come . . . —in the most thoroughgoing attack on privacy; the [contemporary] glorification of the individual, in his annihilation" (Lasch 1978, 70). "The infinitude of the private man," although in its inception a superficial and ambiguous glorification of the individual, belongs to the history of the growth of the state—hence to the eventual annihilation of the individual—because it sanctions the reckless attack on the very idea of public life. The main features of this complex socio-intellectual development are only ludicrously caricatured in the sledge-hammer categories of the history of ideas, the most familiar of which are talismanic phrases like "the legacy of individualism" and "the perfectability of man." And they are only entombed if left to academic literary study, which is itself being steadily marginalized in the political economy of the university and the wider society. Moreover, no single academic discipline is sufficiently comprehensive to take in the full scope of this Emersonian tradition: what gets left out in any given attempt is often as significant as what is included, the criteria for selection often being purely a matter of disciplinary bias.

In recent years, interpretations of American literary and intellectual history—Larzer Ziff's *Literary Democracy: The Declaration of Cultural Independence in America* (1981); Abraham Kaplan's *Democratic Humanism and American Literature* (1972); George Fredrickson's *The Inner Civil*

War: Northern Intellectuals and the Crisis of the Union (1968); Irving Howe's *The American Newness: Culture and Politics in the Age of Emerson* (1986); and Alfred Kazin's *An American Procession* (1984), to name several prominent studies—either overlook the political meaning of Emersonian privatism or beg the question of the relation of literature and democracy. Ziff's book exemplifies the best of this scholarship, which is to say that, like the others, it is a book worth arguing with. Ziff attempts—successfully, in my view—a history of American letters that surpasses both Van Wyck Brooks's exo-histories, *The Flowering of New England* (1936) and *The Times of Melville and Whitman* (1947), and F. O. Matthiessen's aesthetically oriented *The American Renaissance* (1941). Just as Brooks stressed the external details of social and cultural life and ignored the inner workings of American literary masterpieces, so Matthiessen reversed this priority. Ziff offers a synthesis of these two approaches. His book examines "certain precise connections, literary as well as biographical, between the American democracy and its first great body of imaginative writing." Ziff is interested in "the process by which the details of the world—especially its cultural anxieties—worked their way into the form and texture of literature" (Ziff 1981, xii).

I share this interest, but I begin from different premises. In the first place, it is far from obvious to me what it means to speak of democracy in nineteenth- or twentieth-century America. Hence it is altogether unclear what has been established by those "precise connections . . . between the American democracy and its first great body of imaginative writing." I take the view that democracy *just is* a leading issue under discussion in such books and not an inert historical fact that can be taken for granted in the way, say, that the existence of a natural phenomenon like the Rocky Mountains or of a factitious entity like the federal judiciary can be. Indeed, to treat democracy as a neutral datum, as a way of life already achieved, is to start from an anti-democratic premise. If full participation in self-government, whether

representative or direct, is the criterion, then it is obvious that
there has never been democracy in America. Partial democracy, in
nineteenth-century America no less than in the Athenian *polis*, is not
participatory democracy. In not being participatory democracy, partial
democracy reveals itself to be the creature of liberal capitalism that it
is. Politics in this "democracy," as Hannah Fenichel Pitkin and Sara
M. Shumer have written, narrows to " 'Who governs,' which means
determining 'who gets what, when, how' " (Pitkin and Shumer 1982,
44). Yet to be achieved is self-government for all. So, to say that democracy is a, perhaps *the*, leading issue under discussion is to cast a
wider net than any available through the conventional disciplines of
literary, intellectual, political, or social history—wider, indeed, than
any available in American public discourse generally, a dismal fact that
is itself a piece of the Emersonian legacy and the object of much of
my attention in the following studies.[1] By this I mean to suggest that
the mental act of converting democracy as a question into democracy
as a neutral datum suitable for quantification or narration takes place
in the liberal mind, which I believe distinguishes itself precisely by this
capacity to retard the actual development of democracy by *picturing* it
as a *fait accompli*. It may be that the mind which Richard Rorty and
other philosophers have said was an invention of the seventeenth century was not just any mind or "the mind" but was "the liberal
mind."[2] Something like the confluence or congruence of liberalism
and radical interiority is a recurring theme of this book.

Second, I believe that nearly seventy-five years of, in Charles Newman's words, the literary professoriat's "worrying the notion of literature's relationship to society" are perhaps enough (Newman 1985, 55).
It is possible there are more interesting things for those who care
about "literature and society" to do—more interesting and conceivably
more useful. Among them, I suggest, are projects that trace the inner
history of America, the history not only of the forgotten lower orders
but of forgotten or unacknowledged patterns of thought and feeling.

The philosophical history of American literature is one such history. American literature does have a philosophical history, just as American philosophy, we are now learning, has a literary history. These transformations in historical perspective encourage new interpretations of old thinkers and artists and *interpretations* of the dominant interpretive criteria themselves. In the spirit of William James, what we need is "a new name for some old ways of thinking," the "old ways" in this line that I borrow from the title page of *Pragmatism* referring to the whole of the literary-philosophical-political record in America. If regarding Emerson as the fountainhead of American literature is today something of a cliché of American literary studies, the waters from the Emersonian font are nonetheless fresh enough to divert attention from what might be called the constitution of American literature. As a constituted body of academic thought and practice, American literature suffers, like its confrere, American history, from a poverty of philosophical ideas. Though American literature, so constituted, is perhaps to be admired for elbowing its way into academic respectability in the 1920s, nostalgia for this Jacksonian upstart lumbering through the neo-Federalist drawing rooms of early-twentieth-century academia cannot make up for its philosophical emptiness. Even defenders of American literature against this positivism fall victim to it. Thus Lionel Trilling wrote in *The Liberal Imagination* (1950), "American literature as an academic subject is not so much a *subject* as an *object* of study. . . . " He then added, by way of explaining his key terms, that as an academic subject American writing "does not, as a literature should, put the scrutinizer of it under scrutiny." But if the academic study of American writing makes this literature into an object of study, by which Trilling means a restful, perhaps insipid, pursuit, then it is at least conceivable that the fault lies with the way in which American writing has been consolidated in the academy. From this fault nothing whatever follows about the origins, aims, effects, and meanings of American writing, least of all Trilling's conclusion that it enforces the audience's "too comfortable sense of complete comprehension" (Trilling 1950, 283).

Thanks to efforts by Stanley Cavell and other contemporary American philosophers, the very idea of a literary tradition has lost some of the intellectual legitimation that professional literary study has conferred on it through its systematic consolidation of T. S. Eliot's "Tradition and the Individual Talent" (1919)—lost it not because literary works do not make a tradition but because a *literary* tradition is by definition a radically incomplete idea. Indeed, *any* discipline-defined intellectual tradition is radically incomplete and stands as a fallacious synecdoche in relation to the traditions it excludes. This criticism of the prevailing modes of academic specialization is, of course, not new; nor, for that matter, is it anything more than an incidental feature of Cavell's work on Emerson and Thoreau.[3] Cavell's principal thesis about Emerson's significance, moreover, threatens equally the received conceptions of both the literary and the philosophical past in America and, *a fortiori*, the literary and philosophical present and near future. Cavell argues that Emerson did nothing less than make *philosophy* possible in America: a thesis at least as startling to professional philosophers as it is to professors of American literature (Cavell 1986). Cavell's work on Emerson in turn makes Emerson available, so to speak—one would like to think unavoidable—to contemporary Anglo-American philosophers, whose training by and large predisposes them to write off Emerson as philosophically uninteresting, i.e., as worthy of only literary attention (Cavell 1981, 123–60). Thus for a literary critic or historian to study Emerson is, prior to the appearance of Cavell's work, to claim a territory no one else with intellectual training was interested in and whose market value rose and fell over the years in accord with the fortunes of the teaching of American literature and history. For a literary critic or historian to study Emerson today, however, is to discover Emerson to be contested terrain. Along with Richard Rorty, Nelson Goodman, and John McDermott, each of whom has contributed significantly to the philosophical investigation of literature, Cavell has re-seen Emerson in the presence of his official academic custodians.

My point is that it is at least possible that much of Emerson's significance has eluded us, that there is a literary-philosophical narrative of Emersonianism to be written, and that the message of that narrative may well hold meaning for our public life; that is, it may hold a political meaning. The recently discovered instability of boundaries, hitherto thought to be well established, demarcating discipline from discipline and genre from genre may reflect major structural changes in the institutions of higher learning and thereby in the central social means of the production, distribution, and very conception of knowledge. Such structural changes, like those that have come before, present new opportunities for rethinking the past. It is worth mentioning that the relentless pulverization and endless recategorization of knowledge since the seventeenth century have always carried public or political meaning, not only in the Foucauldian sense that inventive minds came to be seen as "transgressors," and hence had to be named and publicly identified as the authors of their works, but also in the broader sense that knowledge became goods subject to the requirements of the state and the valuation of the market (Foucault 1977, 113–38). I view the intellectual transgressions of Cavell and others in this light.

But there is an even more immediate sense in which the breakdown of familiar boundaries infuses any study of Emersonianism with political content. Today, as in the nineteenth century, ruptures in the academic division of labor make Emerson and Emersonianism the potential property of America and not the exclusive preserve of American literature. No more so than any other great mind did Emerson fancy himself an item in a future syllabus. Presuming to tell Americans how to live—and witnessing the effectiveness of his efforts—Emerson, the romantic egoist, apostle of self-culture, author of the latest form of infidelity, the sage of Concord, etc., would be altogether chagrined at the paucity of ties between intellectuals and the larger society in contemporary America. (To the objection that Emerson's inclusion in the humanities syllabus makes him available to the general public, I say that the general public died a long time ago and that institutions of higher learning were partly responsible for and wholly complicit in its death.) The religious faith with which Emerson believed in "the infinitude of the private man" sustained him as a public figure with work to do in a time when there still was a public world in which to think and speak and act. That Emerson did not foresee his own contribution to our state of affairs, in which, as Newman has said, the "Man of Letters [has been eradicated] by the professional academic" and the intellectual middle class has been "pauperized," is an irony of history which we should consider carefully as we set about our own intellectual and political projects (Newman 1985, 118, 186). It is a hint that we might follow up, not an occasion for whipping a great soul from the supposedly safe, dead past.

RAISING THE "PEQUOD"

Emersonian anti-politicism is so extreme, and Emerson's ideas themselves have been so influential in American life and thought, that the Emersonian tradition serves as a powerful means of mapping the leading discursive formations of the last 150 years in the United States. Study of Emerson helps disclose, for example, the largely hidden antagonism between liberalism and democracy in American political thought—an antagonism that has only recently begun to be understood through analyses offered by such theorists as Sheldon Wolin, Carey McWilliams, and John Gunnell. The early 1980s' revival of interest in democratic theory—as seen in such journals as *Democracy*, now defunct—would have been inconceivable apart from efforts to disentangle liberal and democratic traditions of thought and practice.

Even so, the use of Emerson's thought in such analyses has been rare: one aim of this study is at least to suggest, though there is not room to develop, the relevance of Emersonian anti-politicism to current discussions of the ways in which liberal social philosophy, believed to be dead but evidently capable of exerting its influence from beyond the grave, acts as a brake on the democratic political imagination.

Re-seeing Emerson also enriches our understanding of the inner history of Modernism. Contrasting European and American modernisms, Charles Newman has written:

> European Modernism and its Avant-Garde was initially an exclusive social and political movement, while America placed an exclusive emphasis on the aesthetics of Modernism. This is why any attempt to see our literary movements as revolutionary always seems overwrought, just as our few attempts at radical political reform seem so hopelessly literary. The missing social and political ingredient of American Modernism, and it was missing from the first, cannot be overemphasized. (Newman 1985, 52)

Because American literature since Emerson and Melville has as much of a claim to being called "modern" as any literature, American or European, in the twentieth century, I believe that exactly the opposite of Newman's generalization in the final sentence above best describes the relation of culture and politics in America. The task of an American literary-philosophical history is, among other tasks, to work out the implications of what is perhaps the major irony in the relation of culture to politics: not merely that the great nineteenth-century writers from Emerson to Twain and James were more "modern" than those who came later, though they were, but that Emersonian conceptions of politics, culture, and the self did in fact, contrary to Newman's generalization, "confront . . . the dominant cultural and political institutions" (Newman 1985, 51) of American society in so far as they were meant to take them over and make them over, in fact to replace these institutions wholesale. Emerson started no revolution, but nor did Mann or Gide or Rilke.

The rhetoric of confrontation, however appropriate it may be for the literary history of European Modernism, is completely irrelevant to the history of American writing. It does not follow, however, that that history is devoid of social and political content. To the nineteenth-century American writer the dominant institutions set up barriers to artistic invention that the artist transformed into opportunities. Henry James's biography of Hawthorne, published in 1866, may be read in this light as a meditation on the artist's relation to society. James slyly refers in this book to the American's secret joke and, though he implies its exact details elude him, he draws the best map we have had of the peculiar social circumstances from which the joke emerged. I refer to his famous description of the missing parts of American life:

One might enumerate the items of high civilization, as it exists in other countries, which are absent from the texture of American life, until it should become a wonder to know what was left. No State, in the European sense of the word, and indeed barely a specific national name. No sovereign, no court, no personal loyalty, no aristocracy, no church, no clergy, no army, no diplomatic service, no country gentlemen, no castles, no palaces, nor manors, nor old country-houses, nor parsonages, nor thatched cottages, nor ivied ruins; no cathedrals, nor abbeys, nor little Norman churches; no great Universities nor public schools—no Oxford, nor Eton, nor Harrow; no literature, no novels, no museums, no pictures, no political society, no sporting class—no Epsom nor Ascot! Some such list as that might be drawn up of the absent things in American life—especially in the American life of forty years ago, the effect of which, upon an English or a French imagination, would probably, as a general thing, be appalling. The natural remark, in the almost lurid light of such an indictment, would be that if these things are left out, everything is left out. The American knows that a good deal remains; what it is that remains—that is his secret, his joke, as one may say. It would be cruel, in this terrible denudation, to deny him the consolation of his natural gift, that "American humour" of which of late years we heard so much. (James 1979, 47–48)

What *does* remain? is still a fair question a century later. And why is knowledge of it a laughing matter? is an equally pertinent question, if even more difficult to answer. Possibly part of the answer to these questions is this: to write when there is nothing (European-like) to write about requires a new literary covenant between author and audience. The key provision of this covenant, to wit, James's insistence that the audience grant the writer his "donnée," turns up as the central argument of "The Art of Fiction" (1884), James's major critical manifesto (James 1984, 56). Social denudation of a particular variety thus serves as the pretext for aesthetic advance—which is to say, for insisting in the name of artistic freedom upon a blank check so long as one's art remains, to use a favorite Jamesian word, "interesting." Aesthetic experimentalism or pragmatism arises on the social ground that is declared *a priori* to be no social ground. From this nothingness comes, via covenant, something. It is according to the same principle that a joke provokes pleasure: the sudden appearance of pleasure when one gets the joke is like getting something for nothing. The American's secret knowledge of what remains in America, once its "un-European" character is admitted, may be knowledge of this sleight of hand. If so, the knowledge has to remain secret.

In other words, perhaps the writer's knowledge of his or her own social purposes, developed in a state of heightened consciousness of the circumstances James enumerates, remained ulterior, and, so to speak, went down like the "Pequod." If so, these wrecks need to be raised. We may find in such native bottoms the "missing social and political ingredient," a cargo which has been present (even if as historians *we* have been missing from the scene *it* would describe for us) but largely unacknowledged: unacknowledged because unseen, and unseen because, as Wittgenstein would have said had he taken an interest in the foibles of literary criticism and history, too typically we have "thought" when we should have "looked" (*Philosophical Investigations* 66).[4] It does not follow, for example, that because American fiction fails to exhibit stylistic and textual features similar to the salient qualities of the British, French, or Russian novel of manners it therefore lacks social or political content. It is true that American writing has stressed an aesthetics of modernism, yet that emphasis, I would argue, has always had embedded in it a Deweyan or experimentalist conception of the aesthetic. R. P. Blackmur, our foremost analyst of modernism, understood his subject in these terms when he wrote: "in the world as it is, there is no way to get a mastery of a subject except in the aesthetic experience . . . and if our account of it is correct, we also discover what our culture is" (qtd. in Newman 1985, 109). Blackmur's critical principle, "poetry is life at the remove of form and meaning . . . not life lived but life framed and identified" (Blackmur 1962, 269) translates Dewey's claim in *Art as Experience* (1934) that aesthetic quality characterizes anything that is *an* experience, that "art, in its form, unites the very same relation of doing and undergoing, outgoing and incoming energy, that makes an experience to be *an* experience."

> A piece of work is finished in a way that is satisfactory; a problem receives its solution; a game is played through; a situation, whether that of eating a meal, playing a game of chess, carrying on a conversation, writing a book, or taking part in a political campaign, is so rounded out that its close is a consummation and not a cessation. Such an experience is a whole and carries with it its own individualizing quality and self-sufficiency. It is *an* experience. (Dewey 1958, 35)

The force of Blackmur's remark about getting "a mastery of our subject" derives, not from an invocation of a socially empty aestheticism, but from an awareness, born of long experience, of the arduousness entailed in mastery. Blackmur was by no means certain that a "correct account" of human experience in the modern age was within our grasp.

The "cult of experience in American writing," diagnosed almost a half-century ago by Philip Rahv, has been only partly a matter of American writing historically alternating between plunges into, and withdrawals from, experience (Rahv 1969, 21–37). Equally significant has been an irrepressible urge toward affirmation. In this respect, American literary-philosophical history may be seen as an expression of what Herbert Marcuse labeled affirmative culture:

> By affirmative culture is meant that culture of the bourgeois epoch which led in the course of its development to the segregation from civilization of the mental and spiritual world as an independent realm of value that is also considered superior to civilization. Its decisive characteristic is the assertion of a universally obligatory, eternally better and more valuable world that must be unconditionally affirmed: a world essentially different from the factual world of the daily struggle for existence, yet realizable by every individual for himself "from within," without any transformation of the state of fact. It is only in this culture that cultural activities and objects gain that value which elevates them above the everyday sphere. Their reception becomes an act of celebration and exaltation. (Marcuse 1968, 95)

Emersonian privatism generally conforms to this description of European culture since the renaissance, and for that reason it would be an ideological distortion to push very hard any claim for American cultural exceptionalism. One of the arguments of this book, however, asserts that it is precisely from the extremism, the extravagance, of American idealism and interiority that new modes of social control, aimed squarely at the "transformation of the state of fact," have acquired much of their intellectual content.

However, social institutions themselves, no matter how congruent they may be with prevailing modes of control or how efficient they may be as instruments of domination, are reducible to their intellectual content only through the alembic of the severest ahistorical idealism. As Martin Jay has argued recently, "although a de-naturalizing consciousness of the subjective origins of the social world may be a necessary moment in the struggle to change society, it is not a sufficient one. Indeed, paradoxically, by assuming that public institutions are merely 'cultural conventions' that can be changed by exposing their artificiality, we may blind ourselves to the deeper more varied sources that generated them and the still potent functions that they now serve" (Jay 1984–85, 140). My purpose is to suggest that the hierarchy which elevates mental over manual labor, high culture over everyday life, is an unstable one in American experience. Whereas European tradition finds T. W. Adorno arguing with Walter Benjamin over, say, the potential revolutionary content of Surrealism, in America no comparable debate has ever occurred. The reason, I suspect, is that under the material conditions of white settlement, conquest, and expansion American idealism loses its critical power. Idealism without negativity, I take it, is mere interiority. Affirmation of "the infinitude of the private man," though overtly cheery, betokens a worry that privacy is desolate, an interior landscape not so different from the objective wilderness. Emerson's magnificent defense of nature is compensatory, as we shall see. Affirmative culture thus affirms ambiguously in America. It promises an inner refuge, but the refuge turns out to be a busy schoolhouse, not a private chapel. The everyday world above which this culture elevates itself ironically occupies the same plane of existence as itself. The question, as Emerson said many times, is whether the observer sees this ironical two-in-one. To miss it either because one is satisfied with exposing the facticity of institutions or because one is patiently awaiting an American version of Adorno versus Benjamin is perhaps to miss what is truly monstrous in American life.

Emersonianism is not a sentimental humanism. If anything, it represents a transformation on native grounds of the peculiar modes of freedom enunciated in the new metaphysic of the modern age. In escaping "the bonds of the Middle Ages," Martin Heidegger wrote in "The Age of the World Picture" (1936), modern man frees himself to himself. In so doing, he becomes "subject" even as he conceives and grasps the world as picture—as a visual entity.

> The interweaving of these two events, which for the modern age is decisive—that the world is transformed into picture and man into *subiectum*—throws light at the same time on the grounding event of modern history, an event that at first glance seems almost absurd. Namely, the more extensively and the more effectually the world stands at man's disposal as conquered, and the more objectively the object appears, all the more subjectively, i.e., the more importunately, does the *subiectum* rise up, and all the more impetuously, too, do observation and teaching about the world change into a doctrine of man, into anthropology. It is no wonder that humanism first arises where the world becomes picture. (Heidegger 1977, 133)

Heidegger notes that *subiectum* translates the Greek *hypokeimenon*, the word for "that-which-lies-before, which, as ground, gathers everything onto itself." As the philosophical program for the activities of the new subject, humanism dignifies the pictorialization of the world and guides the self-pictorialization of the individual. Eventually, it sanctions the masterless man as a weird historical project—the mythical yet real individual—and culminates in Modernism, its final efflorescence. Modernism in turn surrealizes and pluralizes without humanizing, as Newman has observed (Newman 1985, 60). The social monsters to which Emerson alludes in "The American Scholar" may appear quaint in the gothic penumbra enveloping them, but they are not friendly.

Therein is a link between nineteenth-century idealism and twentieth-century pragmatism, and, I should add, between literature and political theory. The oscillation—by essayist, poet, philosopher, or critic—between wild and woolly acceptance of experience and ascetic and "precise scrutiny" of it has not only been underlain by a common affirmation and "an essential Americanism" (Rahv 1969, 27). It has also served as the medium through which the writer has indulged what Sheldon Wolin has called the "architectonic impulse," a powerful drive in the direction of "ordering . . . a disordered world" (Wolin 1960, 294–95). The American writer imagined that what democracy needs is a republic of letters. I believe that a democratic future hinges, in part, on whether this fantasized republic of letters can be transformed, at last, into institutions of culture.

ENVIRONMENTS OF FREEDOM

Twenty years ago, Richard Poirier identified some of these features of American writing in his *A World Elsewhere: The Place of Style in American Literature*. "The most interesting American books," Poirier suggested, "are an image of the creation of America itself." The American writer has heeded faithfully the injunction of Emerson in his essay *Nature* (1836): "Build, therefore, your own world." American books

> are bathed in the myths of American history; they carry the metaphoric burden of a great dream of freedom—of the expansion of national consciousness into the vast spaces of a continent and the absorption of those spaces into ourselves. Expansive characters in Cooper, or Emerson, Melville, Henry James, Fitzgerald or Faulkner are thus convinced as if by history of the practical possibility of enclosing the world in their imaginations. (Poirier 1966, 3)

American writing at its most innovative creates "environments of freedom" within the novel, poem, or essay—an environment composed of language used in such a way as to create a liberated place. One immediately thinks of Thoreau at Walden Pond, Ishmael aloft above the decks of the "Pequod," Huck and Jim on the raft at night. "American books," Poirier suggests, "are often written as if historical forces cannot possibly provide such an environment, as if history can give no life to 'freedom,' and as if only language can create the liberated place." American heroes are free from the pressures of actual life—"from biology, economics, and from the social forces which are ultimately the undoing of American heroes and quite often of their creators." American heroes do not so much revolt against the system which threatens to dominate them as they "tend to substitute themselves" for it. Although the ordinary world is often acknowledged in even the most far-flung of American books, such as *Moby-Dick,* at the same time it is clear that the ordinary world is inadequate as "a source of moral or psychological standards." Furthermore, these books resist translation into ordinary standards, for what they depict is a radical expansion of self, a wholly free "exercise of consciousness." In short, by giving the "illusion of a world elsewhere," American writing at its best presents a world in which consciousness has decisively triumphed (Poirier 1966, 3–5).

I find Poirier's analysis compelling but incomplete. I agree that all American writing starts with Emerson's amazing sentence, "Build, therefore, your own world." But concealed within this seemingly airy notion is an entelechy whose terms are only fully elaborated in Emerson's other essays and elaborated again and again in American literature and thought since the mid-nineteenth century. Emerson inaugurated this intellectual project with his eloquent hope, expressed best in "The American Scholar" (1837), that the day was at hand in the 1830s when "the sluggard intellect of this continent will look from under its iron lids and fill the postponed expectation of the world with something better than the exertions of mechanical skill." The "doctrine" set forth in an "old fable" Emerson admired held that originally there was

> One Man,—present to all particular men only partially, or through one faculty; . . . you must take the whole society to find the whole man. Man is not a farmer, or a professor, or an engineer, but he is all. Man is priest, and scholar, and statesman, and producer, and soldier. In the divided or social state these functions are parcelled out to individuals, each of whom aims to do his stint of the joint work, whilst each other performs his. The fable implies that the individual, to possess himself, must sometimes return from his own labor to embrace all the other laborers. But, unfortunately, this original unit, this fountain of power, has been so distributed to multitudes, has been so minutely subdivided and peddled out, that it is spilled into drops, and cannot be gathered. The state of society is one in which the members have suffered amputation from the trunk, and strut about so many walking monsters,—a good finger, a neck, a stomach, an elbow, but never a man. (Emerson 1957, 64)

Man, originally One, when divided in the social state, is "metamorphosed into a thing, into many things." The individual merges with his social function. Just as the attorney becomes a "statute-book" and the "mechanic a machine," so the scholar becomes "the delegated intellect" (Emerson 1957, 64–65).

In need of discipline, the scholar goes to school to Emerson's three teachers: nature, books, and action. For Emerson, nature is "the first in time and the first in importance of the influences upon the mind." Learn the following lesson, Emerson says:

> Every day, the sun; and, after sunset, Night and her stars. Ever the
> winds blow; ever the grass grows. Every day, men
> and women conversing—beholding and beholden. The scholar

is he of all men whom this spectacle most engages. He must
settle its value in his mind. (Emerson 1957, 65)

Then, put the value of books in exact perspective: *because* they are the
repository of the "mind of the Past" books should be valued not for
their own sake but as inspirations to original thought. "They are for
nothing but to inspire." Finally, if you would be a scholar, refuse to
accept the fashionable definition of the thinker as a recluse. "The so-
called 'practical men' sneer at speculative men, as if, because they
speculate or *see*, they could do nothing." For Emerson, seeing is not
always believing, but it is always doing, always an activity. What the
scholar does is to convert "experience into thought, as a mulberry leaf
is converted into satin. The manufacture goes forward at all hours"
(Emerson 1957, 64–70).

Emerson's essays and journals stand before us like a bright mirror
on which are reflected, not images of ideal selves or real ancestors,
but occasions and possibilities for writing itself. All such occasions
and possibilities, however, take shape and appear to us in the particular social condition in which we find ourselves. "You must take the
whole society," Emerson advised, which lies splintered into pieces
around us and in us, "to find the whole man." This directive defines
the peculiar Emersonian mode of being in the world. It is a mode of
being limned by the scholar's efforts to trace a line in between two
alternatives: on the one side, transcendental reconstitution of the broken whole; on the other, remedial political action. This line in between is the line of the scholar's true interest. The scholar *takes*
society, then, neither as a silent visionary, frozen in transcendental
self-attention, nor as a political actor seeking to bend the given social
world to his will, but as Man Thinking. In between being and
doing, Emerson's own example suggests, Man Thinking finds himself using words. The finding is simultaneously a making. The social
whole thus re-envisioned is something new, not something re-done.

The monsters remain on the social landscape, and they are ours as much as Emerson's or any later writer's.

Whether he feigns standing alone or eagerly cultivates the social whirl, the American writer in the nineteenth century stays within the social ontology of Emerson's American Scholar. Writing becomes the experience that comes before experience, not in the order of time but in the order of value, to adapt a line from George Orwell. The American writer—Hawthorne, Melville, Thoreau, Whitman, Dickinson, Twain, Henry James—is compulsively experimental, as has often been remarked, writing against the day when the ground Emerson had staked out will be reclaimed by the "sluggard intellect" and "exertions of mechanical skill." The case of Hawthorne—in many obvious, important ways an anti-Emersonian writer—is nevertheless instructive. In a melancholy lament, voiced in his letter of June 4, 1837, to Longfellow, he wrote: "I have not lived, but only dreamed about living" (Hawthorne 1977, 670). This exclamation betokens Hawthorne's power as an imaginative writer, not his weakness, much less his remorse at being cut off from the allegedly real world. Had he "lived"—according to whatever extravagant terms he must have been imagining—he might never have written *The Scarlet Letter*, pretending in the introduction to that book that he had only found and not made the story of Hester Prynne.

Thoreau, the most celebrated American writer to affect standing outside the common lot, says that he went to Walden Pond

because I wished to live deliberately, to front only the essential facts of life, and see if I could not learn what it had to teach, and not, when I came to die, discover that I had not lived. I did not wish to live what was not life, living is so dear; nor did I wish to practise resignation, unless it was quite necessary. I wanted to live deep and suck out all the marrow of life, to live so sturdily and Spartan-like as to put to rout all that was not life, to cut a broad swath and shave close, to drive life into a corner, and reduce it to its lowest terms, and, if it proved to be mean, why then to get the whole and genuine meanness of it, and publish its meanness to the world; or it if were sublime, to know it by experience, and be able to give a true account of it in my next excursion. (Thoreau 1966, 61)

As Stanley Cavell has noted, the testimony of the text of *Walden* (1854) shows that its author went to the woods in order to have an occasion to write. "It takes a while to recognize that each of [Thoreau's] actions is the act of a writer, that every word in which he identifies himself or describes his work and his world is the identification and description of what he understands his literary enterprise to require" (Cavell 1981, 5). To say that the literary enterprise mattered this much to Thoreau is only to say that he wrote as Man Thinking, as Emerson's American Scholar engrossed in the "manufacture" by which experience is converted into thought, "as a mulberry leaf is converted into satin."

In Henry James the "literary enterprise" retains its original Emersonian purpose but fulfills itself on the ground of a new social order. Whereas the pre–Civil War America of Hawthorne and Thoreau was divided between rich and poor, slave and freeman, the world as it appeared in James's social perception was divided between old money and new money in America and Europe. "I do not see," Emerson had complained in "The American Scholar," "how any man can afford, for the sake of his nerves and his nap, to spare any action in which he can partake. It is pearls and rubies to his discourse. Drudgery, calamity, exasperation, want, are instructors in eloquence and wisdom" (Emerson 1957, 70). James appears to have followed this advice to the letter. R. P. Blackmur tells the following story of the artist gathering his materials:

> Once, in the nineties, while James was staying in an English country house, the only child of a neighbor died of a sudden illness; and although

James had quarrelled with the neighbor and they had not been on speaking terms he announced to his host that he would attend the funeral of the little boy. His host argued that, in the small church in the small village, it would be conspicuously unseemly for him to go—the bereaved parents could only take it as an affront; but James was obstinate. When he returned, his host asked him how on earth he could have brought himself to go, and to sit, as he had, in the pew directly behind the mourners. James brushed all argument aside and, with that intensity in his eyes which made his face seem naked, stated firmly: "Where emotion is, there am I!" (Blackmur 1963, 1039)

James's host had, of course, asked a nosy psychological question, to which James gave an answer that succinctly revealed his purpose as a writer. His novels embody that purpose in the form of an absorbing interest in presenting historical, or social, tension as private emotion. It is precisely in the smallest details of social life that James could imagine what he took to be the totality of social relations. For him to forego, out of a sense of bourgeois decorum, attending the funeral and taking in the scene would have been the greater affront. "Live all you can; it's a mistake not to," Lambert Strether tells Little Bilham in an oft-quoted passage from *The Ambassadors* (1908).

"It doesn't so much matter what you do in particular, so long as you have your life. If you haven't had that what *have* you had? . . . What one loses one loses; make no mistake about that. The affair—I mean the affair of life—couldn't, no doubt, have been different for me; for it's at the best a tin mould, either fluted and embossed, with ornamental excrescences, or else smooth and dreadfully plain, into which, a helpless jelly, one's consciousness is poured—so that one 'takes' the form, as the great cook says, and is more or less compactly held by it: one lives in fine as one can. Still, one has the illusion of freedom; therefore, don't be, like me, without the memory of that illusion." (James 1964, 132)

The absence of freedom in the actual world is overcome only by the illusion of freedom in art. It is, James thought, a compensation fully large enough.

THE LITERARY APPEARANCE OF PHILOSOPHY

American writing since Emerson has been saturated with social content—its often-noted avoidance of social reality notwithstanding. Emerson's "Build, therefore, your own world" expresses a social ideal—the ideal of bourgeois individualism—no less than a stylistic practice. Indeed, to name it a social ideal is the same as to name it a stylistic practice, or family of stylistic practices. Such is the nature of idealized interiority American-style, however, that the Emersonian injunction engenders, and with complete consistency, its seeming opposite, namely, Dewey's hard-won conclusion, grounded in exactly the same tradition of experimentalism, that "What is called inner is simply that which does not connect with others—which is not capable of free and full communication" (Dewey 1966, 122). From Emerson to the land that lies beyond Ellison may be a trek into a territory in which literature and democracy alike are unknown. For in the American tradition of literature, philosophy, and politics, "The work of art is, after all, an act of faith in our ability to communicate symbolically," as Ellison reminds us in his latest book, *Going to the Territory* (Ellison 1986, 15). The Deweyan "What is called inner" is first of all a matter of world-building, or what Nelson Goodman calls worldmaking, an activity that does not necessarily eventuate in either a society of one or an apolitical order (Goodman 1978). It *could* help us envision and bring about a *modus vivendi*.

The social saturation of great American works has been now mundane, now sublime. Consider Melville: if all our knowledge of whales and whaling were suddenly expunged in a bizarre disaster, the essential knowledge could be recovered and the whaling industry re-established by a careful reading of *Moby-Dick* (1851). Or Hawthorne: more finely wrought than *The House of the Seven Gables* (1851) or *The Blithedale Romance* (1852), *The Scarlet Letter* (1850) not only stands as his most sustained effort to bury the past of his forefathers but also gives us many glimpses of the America of his own day. The subtlety of Hawthorne's prose ridicules in advance the positivism informing his inferior later works and leaves us with a profound conception of mass society. I think of the opening scenes of *The Scarlet Letter* as a parable of the American writer's peculiar relation to American society—a parable of social perception which figures in each of the studies in this book. Recall Hester Prynne's dilemma at the beginning of Hawthorne's book. Hester has assumed her position on the scaffold in the full glare of public disgrace. "Of an impulsive and passionate nature, she had fortified herself to encounter the stings and venomous stabs of public contumely," Hawthorne says, but she soon discovers that she is to suffer an even worse punishment: "the leaden infliction" of utter silence on the part of the assembled townspeople. The "heavy weight of a thousand unrelenting eyes, all fastened upon her, and concentred at her bosom" is almost unbearable, and Hester imagines she will "go mad at once." But only minutes later, when Hester spies Chillingworth at the back of the crowd and is certain that he has recognized her, the crowd suddenly becomes a sanctuary:

> Dreadful as it was, she was conscious of a shelter in the presence of these thousand witnesses. It was better to stand thus, with so many betwixt him and her, than to greet him, face to face, they two alone. She fled for refuge, as it were, to the public exposure, and dreaded the moment when its protection should be withdrawn from her. (Hawthorne 1962, 57, 63)

Hester had earlier set herself apart from the mass by an act of passion and defiance—daring to think and live by a radically different code—but now she seeks and finds refuge in the democratic anonymity that only the mass can provide. Alternately threatening and comforting, tyrannical and merciful, the mass appears to Hester as at once a public and a private refuge. Hester Prynne's dilemma, in turn, appears to the retrospective historian of American writing as an emblem of interesting political confusion.

Walden teaches us to build a hut and plant beans—and to see how we use language to convert nature into property, and to feel the costs of that appropriation. Such are the social riches residing in "the poverty of our nomenclature" that through the act of naming—as though Americans were a race of scholastic realists—we create the legal fiction of ownership and make the fiction come true. "*Flints' Pond!*" Thoreau exclaims, indignantly. "What right had the unclean and stupid farmer, whose farm abutted on this sky water, whose shores he has ruthlessly laid bare, to give his name to it?" (Thoreau 1966, 131). *Walden* provides the answer to this rather misconceived question: it is not a matter of rights at all but an affair of the human imagination.

> For the most part, we are not where we are, but in a false position. Through an infirmity of our natures, we suppose a case, and put ourselves into it, and hence are in two cases at the same time, and it is doubly difficult to get out. (Thoreau 1966, 217)

Property—indeed, the entire reified world—originates in that infirmity, that locus of desire which provokes us to suppose a case; human social existence at its meanest is strung out between the supposed case of property and what Thoreau calls "the case that is" (Thoreau 1966, 218).

Although *Walden* answers its author's question, the answer is interestingly incomplete, partly because Thoreau's polemic against the skinflint Flint is incomplete. Let us return to the polemic. Thoreau would call the pond in question "Sandy Pond." Ownership by the farmer has led to the use of the name "Flints' Pond." Thoreau implies that "Sandy Pond" is better because it connects more completely with the distinctive features of this particular body of water. "Flints' Pond," by contrast, connects with none of these features but quite well with the distinctive features of the farmer: his greed, presumptuousness, egotism, stupidity, etc. Thoreau recognizes that the different names have different meanings: did he not, he would have nothing to say about property, or about a good many other topics in *Walden*. But he also recognizes that the thing in question—*this* body of water—is one and the same under both names. It is at this strategic point that Thoreau's polemic ends. (If *Walden* were a sphere, this point would be its center.)

The conclusion just around the corner is that *because* the meanings are different, they *must*, if Quine is right (Quine 1980, 8–9), be other than the thing—i.e., not organically connected at all, neither to the pond nor to the farmer. In his analysis of Thoreau's project of refounding language on its supposed "natural physical base," Larzer Ziff stops where Thoreau stops and takes him at his word, so to speak. Ziff thinks that the baroque idealism in Thoreau's attempt to unite word and thing in passages like the following from "Spring," the penultimate chapter of *Walden*, typifies Thoreau's assumptions about language. Thoreau is describing the sudden appearance of vegetation on the banks of Walden in the spring:

> You find thus in the very sands an anticipation of the vegetable leaf. No wonder that the earth expresses itself outwardly in leaves, it so labors with the idea inwardly. The atoms have already learned this law, and are pregnant by it. The overhanging leaf sees here its prototype. *Internally*, whether in the globe or animal body, it is a moist thick *lobe*, a word especially applicable to the liver and lungs and the *leaves* of fat, ($\lambda\epsilon\iota\beta\omega$, *labor, lapsus*, to flow or slip downward, a lapsing; $\lambda o\beta os$, *globus*, lobe, globe; also lap, flap, and many other words,) *externally* a dry thin *leaf*, even as the *f* and *v* are a pressed and dried *b*. The radicals of lobe are *lb*, the soft mass of the *b* (single lobed, or B, double lobed,) with a liquid *l* behind it pressing forward.

In globe, *glb*, the guttural *g* adds to the meaning the capacity of the throat. (Thoreau 1966, 202)

Thoreau himself, however, indirectly acknowledges what a circus-freak such writing is. It not only fails to qualify Thoreau as a "linguistic scientist," as Ziff correctly remarks (Ziff 1981, 202, 209); more important, it perfectly exemplifies that "infirmity of our natures" which leads us simultaneously into two or more cases from which there may be no escape. For it is that infirmity which, according to Thoreau, sets up the vain project of attempting to unite word and thing in perfect organic wholeness.

Recall that Thoreau had stopped short of concluding that because meanings carried by different names for the same thing are different meanings there *can* be no such organicism. The passage on "the infirmity of our natures," which I have called the answer to the problem set up by the polemic against the farmer, is likewise silent on this matter: it, too, does not say that because meanings carried by different names for the same thing differ there *can* be no such organicism. Yet this passage depends on just this premise in order to get going, just as the polemic against Flint derives its amusing and indignant tone from the absence of the same premise. The conspicuous absence of this premise is a matter to which I will return below. For now, I want to stress the sense in which the second passage finds Thoreau in effect admitting defeat, for this passage says that "the infirmity of our natures" is such that there simply is no curtailing the proliferation of meanings. They tumble out of the human imagination continually and always in the guises of new names. They obscure, perhaps permanently, "the case that is." At the same time—and this is the specific function of one such squadron of meanings—they conceal the very distinction between meaning and naming. Thoreau's project is first of all to salvage that distinction and, second, to use it in apprehending "the case that is." To *imagine* what exists, he insists, is exactly the wrong thing to do; Ziff's analysis, in a chapter called "Imagining What Exists: Henry David Thoreau and the Language of Literature," seems to me, therefore, to be mistaken (Ziff 1981, 202ff.). Thoreau's flight of *naming* in the paragraph from "Spring" above confuses *naming* with *meaning*: "In globe, *glb*, the guttural *g* adds to the meaning the capacity of the throat." It does nothing of the sort. Thoreau supposes a case here, the case called "trivial onomatopoeia," and puts himself into it. He gets out of this false position and writes about it from experience in his dilation on "the infirmity of our natures." And it is from this *true* position that he formulates his critique of the origins of property.

The origins of property, however, are obviously not the whole of property; Thoreau's moral eloquence and linguistic insights tell us a bit about ownership but little else about property relationships. *Moby-Dick* tells us a good deal. Melville's condemnation of Christian capitalist civilization, while dramatizing a few moments of happiness and brotherhood, is mainly a story of terror, exploitation, mystification, failure, and loss. Ruling this life are the two laws of the whale fishery, "Fast-Fish and Loose-Fish," synopsized in Chapter 89.

I. A Fast-Fish belongs to the party fast to it.
II. A Loose-Fish is fair game for anybody who can soonest catch it. (Melville 1964, 507)

The first law in effect says that (1) a thing belongs to you if in some way you control it or are attached to it and that (2) the "party fast to it" is the party fastest in getting to it. In other words, there is nothing in the world that is not either your property already or potentially your property. By the same token, there is nothing in experience, *not excluding* anything which you claim as yours, that is not at least potentially someone else's property. The second law of property, the law of "Loose-Fish," enjoys the status of a separate and distinct rule in the discourse of the law. In fact, it is already implicit in the law of "Fast-Fish" by dint of the unresolved, programmatic ambiguity sanctioned in that law.

Melville's commentaries on "Fast-Fish" and "Loose-Fish" show, respectively, the particulars of property relations and the distinctive character of both material and spiritual domination. Illustrative of "Fast-Fish" are the feudal social system, in which the "sinews and souls of Russian serfs" are "Fast-Fish" owned by their Russian masters, and the American slave system, in which the "sinews and souls of . . . Republican slaves" are owned by American slave-masters. Illustrative of "Loose-Fish" are various material forms of domination—of America by Spain in 1492—and various objects of spiritual domination—the "Rights of Man," and "all men's minds and opinions," which are there for the taking or molding. Melville's remarkable catalog of legally stable and relentlessly predatory property relationships culminates in this remark about the reader of *Moby-Dick*: what is he or she, Melville asks, if not *both* a "Fast-Fish" and a "Loose-Fish"? A "Fast-Fish" in the sense that the authorially constituted reader *feels* autonomous and self-possessed and a "Loose-Fish" in the sense of *being* a prey for others, first among them the parodic author himself (Melville 1964, 509–10).

In the foregoing discussion of Thoreau on property I pointed out that both the polemic against ownership and the doctrine of "the infirmity of our natures" depend, each in its own way, on a particular premise about words and things which Thoreau simply skips over—not, to be sure, out of sloppiness but, most likely, because the premise itself had not yet been coined. Similarly, in Chapter 89 of *Moby-Dick* Melville is eloquently silent about the disjunction between the reader's inner, *felt* autonomy and the reader's actual vulnerability. These missing ideas are what I call *philosophical appearances*. By *philosophical appearance* I mean the evocation or dramatization *but not statement* of a philosophical idea. A philosophical appearance is not an idea but the shadow of an idea; it is a "virtual idea," to adapt Suzanne Langer's

term in *Problems of Art*. Philosophical appearances in literature cannot
be strung together to form literary philosophy, which does not exist,
but instead make possible the text as symbol. The mode of evocation
or dramatization—more generally, the mode of philosophical presence—traps each such appearance within the work's overall illusion of
concrete immediacy, which is the stuff of literature. Both philosophical appearance and artistic illusion vanish as soon as the author turns
explicitly "philosophical" and makes (often) grandiose truth- or
knowledge-claims.

A philosophical appearance, then, is that about which the author is
conspicuously or strategically silent. The silence both informs and sur-
rounds the text, allowing it to stand forth as symbol, as *an* experience,
in Dewey's terms. Without this animating, enveloping silence apprehended in the act of reading, the text would be indistinguishable from
the continuous occurrence of experience (Dewey 1958, 35), just as in
Langer's account of pictorial art, pictures "create a picture space,"
without which "we would not see them as pictures, but as spotted
surfaces" (Langer 1957, 35). In answer to the challenge to literary
study, laid down by René Wellek and Austin Warren in *Theory of Literature* forty-five years ago, to explain "how ideas actually enter literature," I would say, first, that the image of "entering" is misconceived
and inappropriate. The work, no more so than the writer's mind, as
Trilling said in his rejoinder to Wellek, Warren, and T. S. Eliot, is not
a Clarissa Harlowe being violated by an idea in the figure of Colonel
Lovelace (Trilling 1950, 276). The platitudinous truth is that everything imaginable somehow finds its way into literature. Hamlet's remark to Horatio, "There are more things in heaven and earth, Horatio, / than are dreamt of in your philosophy" (1.5.166–67), is as
true as it is pat. It is idle to ask how ideas "enter" anything. A revision of Wellek and Warren's question would direct us to understand
the literary appearance of philosophy. For it is a fact that philosophy
can appear literary, and literature can appear philosophical. In neither

case is the only—or even main—question Wellek and Warren's question of "how ideas actually enter into literature."

Wellek and Warren say:

> It is obviously not a question of ideas in a work of literature as long as these ideas remain mere raw material, mere information. The question arises only when and if these ideas are actually incorporated into the very texture of the work of art, when they become "constitutive," in short when they cease to be ideas in the ordinary sense of concepts and become symbols, or even myths. (Wellek and Warren 1956, 122)

Flaws in this conception of the issue abound. "Ideas," "information," "raw material," "mere information," "ideas in the ordinary sense of concepts," "symbols," "myths": this potpourri gets us nowhere. Yet the question of how to characterize the philosophical constituents of a literary work is important. I argue that the philosophical appearance shapes the whole of which it is a part: the silence foregrounds the sound and sense of the work. This premise would be a truism were the silence the same for all works, as though it were an entity like the paper of which a book is made or a monochromatic abstraction like Truth. But the silence that shapes the work is particular. It is as much the author's creation as the description of a character's coat or the account of her reflections. Trilling was correct to criticize Wellek and Warren and, by implication, the entire New Critical program, for mounting a "defense of the autonomy of poetry" which forgot that "poets too have their effect in the world of thought" (Trilling 1950, 278). Poets have that effect, I argue, partly because they produce in their works philosophical appearances. Philosophical appearances in literature comprise the vast other side of Wittgenstein's momentous conclusion to the *Tractatus*: "What we cannot speak about we must pass over in silence" (Wittgenstein 1974, 7). From this remark it does not, of course, follow (nor did Wittgenstein imply) that everything so passed over in silence falls under the heading of "what we cannot speak about." Literature recognizes no such prohibition. It is as though the habits of literary invention silently repudiate Wittgenstein's austere pronouncement. The ghost of the early Wittgenstein haunts literature and antedates the appearance of Wittgenstein himself on the philosophical scene.

A philosophical appearance differs from overt philosophizing in roughly the way that, according to Richard Rorty, in his *Consequences of Pragmatism*, pragmatism differs from philosophy. Whereas the latter, beginning with Plato, dedicates itself to discovering the true nature of "the True or the Good" and in many of its twentieth-century versions concentrates on defining "the word 'true' or 'good,' " pragmatism "does not think we should ask those questions anymore."

> When [pragmatists] suggest that we not ask questions about the nature of Truth and Goodness, they do not invoke a theory about the nature of reality or knowledge or man which says that "there is no such thing" as Truth or Goodness. Nor do they have a "relativistic" or "subjectivist" theory of Truth or Goodness. They would simply like to change the subject. (Rorty 1982, xiv)

Authors of what we call literary works, I might add, are always changing the subject in this Rortyan sense of that expression. Rorty continues, drawing out his key distinction between pragmatism and Philosophy.

> All this is complicated by the fact that "philosophy," like "truth" and "goodness," is ambiguous. Uncapitalized, "truth" and "goodness" name properties of sentences, or of actions and situations. Capitalized, they are the proper names of objects—goals or standards which can be loved with all one's heart and soul and mind, objects of ultimate concern. Similarly, "philosophy" can mean simply what Sellars calls "an attempt to see how things,

in the broadest possible sense of the term, hang together, in the broadest possible sense of the term." Pericles, for example, was using this sense of the term when he praised the Athenians for "philosophizing without unmanliness." . . . In this sense, Blake is as much a philosopher as Fichte, Henry Adams more of a philosopher than Frege. No one would be dubious about philosophy, taken in this sense. But the word can also denote something more specialized, and very dubious indeed. In this second sense, it can mean following Plato's and Kant's lead, asking questions about the nature of certain normative notions (e.g., "truth," "rationality," "goodness") in the hope of better obeying such norms. The idea is to believe more truths or do more good or be more rational by knowing more about Truth or Goodness or Rationality. (Rorty 1982, xiv–xv)

Philosophy with a capital "P" is philosophy in this second, dubious, prevalent sense.

> Cordelia: Nothing, my lord.
> Lear: Nothing?
> Cordelia: Nothing.
> Lear: Nothing will come of nothing.
>   Speak again.

The "nothing" that comes of Cordelia's "Nothing" is, of course, *King Lear*, the play itself. In somewhat the same way a philosophical appearance relates to its environing illusion in the literary work. Each makes the other possible; they are mutually enabling apparitions. A philosophical appearance in literature transacts its business, interacts with its environing illusion, in the manner of philosophy with a small "p"—in fact, interacts *as* pragmatism. The discourse on property in *Walden* exposes not only the desecration of nature; it also exposes Thoreau's own analogous excesses. Similarly, the presentation of the reader of *Moby-Dick* as both "Fast-Fish" and "Loose-Fish" strikingly

contrasts with the ponderous metaphysical pathos of, say, Ahab's
quarterdeck speech to the crew of the "Pequod" in Chapter 36. Moreover, note that in Chapter 89 the philosophical appearance is socially
grounded at both ends—in the subject matter of Ishmael-Melville's
discussion of property relationships and in the reader's pretensions to
autonomy (i.e., in the author's presuppositions about the reader's self-
conception). The gap between *feeling* and *being* divides the book from
the world, and into the chasm thus opened up disappears one *habit* of
reality: namely, the fictions of property, including the reader's own
assumed property in himself or herself. As Nelson Goodman says in
his *Ways of Worldmaking*, "reality in a world, like realism in a picture,
is largely a matter of habit" (Goodman 1978, 20). One habit gone, the
way is cleared for something more serious: the dissonant truth by
means of which Melville takes to its logical conclusions William
Blackstone's central claim about property: namely, that there is no
foundation in nature such that one set of words on parchment can
confer ownership.[5] Social relationships founded on this null foundation are characterized, for Melville no less than for Blackstone, by
fear. Philosophical shadows appear in our great books often bearing,
as here, a heavy weight of political meaning.

EPISODES IN AMERICAN LITERARY–PHILOSOPHICAL HISTORY

To appreciate the influence of Emerson's idealized privatism requires
first of all that we situate the idea in Emerson's own intellectual development. The burden of Chapter One of this book, accordingly, is an
intellectual history of his idea of "the infinitude of the private man."
Emerson described himself as a man of one idea, but if he was a man
of one idea he was not a one-idea man. I try to show in this chapter
that Emersonian privatism, far from being a unit idea that may be
conveniently translated as "the perfectibility of man" or "romantic individualism," names an entire project of the spirit which dissolves na-

ture, culture, and politics *as* unit ideas and refashions them in a vision of a politically sanitized world.

With Whitman the focus of the next chapter, I am aware that the reader may be misled into expecting yet another study of Emerson's literary influence, and I would like to dispel that impression now. A study of Emerson's effect on Whitman might well seem the appropriate sequel to Chapter One: Emerson, Whitman acknowledged in 1855, "brought him to a boil." And when Whitman boiled, he created the most expansive character in American literature and the epitome of Emersonian privatism: the speaker in "Song of Myself." Nevertheless, it is not Emerson's influence on Whitman that interests me in Chapter Two. In this essay I examine Whitman's social criticism in *Democratic Vistas* (1871), a book I have long been interested in because of its extraordinary valuation of literature and of the democratic man of letters, and above all because of Whitman's comprehension of the expansionist tendencies inherent in the American democratic principle. *Democratic Vistas* is a book about the radical expansion of the nation, not of the self. Whitman's understanding of the true character of the democratic idea appears in this book as a wild fantasy of the democratic man of letters, sole legatee of the democratic hope. Whitman's powerful criticism of post–Civil War American life enhances, while concentrating, the hope but spares the American version of the democratic idea itself.

William James's battle against the absolutist hypothesis in philosophy is the subject of Chapter Three. I try in this chapter to draw out from James's critique of absolutism a key feature of James's incipient philosophy of pluralism. I suggest that the leading twentieth-century radical critique of instrumental reason only mirrors rather than refutes the main tenets of Jamesian pragmatism. If absolutism is irrational on James's account, the account itself covertly points to pragmatism's own fatal weakness: its remarkable suitability as a subpolitical public philosophy. There is a sense in which that face of pragmatism which is a public philosophy of freedom, as distinguished from instrumental reason (the soul of modern modes of social control), may be apprehended only in its vanishing. A political renewal would alter this philosophical-political link to the romantic past. The infinitude of the private man, of which James's pluralism is a latter-day philosophical expression, would fulfill itself as democratic praxis.

Chapter Four presents the literary criticism and social thought of R. P. Blackmur as an extension and critique of idealized privatism since Emerson. In this chapter I begin by contrasting two prominent ways in which this legacy has been taken in by twentieth-century American writers—the way of Robinson Jeffers and the way of Blackmur. Jeffers' pseudo-philosophy illustrates what happens to poetic talent when Philosophy becomes more attractive to the poet than philosophy, when ideology crowds out literary pragmatism. Blackmur's work, on the other hand, begins at the beginning of the literary-philosophical road with a scrupulous examination of names and naming in modern literature. Blackmur's criticism begins in skepticism in order to end in invention. This critical project, which Blackmur came to call bourgeois humanism, took shape as a cultural version of Adam Smith's Invisible Hand, the guiding force Blackmur believed essential to a human existence in mass society.

Chapter Five, though mainly concerned with Ralph Ellison's two books of autobiographical essays, *Shadow and Act* (1964) and *Going to the Territory* (1986), considered as political education, opens with a taxonomy of public discourse today in Heller's *Catch-22*. The world built in this novel comprises a terrifying whole, its terror predicated on the conquest of political space by the bureaucratic state. At the opposite end of this spectrum, which describes the final legacy of American privatism, stands Ellison. As one of the last citizens of the republic of letters founded by Emerson and Whitman, Ellison, like his "little man at Chehaw Station," "senses that American experience is of a whole and . . . wants the interconnections revealed. And not out of a penchant for protest, nor out of petulant vanity, but because he sees his own condition as an inseparable part of a larger truth in which the high and the lowly, the known and the unrecognized, the comic and the tragic, are woven into the American skein" (Ellison 1986,14). To sense, as Ellison does, the wholeness of American experience and to ask that literary art disclose its interconnections is not to sanctify a kind of literary monism, or to long for a chauvinistic transcendental signified. It is to acknowledge the power of art to assume a public role, a political (not to say ideological) power as one of the institutions of culture. Ellison's major theme of identity in a world of constantly shifting appearances rounds out a tradition that begins with the main ideas of Ellison's namesake. "[M]y middle name, sadly enough," he wrote in "Change the Joke and Slip the Yoke" (1958), "is Waldo" (Ellison 1964, 72).

As symbol, the Afro-American of white fantasy is, in the account Ellison gives of his literary life, a fully enfranchised but publicly invisible citizen of the American polity. The *being* thus symbolized accordingly forever stands in peril of being taken as a *thing*. Inasmuch as the difference between beings and things is, as Cavell has said, *the* philosophical difference (Cavell 1979, 468), the problems of American politics and the problems of American literary genius may be said to belong to the same family of problems. The members of this family, past and present, exhibit various transformations of the ancestral idea of Emersonian infinitude and privacy. Such, at any rate, is the lesson I draw in these studies and offer as the main argument of this book.

"The Infinitude of the Private Man": Emerson's Ideas of Nature, Culture, and Politics

★   ★   ★

THE PROMISE OF *Nature*

"The word of ambition at the present day is Culture," Emerson announced in his essay "Culture," published in *The Conduct of Life* in 1860 (*Works* 6:131). The date of this essay is itself significant: Emerson's "Culture" appeared seven years before Matthew Arnold wrote "Anarchy and Authority" for *Cornhill Magazine*, an essay reprinted in 1869 as *Culture and Anarchy*, perhaps the most influential statement in English of the social and moral role of literature. The target of Arnold's analysis was the "Philistinism" of the newly empowered British bourgeoisie, and his book was in part an expression of his own awareness of social class. By contrast, although the target of Emerson's essays in *The Conduct of Life* and previous works was also social, it was much less clearly defined and only vaguely informed with class awareness. This difference between Arnold and Emerson directly reflects the different social conditions of the two countries: England's relatively clear class divisions as opposed to the mass society of America. The conflict between "culture and society," to borrow the pair of terms used by Raymond Williams in his study of English thought from the

Romantic movement to George Orwell, also manifested itself in American thought in the nineteenth and twentieth centuries but played itself out over comparatively amorphous historical circumstances. The English Romantic poets, along with Carlyle and, later, Arnold, readily identified their adversaries in social no less than in ideological terms (Williams 1966). The evolution of class relationships was the stuff of everyday social experience, as E. P. Thompson has shown in his compendious *The Making of the English Working Class*. Shifts of class power proceeded smoothly, with relatively little violence, as the bourgeoisie registered decisive victories through the Reform Bills of 1832 and 1867, and as the "working class reproduced itself" with "relative national homogeneity" up to the mid-twentieth century (Gutman 1976, 14).

In America, on the other hand, gentry social perception tended to disclose a welter of mass social conditions rather than class divisions, much less class antagonisms, as Stow Persons has suggested (Persons 1973). Periodic influxes of immigrants, along with relentless movement westward, internecine sectional conflict, and white racism vastly complicated social perception. The more or less uniform, if harrowing and, to some, repugnant, development of capitalist society in England did not duplicate itself in America; America was not the social science laboratory that England was for Karl Marx. A confusing zig-zag transition from pre-industrial to industrial or capitalist conditions occurred in the United States. Moreover, capitalism developed, not as an agent of democratization, as in England, but in the context of a pre-existing and vigorous democratic ethos (Gutman 1976, 3–78; Kovel 1971). Tocqueville observed some of these features of American society and in his analysis of its distinctively mass character suggested in *Democracy in America* a causal connection between mass social conditions and social perception, noting in particular the American tendency toward abstract thought. "As . . . Americans never know whether the idea they express today will be appropriate to the new position they may

occupy tomorrow, they naturally acquire a liking for abstract terms."
"An abstract term," he wryly added, "is like a box with a false bottom; you may put in it what ideas you please, and take them out
again without being observed" (Tocqueville 1945, 2:74). Such was the
case with Emerson's ideas of culture and nature.

These two ideas developed in parallel, forming a crucial dualism in
Emerson's thought from *Nature* (1836) to *The Conduct of Life* (1860).
What makes the dualism crucial is that from it Emerson derives his
definition of man, of human nature. "What we are," he concludes, at
the close of Chapter Eight of *Nature*, "that only can we see."' That
which makes us "what we are," the soul, "is a watcher more than a
doer, and it is a doer only that it may the better watch" (*N*, 28). At
bottom, then, human nature is predicated on the faculty of perception,
whose object is nature. But in the Introduction to *Nature*, Emerson
presents a suspicious-looking set of distinctions. First, there is the division between Nature and the Soul. Through this division, the term
"nature" acquires what Emerson calls its "philosophical definition" as
the "NOT-ME"; in this sense, "nature" designates "nature and art, all
other men and my own body." Second, there is the distinction between two senses of "nature": on one side, the foregoing definition
(the "NOT-ME"); on the other, what Emerson calls "the common
definition" as "essences unchanged by man." The paired opposite of
"nature" in the common definition is "Art": a term "applied to the
mixture of [man's] . . . will with the same things [i.e., with "space, the
air, the river, the leaf "], as in a house, a canal, a statue, a picture."
Rather than jettisoning one definition or another of "nature," Emerson boldly asserts he will use the word in *both* senses, assuring us that
any resulting "inaccuracy" will not matter. And why will it not matter? Presumably because artifice or culture itself is inconsequential
alongside Nature and the "grand" "impression" that Nature makes
upon the human mind. Culture does represent a transformation of nature through man's mixing of his will with it, as in the creation of a

house from wood. But the sum total of man's transformations, of his culture, is a small thing, "a little chipping, baking, patching, and washing"; and so too is the inaccuracy that will come from Emerson's use of these two conflicting definitions of "nature" in *Nature* (*N*, 5). Clearly, though he promises to use "nature" in both senses, resulting in an inaccuracy so trivial as hardly to be worth mentioning, it is the first sense of the term that Emerson intends to stress. He purports to inquire into the relation of nature and the soul, to study the grand impression that Nature makes upon the human mind.

To introduce two distinct but partly overlapping senses of his key term and then to forewarn the reader of inaccuracies to come about which he need not worry is an intriguing strategy. To suggest that civilization hitherto has amounted to next to nothing deepens one's curiosity. Not known for his irony, Emerson opens his first major philosophical essay with a strategic irony whereby he simultaneously exalts Nature and denigrates all Art save his own. *Nature* swiftly mythicizes the natural given while dwarfing everything factitious—everything except the very distinctions Emerson makes between the two senses of "nature" and the division upon which each sense depends: in the first sense the division between the me and the not-me, in the second sense the division between art and nature. Getting rid of Art— which on Emerson's definition includes philosophy—in order to study the relation of nature and the soul is harder to do than it is to write. That relation, moreover, though it almost seems an inert, "found" thing when Emerson authoritatively names it—"Philosophically considered, the universe is composed of Nature and the Soul"—is highly changeable and unfinished. It is not a mere *fait accompli* that Emerson, the nearly presuppositionless philosopher, only happened upon. Nor does it turn out to be an unmediated relation: the several chapters of *Nature* lay out the various mediations. Finally, it is the character of these very mediations that, more than anything else, Emerson believes should be changed. Not an unmediated relation of man and nature but altogether new mediations are what is wanted: not merely the *wish* for "an original relation to the universe" but a plan for achieving it which Emerson believes is within human power to fashion. The implied question with which *Nature* closes is whether man is a passive pupil, the fortunate beneficiary of Nature's unerring tutelage, or a new being, empowered to make a new world.

The irreconcilable antagonism between these two definitions of his key term accounts for Emerson's ambiguous treatment of "Idealism" and "Spirit" in Chapters Six and Seven of *Nature*. "Idealism" is at once the most muddled and the most instructive chapter in the essay, and though its meaning can be discerned, it becomes intelligible only with the addition of "Spirit," which offers Emerson's final statement on idealism and the conclusion to his inquiry into "the effects of culture" as if it were an afterthought (*N*, 24). These chapters of the essay stand apart from the others in several ways. They are neither as daring and revolutionary in tone as the Introduction nor as sublime in feeling as "Prospects," the final chapter of *Nature*. Both lack the clarity borne of unified purpose running through the middle four chapters (Two-Five), which recount the several uses of nature. Taken together, "Idealism" and "Spirit" constitute Emerson's defense of nature, in the two mingled senses of the term, against culture.

"Idealism" opens with the central question of philosophical empiricism: the question whether nature has objective existence. Acknowledging his "utter impotence to test the authenticity of the report of . . . [his] senses," Emerson dispenses with the "noble doubt" bequeathed by the empiricist tradition by proclaiming that it does not really matter whether nature exists outwardly or only as a mental apparition: "it is alike useful and alike venerable to me." In a word, it is "ideal." But this sense of the term "ideal" is to be distinguished from the sense of "ideal" that crops up next, in the delightful critique of "the frivolous [who] make themselves merry with the Ideal theory, as if its consequences were burlesque; as if it affected the stability of nature." For, in this second sense of "ideal," nature is wholly spiritualized, made over as accident rather than substance (N, 23). This is the Idealist or cultured view of nature. If this view is wrong, as Emerson attempts to argue in the bulk of this chapter, does nature then exist absolutely, as we are led to believe if we follow our "instinctive belief" which arises from our senses and "unrenewed understanding"? That is, can nature be shielded from the dissolving effects of "frivolous" Idealism only by the philosopher's resorting to verification by the senses, a procedure deemed moot at the opening of the chapter? Emerson answers no, this naive view is also false. In sum, neither the naive view nor the "cultured" or Idealist view establishes the correct relationship between man and nature. To understand this in detail, it is necessary to examine "the effects of culture," of which there are five (N, 23–24).

1. The Training of the Sensual Man. The first premise of Idealism, or the first effect of culture—the subject-object dualism—appears as "a hint from nature herself." The experience of simple motion, changing one's physical position and therefore one's point of view, "gives the whole world a pictorial air." "Turn the eyes upside down, by looking at the landscape through your legs, and how agreeable is the picture, though you have seen it any time these twenty years." Thus ordinary experience makes us aware of the gap "between the observer and the spectacle,—between man and nature": this first premise of Idealism is ontologically lodged in nature. The corollary to this premise is that as man learns to appreciate the variegated spectacle of the world through an infinitude of perceptions, he intuits an inner stability, as if by a common sense inference.

But over against this imagined inner stability there occurs a subtle cancellation of nature as substance, a transformation of the perceptual object into an appearance.

A man who seldom rides needs only to get into a coach and traverse his own town, to turn the street into a puppet-show. The men, the women,—

talking, running, bartering, fighting,—the earnest mechanic, the lounger, the beggar, the boys, the dogs, are unrealized [i.e., made unreal] at once, or at least, wholly detached from all relation to the observer, and seen as apparent, not substantial beings.

The subject-object dualism, Idealism's first tuition to the pupil man, betrays its ontological origins and takes revenge upon nature, ironically serving as an instrument of its dissolution. Just as subject and object name different domains, so, too, appearance splits off from substance and becomes *mere* appearance. It is fitting that an empiricist epistemology accompanies the quotidian awareness of the subject-object split: "The sensual man conforms thoughts to things." Language is simplistically referential, rationality instrumental (*N*, 24–25).

2. Activities of the Poet. In direct contrast to the sensual man, the poet "conforms things to his thoughts." Whereas nature was "rooted and fast" to the sensual man, it is "fluid, ductile, and flexible" to the poet. More than a mere spectator, the poet begins with perception but quickly conquers "the refractory world" through exercising his imagination. Thus "the imagination may be defined to be, the use which the Reason makes of the material world." The poet's perception of the world is in effect a poetic creation or re-creation of the world. In a fine inversion of the Platonic prejudice, Emerson identifies the poet as a discoverer of the "real affinities between events, (that is to say, of *ideal* affinities, for those only are real)." The second effect of culture, issuing from the domain of the poet, accordingly "assert[s] the predominance of the soul" over nature (*N*, 25–26).

3. Effects of Natural Philosophy. A similar predominance of spirit over matter results from natural philosophy's pursuit of truth. Natural philosophy is ruled by the assumption that the universe is lawful and by the promise that, once the law is discovered and the absolute ground of all being disclosed, then "the phenomena can be predicted." But this rationalist project, whether in the form of ancient philosophy

(Plato and Aristotle) or in the form of modern physics, has the effect of banishing the world, of eliminating experience, as nature is "transferred . . . into the mind," leaving "matter like an outcast corpse." The law discovered, "the memory disburthens itself of its cumbrous catalogues of particulars, and carries centuries of observation in a single formula" (N, 26–27).

4. Effects of Metaphysics. Metaphysics, too, either proceeds from, as in Cartesianism, or begets, as in Platonism, "a doubt of the existence of matter." By such methods we are hoisted into a trans-material realm, where "we become physically nimble and lightsome; we tread on air; life is no longer irksome, and we think it will never be so." From this vantage, we learn that "time and space are relations of matter," not of the Ideal, and that indeed with "a perception of truth, or a virtuous will, they have no affinity" (N, 27). Rationality and morals, fact and value, part company.

5. Effects of Religion and Ethics. The degradation of nature, together with the rationalization of its dependence upon spirit, are taught to the mass of men by religion and ethics, which Emerson calls "the practice of ideas, or the introduction of ideas into life. . . ." Religion and ethics "put nature under foot." Religion proclaims the object of sense to be merely temporal and the unseen world to be eternal; ethics makes a similar proclamation but lacks "the personality of God" to legitimate "this affront upon nature." Thus religion and ethics function for the mass of men in the same way that philosophy functions for the intellectual elite (N, 27–28).

This catalogue of betrayals of nature by culture establishes the intrinsic idealist core of culture, a force standing against nature and assaulting it from five sides. Simple sense perception transforms nature from substance into mere appearance no less than do formal systems of ideas, common codes of conduct, and bibles of religious belief. Clearly, culture affords man no basis wherein to establish "the true position of nature in regard to" him, for the manifold effects of culture are to negate nature at the start. No such "true position of nature" is possible if man's "convictions of the reality of the external world" are undercut at every turn (N, 28). In its common definition ("essences unchanged by man") nature succumbs to the ravages of simple sense perception and to the vicissitudes of human movement: Emerson shows that there are no essences unchanged by man, for man *qua* man insidiously re-makes the substantial world into an apparent one simply by virtue of perceiving it from multiple points of view. Similarly, in its philosophical definition ("NOT-ME") nature dissolves into spirit.

To redeem nature as a basis in which to anchor his definition of man, or of human nature, Emerson must somehow circumvent these effects of culture. He must find a philosophical justification for his own lack of "hostility to nature," for his "child's love to it," for his desire to "expand and live in the warm day like corn and melons" (N, 28). At the same time, however, he would cling to the Ideal theory. Yet Idealism answers but the first of the following three questions: "What is matter? Whence is it? and Whereto?" And its answer, *matter is spirit*, "does not satisfy the demands of the spirit" itself and cannot logically be prevented from "denying substantive being to men and women" themselves. Emerson concludes his inquiry by in effect surrendering for the time being to the quandary he has analyzed, declaring the Ideal theory "a useful introductory hypothesis, serving to apprize us of the eternal distinction between the soul and the world" (N, 30). That is, he attempts to limit the spiritualizing effects of idealism by subsuming it under his doctrine of use, developed in the middle four chapters of *Nature*. But his efforts in the chapters on "Idealism" and "Spirit" nevertheless do yield his definition of man as a watcher of nature and learner of its lessons, a seemingly passive being who "accepts whatever befalls, as part of its lesson" (N, 28).

One may well ask at this point whether this passive being is any the less given to reducing the world to spirit than his implied counterparts whose five departments of culture only equip them with various instruments of mental aggression. This issue is explored in "Prospects," the concluding chapter of *Nature*. Emerson's solution to the problem rests on a new definition of the relationship between the ego and the world. His critical review of culture has in fact not ended on a note of permanent passivity. Rather, it has enabled him to locate in the ego a "tyrannizing unity" that inexorably drives it to empty the world of its vast multiplicity, such that every "thought of multitude," whether simple as in mere sense perception or complex as in philosophical speculation, is "lost in a tranquil sense of unity" (*N*, 32). Such tranquillity, he argues, is not worth the price: the daily falsification of experience. This distortion of nature, this self-perpetuating crime against it which springs from the original subject–object dualism and replicates itself *ad infinitum* through the ego's several efforts to unify the world it itself has divided, is the inevitable consequence of the fateful antagonism between the ego as *abstract monad* and nature. But: the ego is not an abstract monad, at peace with itself. On the contrary, "The reason why the world lacks unity, and lies broken and in heaps, is, because man is disunited with himself " (*N*, 34).

The doubleness, residing in the subject–object dualism, is but a reflection of the structure of the ego itself. The problem of knowledge therefore perfectly coincides with the problem of man. Emerson's solution to this two-sided problem lies in finding a new direction for the ego's thrust toward "dominion." In place of seeking to unify the world it must somehow unify itself. Nature provides useful hints and clues to aid in this effort: "Know then, that the world exists for you"—but not as object, rather as "the perfect phenomenon." Emerson promises an inner dominion "as great as" Adam's and Caesar's. Sense perception remains as central at the conclusion of *Nature* as it was at the beginning, but it has been given a new purpose in so far as the perceiving ego now looks outward only as a necessary gesture toward inner perfection.

"Build, therefore, your own world. As fast as you conform your life to the pure idea in your mind, that will unfold its great proportions. A correspondent revolution in things will attend the influx of the spirit. So fast will disagreeable appearances, swine, spiders, snakes, pests, mad-houses, prisons, enemies, vanish; they are temporary and shall be no more seen. The sordor and filths of nature, the sun shall dry up, and the wind exhale. As when the summer comes from the south, the snow banks melt, and the face of the earth becomes green before it, so shall the advancing spirit create its ornaments along its path, and carry with it the beauty it visits, and the song which enchants it; it shall draw beautiful faces, and warm hearts, and wise discourse, and heroic acts, around its way, until evil is no more seen. The kingdom of man over nature, which cometh not with observation,—a dominion such as now is beyond his dream of God,—he shall enter without more wonder than the blind man feels who is gradually restored to perfect sight." (*N*, 35–36)

In this famous passage, the NOT-ME is miraculously transformed into a beautiful spectacle *without*, however, being subjugated in the process. How can this be? Presumably the divided ego, in conforming itself to its own "pure idea," thereby overcomes its predacity toward nature. In exchange for the ego's renunciation, nature voluntarily presents itself as the object of dominion that the previously divided ego once longed for. It would seem, therefore, that Emerson objects, not to the idea of the "kingdom of man over nature," promised in the final sentence, but to that kingdom's issuing from the union of observation and domination. The kingdom "cometh not" in that way, he insists. Varying the metaphor, we may say the NOT-ME functions in *Nature* as a lover to be wooed but not defiled, as the dialectic of self and nature meanwhile yields lesson after lesson to the watcher man.

This is a significant departure from post-Cartesian idealism. Whereas German Idealism perfected the dialectic of essence and appearance as an abstract expression of reason's freedom, Emerson, at most a superficial Kantian (Wellek 1943, 45), feared the "tyrannizing unity" striven for by the divided ego and, as an antidote, tried to establish what may be called nature's freedom. Emerson in effect rejected the European Enlightenment's ruling assumption of "the disenchantment of the world," Max Weber's phrase for the "liberating demystification of experience," which was a central attribute of Enlightenment thought (Horkheimer and Adorno 1972, 3; Jay 1973, 259). Emerson appears to have seen in this assumption a pretext for unbounded aggression by the ego in its quest for dominion. To Emerson, not the world but the ego itself is disenchanted, a condition that can be alleviated only by its going to school to nature. The essential freedom of nature, and that alone, guarantees man's freedom.

Emerson's rescue of nature from culture is predicated on an insight into the character of abstraction: its inherent tendency toward domination. Emerson would agree with Max Horkheimer and Theodor W. Adorno that "abstraction, the tool of enlightenment, treats its objects as did fate, the notion of which it rejects: it liquidates them." The "leveling domination of abstraction . . . makes everything in nature repeatable," a tendency against which Emerson vigorously protested in the name of the lush plurality of experience. The "distance between subject and object" corresponds to "the distance from the thing itself which the master achieved through the mastered"—a point for which Horkheimer and Adorno are indebted to Hegel's analysis of "Lordship and Bondage" in *The Phenomenology of Mind* and which Emerson appears to have vaguely approached in his critique of the subject-object dualism. The "effects of culture" criticized by Emerson correspond to what Horkheimer and Adorno characterize as Enlightenment. As used by these philosophers, "Enlightenment" refers not only to the period in the history of bourgeois theory bounded by Bacon on one end and by Kant on the other but, more broadly, to western intellectual culture since Homer, whom they regard as the earliest observer of "the divorcement between God and man." Within this "divorcement," the self "awakens"—an awakening "paid for by the acknowledgement of power as the principle of all relations."

The "unity of this *ratio*" of the awakening self and the principle of domination becomes, in Horkheimer and Adorno's view, the philosophical program by which man, in his likeness to God as sovereign lord and master, transforms "myth . . . into enlightenment, and nature into mere objectivity" (Horkheimer and Adorno 1972, 9). Horkheimer and Adorno's critique of Enlightenment's insistence upon unity also resembles Emerson's:

> in advance the Enlightenment recognizes as being and occurrence only what can be apprehended in unity: its ideal is the system from which all and everything follows. Its rationalist and empiricist versions do not part company on that point. . . . Bourgeois society is ruled by equivalence. It makes the dissimilar comparable by reducing it to abstract quantities. To the Enlightenment, that which does not reduce to numbers, and ultimately to the one, becomes illusion; modern positivism writes it off as literature. (Horkheimer and Adorno 1972, 7)

Emerson's thought originates in negativity—in an extraordinarily advanced critique of culture coupled with a defense of nature—inasmuch as it exposes what Horkheimer and Adorno call the self-destruction at the heart of Enlightenment, its hidden alliance with domination, indeed the union of domination and liberation.[2] Nor is Emerson's critique of culture characteristically romantic; it does not reproach "analytical method" and urge a "return to elements." Rather, it makes the same point about culture as the work of Horkheimer and Adorno makes about Enlightenment: in Enlightenment, "the process is always decided from the start." That is, Enlightenment is intrinsically tautological, after the manner of mathematics. The confounding of "thought and mathematics," which leads to the mathematicizing of the world, entails transforming the unknown into the "unknown quantity" of mathematical equations (Horkheimer and Adorno 1972, 24).

But Emerson's remarkable beginning quickly nullifies itself, as the splendid negation turns into that blindness which he valorizes at the end of *Nature* as " 'perfect sight.' " Extremes meet, as Emerson himself once quipped. The private vision he promises his readers, though it in no way threatens either nature or the self with devastating spiritualization, extracts another and higher price: a spiritualization of *social* existence. Stated differently, Emerson's theory of human nature is drawn exclusively from nature, the only "environment of freedom," to recall Poirier's phrase, he could imagine. In the history of western political thought since Aristotle, Emerson's theory of human nature stands as the direct antithesis of the Aristotelian idea that outside human association the individual is either a beast or a god but not a man. Having transferred to nature the mediating and humanizing capacities of human society, Emerson implicitly denies that it is only through the human community that man may become what and who he truly is. In the bosom of nature thus conceived, Emersonian man learns to suppress as merely spurious his own awareness of social facticity (" 'mad-houses, prisons, enemies' "), of social entanglements, an internalized lesson which marks him an anti-social and pre-political being.

Emerson gambled on nature as against culture, society, and politics in *Nature*, but it was only the first of two such gambles, as I shall explain below. In *Nature* Emerson elaborated a theory of human nature in which the self enjoys the splendors of its poetic appropriation of experience, a stance of seeming indifference toward *real* appropriation. The critique of Enlightenment is paid for by the penalty of inaction. Emersonian man remains fixated in a posture of total wonderment before nature, that "fresh green breast of the new world" of which Nick Carroway in *The Great Gatsby* suddenly becomes aware following Gatsby's death:

> Its vanished trees, the trees that had made way for Gatsby's house, had
> once pandered in whispers to the last and greatest of all human dreams;
> for a transitory enchanted moment man must have held his breath in the
> presence of this continent, compelled into an aesthetic contemplation he
> neither understood nor desired, face to face for the last time in history
> with something commensurate with his capacity for wonder. (Fitzgerald
> 1925, 182)

Emersonian man remains in his posture of wonderment—indeed, finds
it an inexhaustible tonic resource, a tailor-made, personal version of
the seemingly boundless frontier—when confronted by social existence
and social calamity. Thus even the virgin timber is thought here to
have cooperated in its own destruction, above which contemplative
Emersonian man hovers, spellbound in his private, blissful, enchanted
moment.

THE WORD OF AMBITION

Emersonian affirmation of nature entails an uncritical and frequently
unconscious acceptance of America. I hasten to add that this acceptance is neither crude nor obvious, as is the case in expressions of cultural chauvinism in, for example, Mason Weems's influential tales,
McGuffey's readers, and popular oratory. In spirit, Emersonian affirmation and acceptance are aspects of literary nationalism in the northeast at mid-century, a movement to which Emerson, Melville, and
other writers and editors contributed and whose pretensions Poe tire-
lessly lambasted in his literary criticism (Miller 1956). Richard Poirier
alludes to these affirmative habits in his characterization of the American writer's predicament:

> The greatest American authors really do try, against the perpetually greater
> power of reality, to create an environment that might allow some longer

existence to the hero's momentary expansions of consciousness. They try even when they are sure of failing, as Hawthorne was; they struggle for years in the face of failure, as Mark Twain did with his finest book, and as Melville did with most of his; and when they succeed, as James sometimes does, it is only that they may then be accused of neglecting the "realities" of sex, economics, or social history. (Poirier 1966, 15)

In other words, there is a tension between the American writer's keen awareness of the overwhelming spaciousness of America, on the one hand, and his extreme commitment to creating through language "environments of freedom" in the domain of consciousness, on the other. Underlying this tension is a subtle harmony between the creation of America, an historical process shrouded in mythology since the time of Columbus, and those images of America's creation which we know as our greatest books. The modernist impulse in American literature, even in its most denunciatory enactments, inexorably validates and perpetuates the American myth.

An argument along similar lines is offered by Sacvan Bercovitch in his study of the American literary appropriation of the revolutionary experience. Noting the "uneasy association of America with revolution," Bercovitch observes that "directly or indirectly the writer converts revolution into the service of society." This attitude toward revolution obtains irrespective of the writer's other social ideas.

Whether the writer focuses, like Thoreau, upon the individual, or like Hawthorne upon history—whether he denounces society, as Melville does, or like Emerson wavers between praise and blame, or like Whitman simply ingests society into the self—the radical energies he celebrates serve to sustain the culture, because the same ideal that releases these energies [the ideal of America] transforms radicalism itself into a mode of cultural cohesion and continuity. (Bercovitch 1976, 599)

It is cohesion and continuity spread over an ever-extending future. American writing is futuristic because it is suffused with the myth of America, the land of the future. Even our conservative writers— Cooper and Hawthorne—are only conservers of John Locke, that is, are liberals, to adapt Louis Hartz's thesis. Like Fitzgerald's Gatsby, the American writer fixes his eye on the green light at the end of Daisy's dock.

This residual endorsement of the future derives from the European and American myth of America, a myth too familiar to require more than a few illustrations here. Probably the most succinct articulation of European expectations of America comes from Locke in the *Second Treatise*: "in the beginning all the world was America," a peaceful state of nature outside time and untainted by money (Locke 1963, 343; sec. 49). To Hegel America also lay outside history, if not time, even as the nineteenth century opened before him:

> If the forests of *Germania* had still existed, there would have been no French Revolution. . . . America is thus the land of the future in which, in times to come, possibly in a fight between North and South America, some world-historical significance is to be revealed.

As Walter Kaufmann has suggested, Hegel seemed to be reserving America's entrance into world history "until the frontier had been conquered" (Kaufmann 1966a, 4). And to Lincoln, in his Annual Message to Congress, December 1, 1862, America was "the last, best hope of earth," a statement belonging, in Sidney Mead's words, to "the American dream of destiny and democracy" (Mead 1963, 74). The myth was still alive in William Carlos Williams' imagination over half a century later in *In the American Grain* (1925). Looking back on the Civil War, Williams noted "the brutalizing desolation of life in America . . . yet perversely flowering," and saw "Lincoln pardoning the fellow who slept on sentry duty . . . , a woman in an old shawl—

with a great bearded face and a towering black hat above it, to give unearthly reality. Failing of relief or expression, the place [America] tormented itself into a convulsion of bewilderment and pain—with a woman, born somehow, aching over it, holding all fearfully together" (Williams 1956, 234).

The obverse of the American myth is disdain for tradition, a theme Emerson announces with fanfare in the first paragraph of *Nature*, where American man is portrayed as "grop[ing] among the dry bones of the past," lacking "an original relation to the universe" (*N*, 5). Unlike Kierkegaard, Marx, and Nietzsche, who revolted against tradition by daring, as Hannah Arendt has said, "to think without the guidance of any authority whatsoever: yet, for better or worse, . . . were still held by the categorical framework of the great tradition" (Arendt 1968, 28), Emerson sought to dispense with tradition altogether in two important respects. The first has been discussed above: namely, Emerson's indictment of "culture" for its transgressions against nature, a radical critique of the traditional relationship between thought and reality. I regard Emerson's insight as the chief, and by no means inconsequential, negative element in American culture which is otherwise mainly affirmative. As I have tried to show, the affirmative strain evolved out of this brief and unsustained insight. Moreover, it is clearly traceable to and congruent with Emerson's effort to throw off tradition in the name of American possibilities.

In Emerson's thought, affirmation of nature was not enough. He went on to mount an ideological assault upon politics and the political. "Every actual State is corrupt," he proclaimed in his essay "Politics" (1841–1843). "What satire on government can equal the severity of censure conveyed in the word *politic*, which now for ages has signified *cunning*, intimating that the State is a trick." But of course the word "politic" has not "for ages . . . signified *cunning*"; only in the liberalist era, itself best characterized as the period in which political things drastically declined in prestige, has it been so regarded.

Hence the manifestly ideological content of Emerson's attack upon politics.

In America all tradition—whether intellectual, social, or political—bows before the pulverizing demands arising from mass social conditions. Perception, cognition, and memory take shape on this shifting ground. Tocqueville was the first to outline this relationship between society and thought:

> Although the revolution that is taking place in the social condition, the laws, the opinions, and the feelings of men is still very far from being terminated, yet its results already admit of no comparison with anything that the world has ever before witnessed. I go back from age to age up to the remotest antiquity; but I find no parallel to what is occurring before my eyes; as the past has ceased to throw its light upon the future the mind of man wanders in obscurity. (Tocqueville 1945, 2:349)

Equal social conditions simultaneously destroy the sense of the past and engender a new social character, a novel way of thinking about one's place in the social scheme of things:

> Among democratic nations new families are constantly springing up, others are constantly falling away, and all that remain change their condition; the woof of time is every instant broken and the track of generations effaced. Those who went before are soon forgotten; of those who will come after, no one has any idea: the interest of man is confined to those in close propinquity to himself. As each class gradually approaches others and mingles with them, its members become undifferentiated and lose their class identity for each other. Aristocracy had made a chain of all the members of the community, from the peasant to the King; democracy breaks that chain and severs every link of it.
>
> As social conditions become more equal, the number of persons increases who, although they are neither rich nor powerful enough to exercise any

great influence over their fellows, have nevertheless acquired or retained sufficient education and fortune to satisfy their own wants. They owe nothing to any man, they expect nothing from any man; they acquire the habit of always considering themselves as standing alone, and they are apt to imagine that their whole destiny is in their own hands.

Thus not only does democracy make every man forget his ancestors, but it hides his descendents and separates his contemporaries from him; it throws him back forever upon himself alone and threatens in the end to confine him entirely within the solitude of his own heart. (Tocqueville 1945, 2:105–6)

The principal contradiction within the mass society—isolation amid great numbers, atomization spewing forth from solidarity, community forever elusive—fills men with illusions of self-sufficiency, myths of the masterless man.

Thinking, says Hannah Arendt, opens a gap in indifferent time, and "only insofar as he thinks, and that is insofar as he is ageless . . . does man in the full actuality of his concrete being live in this gap between past and future."

The trouble, however, is that we seem to be neither equipped nor prepared for this activity of thinking, of settling down in the gap between past and future. For very long times in our history, actually throughout the thousands of years that followed upon the foundation of Rome and were determined by Roman concepts, this gap was bridged over by what, since the Romans, we have called tradition. That this tradition has worn thinner as the modern age progressed is a secret to nobody. When the thread of tradition finally broke [in the early twentieth century], the gap between past and future ceased to be a condition peculiar only to the activity of thought and restricted as an experience to those few who made thinking their primary business. It became a tangible reality and perplexity for all; that is, it became a fact of political relevance. (Arendt 1968, 13–14)

If anyone in American literature or philosophy made thinking his "primary business," it was Emerson. But for Emerson neither thinking nor any other human activity opens a gap in time, unless it is the gap between the present and the future. Not tradition but thinking itself bridges *this* gap. Thus for Emerson tradition has not worn thin; it simply has not worn at all. Thinking *confers* "agelessness" rather than, as in Arendt's analysis, proceeding from it or expressing it. Moreover, "So far as a man thinks, he is free," Emerson writes in his essay "Fate" (1851; 1860), echoing the doctrine of Man Thinking first articulated in "The American Scholar" (1837) and again in "Self-Reliance" (1841) (*Works* 6:23). For Emerson, freedom is contingent upon thought. Thought, in turn, thinks of itself as a mode of praxis, even as it disdains praxis. Thought, in other words, is instrumental, and to think is to experiment, as he says in "Circles": "No facts are to me sacred; none are profane; I simply experiment, an endless seeker with no past at my back" (*Works* 2:318).

Not the activity of thinking but the fact of America itself, its sheer novelty in human history, is what divides past from future; but—and this is the crucial point—it is America's novel capacity for dynamic renewal that causes the past to be obliterated at the very moment of its inception, "the woof of time . . . [to be] every instant broken," in Tocqueville's words. Not for long does the "mind of [Emersonian] man wander in obscurity" under these conditions, for it is immediately driven back upon itself in a desperate affirmation of inner freedom. The political category of freedom is therewith absorbed into the self, true to the pattern of American writing, but with this difference: it is offered in this internalized form by Emerson as a solution to public problems. That is, freedom is first shorn of its distinctively political meaning and then, under faintly Hegelian guise as the fulfillment of consciousness, it re-emerges in Emerson's thought as the idealization of American public life. By the time the thread of tradition finally snapped in the twentieth-century European mind, Emersonianism it-self had become an American tradition of thought and practice.

The idea of public happiness—that "treasure" of modern revolutions which Arendt argues is always lost because tradition is so weak in the modern age that it no longer names, selects, preserves, and foretells the appearance of the treasure—is not lost to Emerson but, more sig-nificantly, is seized and transformed. It is deprived of its political meaning. A new idea of culture, reinvigorated by his defense of na-ture, emerges in Emerson's later essays as the model for the redefini-tion of public life in America. Culture displaces politics as the vehicle for the realization of public happiness. Whereas Locke had despaired of the existence of a rational ethic, or natural law, accessible to the majority of men, Emerson is prepared through his defense of nature to affirm its existence unconditionally. Emerson turns Locke's defeat into a victory: he turns English liberalism on its head. At the heart of his victory lies the basic contradiction in the liberal tradition in politi-cal theory from Locke through Herbert Spencer: the assumption that political theory could dispense with a concept of the political. But whereas English liberals attempted to substitute social-economic activ-ity, under the aegis of the market mechanism, for political activity, Emerson endeavors to substitute culture for both politics and society, the latter especially odious because it is, as he says in "Self-Reliance," "everywhere . . . in conspiracy against the manhood of every one of its members" (Wolin 1960, 286–305; *Works* 2:50).

Emerson's well-known contempt for the leveling tendencies of de-mocracy, though vaguely Tocquevillean in spirit, contrasts radically with Tocqueville's solution to the dilemma of early democratic man. Equality for Tocqueville is not only the name of the new social condi-tion; it also designates one pole of a dialectic, the other pole being po-litical freedom. Action in the world by free men was still a possibility in democratic society, Tocqueville argued. Civility, threatened by the radical privatizing tendencies of mass society, could nevertheless reasonably be expected to take a democratic form—hence Tocqueville's peculiar ambivalence about democracy. Emerson's profoundly anti-political imagination could only apprehend the "riot of mediocrities" in trade and politics. Shortly after a visit to the Midwest, he wrote to Carlyle on April 19, 1853:

> The Prairie exists to yield the greatest possible quantity of adipocere. For corn makes pig, pig is the export of all the land, & you shall see the distant dependence of aristocracy and civility on the fat four-legs. Workingmen, ability to do the work of the River [Mississippi], abounded, nothing higher was to be thought of. America is incomplete. Room for us all, since it has not ended, nor given a sign of ending, in bard or hero. Tis a wild democracy, a riot of mediocrities, & none of your selfish Italies and Englands, where an age sublimates into a genius, and a whole population is made into paddies to feed his porcelain veins, by transfusion from their brick arteries. Our few fine persons are apt to die. (Slater 1964, 486)

As this passage suggests, Emerson's ambivalence about democracy centered not on the possibilities of civility but on the negative example of an age "sublimating" into genius, as in Europe, resulting in something "higher" than greater and greater yields of "adipocere." Emerson's ambition was to find a way of producing something "higher" for the many and not, as the history of Europe showed, just for the few. That is, the collapse of tradition which he himself encouraged, became, in Arendt's terms, "a tangible reality and perplexity for all . . . [,] a fact of political relevance." But politics in America offered little more than "a new version of Oxinstiern's little wit [paucity of wisdom governing political life]," as he had written to Carlyle sixteen years earlier (March 31, 1837), and New England town meetings at best dealt only with local economic issues (Slater 1964, 162). Jeffersonian localism and agrarianism provided no solution to what Emerson

believed was a national crisis, no program for "the conduct of life."
Culture provided the solution.

What is culture? In *The Conduct of Life*, culture is the mechanism for
"cultivating" what Emerson called in his essay "Fate" "the double
consciousness." By means of the double consciousness man solves the
problem of Fate and Freedom, "the mysteries of the human condition" (*Works* 6:47; cf. 1:353). "Fate is the freedom of man," and
"though we know not how, necessity does comport with liberty"
(*Works* 6:23, 4). The double consciousness grasps these paradoxes and
resolves them naturalistically: freedom is to fate as "pusher" is to
"pushed" (*Works* 6:43). That is, nature stands behind the double consciousness, setting the boundaries of its motions and dictating its conclusions in advance.

As an abstract proposition, the notion that "fate is the freedom of
man" is straight Kantianism: freedom means freedom under the rule
of coercive law. Kantian ethics, in turn, only secularized the Christian
conception of inner freedom developed by Luther and Calvin, substi-
tuting secular bourgeois authority, the source of outer coercion, for
their idea of divinely ordained earthly authority. Continuing into
Kant's ethics, however, is the anti-authoritarianism of the Christian
idea of freedom, its transcendental rejection of all earthly authority.
To this notion Emerson's earlier doctrine of self-reliance bears close
resemblance, especially in so far as both Emerson and Kant regarded
mere social conformity as a form of self-inflicted punishment, for
which Emerson prescribed self-reliance as the corrective. But the anti-
authoritarian strain is mitigated in Kant's ethics; for, although "the
public use of man's reason must always be free," by "public" Kant
means the world of learning and ideas: "By the public use of one's
own reason I mean that use which anyone may make of it as a man of
learning addressing the entire reading public." Thus the link between
inner freedom and outer authority is maintained in new form, and, as
Herbert Marcuse says, Kant's " 'intellectual world' is given the ap-

pearance of being actually public and free but is separated from public and free action, from real social praxis" (Marcuse 1972, 81, 80–94). This perfectly describes the world of culture that Emerson advocates as the replacement for politics.

The mechanism of culture's authoritative discipline, the double-consciousness, reverses Emerson's earlier notion of the ego as an entity divided against itself and thereby the subjective source of nature's fundamental adversary, the subject-object dualism. The idea of the double-consciousness in effect negates the critique of culture and prepares the way for the reinstatement of culture. Unity, heretofore condemned as "tyrannical," becomes "Blessed Unity" in the essay "Fate," the idol to which man is urged to "build altars." The multiplicity of experience is subjugated in the interests of "the Blessed Unity which holds nature and souls in perfect solution." A bland and repressive reconciliation settles over all: "Let us build to the Beautiful Necessity, which secures that all is made of one piece; the plaintiff and defendant, friend and enemy, animal and planet [sic], food and eater are of one kind" (*Works* 6:48–49). In return for this falsification of experience, Emerson promises "the infinitude of the private man," a multitude of private visions conceived as boundless self-development.

Mankind is sick. Egotism abounds, for "it is a disease that like influenza falls on all constitutions," Emerson says in "Culture." Egotism is "a metaphysical variety" of the malady known as chorea, which causes some of its victims to "spin slowly on one spot." "Sufferers parade their miseries, tear the lint from their bruises, reveal their indictable crimes, that you may pity them": extreme selfishness thus is self-perpetuating, instilling in the "private person a high conceit of his weight in the system." But "this goitre of egotism is so frequent among notable persons we must infer some strong necessity in nature which it subserves; such as we see in the sexual attraction." Emerson concludes that "egotism has its root in the cardinal necessity by which each individual persists to be what he is." In other words, though

egotists are "the pests of society," egotism shares a common root in
nature and necessity with individualism and therefore requires a cure
that eliminates the disease while preserving its always beneficent natural origins. The "private person" must be taught, not the origins or
limits of his privateness, but the means of perfecting and extending it
(*Works* 6:132–34).

Culture provides this means, for it is a form of tutelage issuing
from nature; culture is simply a generalized version of nature's lesson
of individuality. A "secular melioration by which mankind is molli-
fied, cured, and refined," culture consists of the development and use
of higher faculties, such as those involved in reading good books, in
travel and social contact with people of merit, in music, eloquence,
and philosophy (*Works* 6:165). Culture cures narrowness, whatever its
origin, and the timing of its curative effects is always right: some children come to books later than do others.

Culture enables the city dweller to overcome his pseudo-
sophistication ("New York is a sucked orange," complains Emerson)
and the country boy, through the advantage of railroad, which puts
him within reach of faraway places, to "have *some chance*" (*Works*
6:146). The ideal place of residence of the cultured individual is what
today would be called a suburb, where he may take advantage of both
small-town solitude and urban variety. One imagines that what Emerson has in mind here as a model suburb is Concord, Massachusetts.
As a cure for provincialism, including urban "provincialism," culture
tends to be a nationalizing, universalizing, and suburbanizing force.

Culture inculcates a bourgeois moral style and an ethic of deferred
gratification:

> There is a great deal of self-denial and manliness in poor and middle-class
> houses in town and country, that has not got into literature and never will,
> but keeps the earth sweet; that saves on superfluities and spends on essen-
> tials; that goes rusty and educates the boy; that sells the horse but builds the

school; works early and late, takes two looms in the factory, three looms, six looms, but pays off the mortgage on the paternal farm, and then goes back cheerfully to work again. (*Works* 6:155)

The end of this ethic is the ideal of individual "self-subsistency" and "self-possession" (*Works* 6:163, 159). At the same time, however, the highest end of culture is not personality but the transformation of personality (presumably always threatening to lapse into egotism) into "channels of power" (*Works* 6:162). Indeed,

> Man's culture can spare nothing, wants all the material. He is to convert all impediments into instruments, all enemies into power. The formidable mischief will only make the more useful slave. And if one shall read the future of the race hinted in the organic effort of nature to mount and meliorate, and the corresponding impulse to the better in the human being, we shall dare affirm that there is nothing he will not overcome and convert, until at last culture shall absorb the chaos and gehenna. He will convert the Furies into Muses, and the hells into benefit. (*Works* 6:166)

Culture is truly "the word of ambition."

Emersonian culture pretends to generate *power.* But by "power," traditionally a distinctively political category, Emerson does not mean political power, though he most emphatically does mean a human capacity or performance having public significance—that is, political significance.[3] Emerson appears to be envisioning a non-political, even anti-political, public realm. Culture is the mechanism that will operate in place of politics in this realm, and culture is synonymous with education.

> Let us make our education brave and preventive. Politics is after-work, a poor patching. We are always a little late. The evil is done, the law is passed, and we begin the uphill agitation for repeal of that which we ought

to have prevented the enacting. *We shall one day learn to supersede politics by education.* What we call our root-and-branch reforms, of slavery, war, gambling, intemperance, is only medicating the symptoms. We must begin higher up, namely in Education. (*Works* 6:140–41)

Culture, formerly the dreaded enemy of nature, becomes in Emerson's later essays the substitute for politics—becomes in effect what Sheldon Wolin would call the sublimation of politics (Wolin 1960, ch. 10). In place of an *age* sublimating into individual genius, after the European manner described by Emerson in his letter to Carlyle, in America politics should sublimate into culture. In this way, "our few fine persons" might be saved, while the cloddish many were being schooled. The Emersonian public realm is now the setting for the activities of the double consciousness. Politics, trade, and other practical activities lack "value" until infused by culture—that is, until "from higher influx" they are given "intellectual quality" (*Works* 6:158, 160). Mind supplants politics. It would be a national gesture rebuking "Oxenstiern's little-wit."

Nor by "education" does Emerson mean "political education," for, as this passage indicates, what he anticipates is the actual supersession of politics. As that human performance whose outcome is at once the least predictable and most fragile, politics is inadequate.[4] This is perhaps the more so when politics is narrowed to reformism, as is suggested by Emerson's examples here, for political reformism is highly aspirational and its consequences, to temperaments that expect definitive results, always disappointing. The disappointment is tempered if, as Emerson wrote in his journal in 1839, "we learn to treat everything . . . poetically,—law, politics, housekeeping, money," for "all human affairs need the perpetual intervention of this elastic principle" (*Journals* 7:329). But to poetize politics is to convert it into a species of mind, to render it unto Man Thinking. The elevation of Emerson's self-reliant, cultured individuals into the public realm is, by Emerson's own admission, tantamount to the triumph of impotence, of inactivity. "And must I go and do somewhat [sic] if I would learn new secrets of self-reliance?" he asks in his journal for October 23, 1840. He answers no. "But self-reliance is precisely this secret,—to make your supposed deficiency redundancy. If I am true, the theory is the very want of action, my very impotency, shall become a greater excellency than all skill and toil" (Emerson 1957, 146).

Emersonian culture, or education writ large, belongs to the history of Americanization and social control. It presumes to make individuals out of mass men by teaching them self-reliance; it also tames and civilizes them. In the essay "Considerations by the Way," Emerson announces his hardheaded approach to the problem of mass society:

> Leave this hypocritical prating about the masses. Masses are rude, lame, unmade, pernicious in their demands and influence, and need not to be flattered but to be schooled. I wish not to concede anything to them, but to tame, drill, divide and break them up, and draw individuals out of them. The worst of charity is that the lives you are asked to preserve are not worth preserving. Masses! The calamity is the masses. I do not wish any mass at all, but honest men only, lovely, sweet, accomplished women only, and no shovel-handed, narrow-brained, gin-drinking million stockingers or lazzaroni at all. If government knew how, I should like to see it check, not multiply the population. When it reaches its true law of action, every man that is born will be hailed as essential. Away with this hurrah of the masses, and let us have the considerate vote of single men spoken on their honor and their conscience. (*Works* 6:249)

The manipulativeness at the center of Emerson's doctrine of culture only fully reveals itself in moments when, as here, Emerson relaxed his own posture of sheer wonderment and gazed steadily and directly at the tumultuous social world of his own time. Here was a spectacle that called, not for wonder, but for "didactics" (contrary to his professed aims at the outset of "Considerations by the Way"). Beginning in the 1830s and continuing until 1860, the first of three distinct periods of unrestricted European immigration, millions of northern and western European peoples entered the United States, the peak years in this first period being 1847–1854 (Hansen 1961, 9–10). In this passage from Emerson is a message repeated to them innumerable times. That the European peasantry flooding into America between 1820 and the close of unrestricted immigration by Congressional action in the laws of 1921 and 1924 did not consist of "individuals" but, to Emerson's way of thinking, amounted to a "calamity" only testifies to his class prejudice and ethnocentrism, which he covers over (but only barely) with the language of education and uplift. To Emerson, "all great men come out of the middle classes" (*Works* 6:259). Like the activist social reformers around him, to whom Emerson is often misleadingly contrasted in order that his alleged "social irresponsibility" may be highlighted, Emerson saw himself as a minister to the heathen, an apostle armed with a doctrine of culture for rehabilitating the masses—that is, for "Americanizing" them.[5]

Sacvan Bercovitch has claimed that nineteenth-century American intellectuals redefined the term "middle-class" in such a way that it ceased to be a class tag at all and became a term for a moral outlook (Bercovitch 1976, 610). This claim will not survive scrutiny. Moral outlooks are themselves the articulated, rationalized expressions of social life. In Emerson's case, it is true, the moral outlook he advocates (his doctrine of culture) is overweening, especially in *The Conduct of Life*, but it is never separable from his social perception. Emersonian moralism is undergirded and frequently stimulated into eloquence by the facts of social life. As perceived by Emerson and other representatives of what Stow Persons calls the American gentry, social life in the nineteenth century was composed of a sprawling mass surrounded by various functional elites, among them the gentry itself. From about the middle of the century on, the gentry felt increasingly beleaguered, as it witnessed the repeated rejection of gentry values by the mass of Americans. As I remarked at the outset, whereas Matthew Arnold could readily identify his social and cultural opponent in class terms, Emerson and his fellow gentlemen were confronted with a much more amorphous social and cultural entity. Perhaps because this was so, twentieth-century commentators like Bercovitch infer that "middle-class" lacked social significance in Emerson's day. Emerson himself, however, well understood the social basis of morality, even if in pointing it out he lacked the precision of an Arnold. There are but two classes of men, Emerson declared: "benefactors and malefactors." He explained that this moral distinction directly corresponds to the immediately apparent social division in America, that between the minority and the majority. Upon making this observation, he was incurious to look more closely at the social world and impatient to get to the vital question of judgment. "Shall we then judge a country by the majority, or by the minority? By the minority, surely" (*Works* 6:248–49). To judge America by the majority in the 1850s was to validate in "the common experience . . . a poor and squalid . . . habit of thought" (*Works* 6:271). The mass is animalistic until and unless redeemed by Emersonian culture. "The mass are animal, in pupilage, and near chimpanzee," but its individual members are "neuters" and are susceptible of cultivation (*Works* 6:251–52).

EMERSON IN THAW

Newton Arvin once attempted to defend Emerson against Yeats's charge that he lacked a "vision of evil" by elucidating the polarity in Emerson's thought between optimism and pessimism, between his extraordinary celebration of human potentiality and his tough-minded insistence upon human limitations (Arvin 1967, 16–38). My aim has not been to re-open this debate; indeed, I find it hard to believe that Yeats's claim, or any other declaring Emerson to be a fatuous optimist, ever was taken seriously by those familiar with his writings. I have sought instead to get beyond this issue by sketching the history of Emerson's ideas of nature, culture, and politics. This history shows that "optimistic" and "pessimistic" (or any other handy tags) do not adequately characterize Emerson's thought; Emerson's definition of man eludes these frozen categories. Such "familiar rubrics of Emersonian thought, the stock in trade of most Emerson criticism," as Joel Porte has written, "though undeniably there, are a positive hindrance to the enjoyment of Emerson's writing" (Barbour and Quirk 1986, 65). They are also a hindrance to understanding it, unless, that is, they are thawed out and poured back into the still-flowing stream of Emerson's thought. Thus, the evidence of "naturalistic pessimism" which Arvin finds in the essay "Fate" does not so much refute Yeats's charge as open up a new issue, which I have examined in these pages (Arvin 1968, 26). And, though I agree with Stephen E. Whicher's characterization of Emerson as a divided man, holding "both to faith and to experience," I disagree that Emerson's remark,

> A believer in Unity, a seer of Unity, I yet behold two,

"epitomizes his intellectual position" (Whicher 1953, 32–33). Emerson's views can only be historicized, not epitomized. To distill them into essences is to miss the twisting inner logic by which doctrines of self-culture evolve into a public philosophy for the anti-political conduct of life.

All his life Emerson thought that we can get by without politics. Nature, after all, guarantees human freedom. The folly of this project is instructive, for there is perhaps no more definitive demonstration of the intrinsically democratic content of the political than Emerson's own longing for better and better modes of social control. If, as George M. Fredrickson has argued, Emerson "lost his contempt for the masses and for crowds of all kinds" when he witnessed the "post-

Sumpter 'whirlwind of patriotism' which was 'magnetizing all discordant masses under its terrific unity,' " it was precisely the idea of that "terrific unity" and not the masses which fired his imagination (Fredrickson 1968, 66). This point is missed, however, if one comes to Emerson thinking he was a harmless visionary given to occasional curmudgeonly expressions of contempt for the lower classes when he ought to have been meeting his social responsibilities as a political actor. The "anti-individualistic tendency of his later thought," brought into the open by the Civil War, did not, contrary to Fredrickson's claim, signify a new social responsibility so much as another move in the Emersonian game of the spirit, a clever gesture toward social control appearing as a token of new-found social responsibility (Fredrickson 1968, 177).

But if Emerson's hopeful mind does not belong to the benign sweet face of the (literary) figure in the American pantheon, neither is it the intelligence of some mythical arch-enemy of American democracy. Emerson, in my account, is much more interesting than any political villain. He is a philosopher whose idealist gyrations led him to the edge of a world in the making: our own world. That he partly approved of means for ridding that world of its riot of mediocrities, its calamitous masses and massive calamities, only puts him in our own quite familiar company. That he had no answer to the riddle of democracy but instead contributed to the deepening of it is, finally, one measure of his stature as a political thinker *malgré lui*.

I have argued that Emerson's unification of "eater" and "eaten" is inextricably connected with his promise of sublime inwardness for each man. Earlier, I showed that Emerson's views of nature and man originate in a critique of culture, thought to be nature's adversary, only to eventuate in the re-instatement of culture as nature's new ally. "The infinitude of the private man" becomes in the course of this intellectual development the basis of the good and, through the mechanism of culture as defined in his later work, of civility itself.

"Come Forth, Sweet Democratic Despots of the West!": Whitman's *Democratic Vistas*

The whole earth, this cold, impassive, voiceless earth, shall be completely justified. . . .

WALT WHITMAN, "Passage to India" (1871)

Whitman's *Democratic Vistas* (1871) is the quintessential fantasy of the would-be democratic man of letters. It is at once stridently critical of mass industrial society in the period following the Civil War and extravagantly hopeful about that society's future. The desperate tone of *Democratic Vistas* expresses this tension: the more cowardly, mean, puerile, and wasteful American life appears to Whitman as his analysis in this book unfolds, the more unconditionally he asserts his personal remedy for American ills. First articulated in the Preface to the 1855 edition of *Leaves of Grass*, his remedy calls for the creation of a national literature commensurate in spirit with the American promise. To an even greater degree than the Preface, however, *Democratic Vistas* discloses Whitman's democratic commitments and more than hints at their political implications. In this book he reveals a subtle understanding of the universalizing, expansionist, and imperialist strains in the American democratic principle.

That Whitman not only sees this aspect of the democratic idea but enthusiastically endorses it as the ideal solution to American and world problems is perhaps to be construed as nothing more than a harmless foible, an idiosyncrasy of the artist which it would be absurd to take seriously. Such an interpretation, though faithful to Whitman the poet, ignores two facts about Whitman's life and work. First, it forgets that as an editorial writer for the *Brooklyn Daily Eagle* during the forties Whitman embraced a radical expansionist position on the Mexican War. In an editorial for September 23, 1847, for instance, he argued vigorously, and with the same fidelity to the logic of his democratic beliefs as one finds in *Democratic Vistas*, for a large-scale invasion of Mexico as a means of democratizing the country and bringing peace to the region (Graebner 1968, 207–9). Second, the apologetic interpretation overlooks the most striking feature of *Democratic Vistas*: its distinctive tone, the tone of Whitman the poet and ex-politico turned social critic, which expresses, in an elaborate oxymoron, denunciation conjoined with regeneration on nearly every page.

Through a clear three-part structure, *Democratic Vistas* articulates three interrelated theories of American civilization: a political theory, a theory of history, and a literary theory. The political theory with which it opens serves Whitman as the vehicle for stating the central problem left him by Carlyle's vitriolic attack on democracy in "Shooting Niagara: and After?" (1867). Political theory gives way to a theory of history, as the author lays the groundwork for his idea of historical transcendence, leading to the fulfillment of the democratic promise. Finally, Whitman articulates in detail his theory of literature, the soul of democracy, which will supervise the forthcoming era of Personalism, a period of world domination stretching indefinitely into the future. If the individual body caged the individual soul in Christian theology, the projected soul of Whitman's democracy rules the *body politic,* taking its form and content from the literary imagination. *Democratic Vistas,* a re-invention of America like most of our best books, invents a soul for the nation. The condemned man of European systems of punishment was already a fully formed object of discipline, as Foucault has written, an *effect* of the soul "in" him, which functioned like the prison guard of the body (Foucault 1979, 29–30). The citizens of Whitman's fantasized future America would comprise a body politic supervised by a literary soul.

POLITICAL THEORY

"We have founded for us the most positive of lands," Whitman says. "The founders have passed to other spheres—but what are these terrible duties they have left us?" Note the complex tone of this passage. America, "the most positive of lands," now only fills the author with a sense of loss, of historical discontinuity, and of "terrible" obligation, all of which creates in *Democratic Vistas* an atmosphere of desperation and confusion.[1] The ambiguous tone indirectly points to a purpose in *Democratic Vistas* other than or in addition to the ostensible one. As the reference to John Stuart Mill on the first page indicates, *Democratic Vistas* seems in substance to be a statement of rather conventional liberal tenets, chief of which is the belief in the supremacy of the individual. But, unlike the liberal political thinkers from Locke through the framers of the American Constitution and the post-revolutionary French intellectuals, Whitman, the text shows, was moved by events to follow what Sheldon Wolin calls the "architectonic impulse," the "impulse toward mastery" awakened in political thinkers during times of "crisis," which "seeks creative release in drawing plans for the ordering of a disordered world" (Wolin 1960, 294–95).

The American history of the architectonic impulse may be sketched in the following way. Prior to the early nineteenth century, liberalism was as much a "defense against radical democracy" as it was the "fighting creed" it is usually believed to have been. "In the early years of the American republic," Wolin shows in *Politics and Vision*, "liberal writers sought a substitute object for the patriotic and political impulses fostered by the ideas and events of the revolutionary war. The Constitution served their purpose, and they succeeded in surrounding it with a wealth of legend and symbol so that in the end the 'myth' of 1789 overcame that of 1776" (Wolin 1960, 294). The architectonic impulse was effectively negated between 1776 and 1789, as the Constitutional tradition in political theory provided no concept of political action. Since its inception in the seventeenth century and especially in the work of the American Founding Fathers, this tradition has extolled "social order, procedural rationality, and the material bases of political association," in short, has been "abstract and systematic in temper," according to Norman Jacobson. The United States Constitution has served the citizenry as the chief instrument of political education, but the "prescriptive theory" it offers has often been at odds with the facts of American political life (Jacobson 1963, 561). At the root of this conflict between political theory and political life is the failure of the Constitutional tradition to provide a concept of political action. In this tradition political action tends to be sublimated, leaving a residue consisting, according to Kirk Thompson, of the following elements: (a) "a science of politics," which seeks the "causes of political phenomena rather than the reasons for political action"; (b) a definition of "the state as a product of artifice" designed "to contain the political life of subsequent generations"; (c) a view of the polity as an "impersonal object" rather than as "a human community"; and (d) a "politics of economic interest" (Thompson 1969, 656–57).

By the mid-nineteenth century, the drive for mastery, though stilled in political thinkers, manifested itself in the literati, in particular Emerson and Whitman, as they witnessed the oddly American spectacle of disorder amid order, of unprecedented social mobility and fluidity overlain by the "myth of 1789." The search for a "substitute object for patriotic and political impulses" (Wolin 1960, 294) became, in Emerson, a search for a substitute for politics itself, leading to a suggested re-definition of American public life. But in Whitman, a more thoroughgoing democrat than Emerson, the search took a different turn. His belief in the individual was as extreme as Emerson's, but his desire for mastery was more focused and intense. Of one thing he was certain at the opening of his pamphlet: "America" and "democracy" are "convertible terms" (*PW*, 363). With this premise the way was clear for him to find his own "formula for controlling the dynamics of change" (Wolin 1960, 294), one that was liberal but not defensive. This was no time for a second American counter-revolution but rather a time for a radical purification of democracy.

Universal suffrage, Whitman wrote, is hardly the solution to the problems of the day but, as Carlyle had said, a manifestation of those problems. "I will not gloss over the appalling dangers of universal suffrage in the United States," Whitman promises. "In fact, it is to admit and face these dangers that I am writing" (*PW*, 363). But Whitman fails to make good on this promise: nowhere in *Democratic Vistas* does he identify any such "dangers." Whereas Carlyle wrote angrily about the perils of democracy on the occasion of the passage of the 1867 Reform Bill, which radically extended the suffrage in England, Whitman in *Democratic Vistas* was actually addressing, not any comparable development in America, but the general social life of masses and oligarchic elites sullying the democratic fabric. Politics, including "the popular superficial suffrage," is neither to be blamed for the problems of the republic nor looked to for their solution (*PW*, 365). On the other hand, unlike Emerson, Whitman did not discredit politics and the political, though he did warn against political parties, which he hated and which, moreover, he believed America had "outgrown" (Fredrickson 1968, 21). He warned just as strongly against "dilettanti and fops" who "decry the whole formulation of the active politics of America"; "America, it may be, is doing very well upon the whole," and "it is the dilettanti, and all who shirk their duty, who are not doing well" (*PW*, 399). However that might be, the main point is that Whitman's response to Carlyle's critique of universal suffrage is ostensible only, not real, for he has his eye fixed on a different object in the American social landscape. Whitman would have understood the paradox of capitalism, as analyzed by Marx: if the world suffers from the development of capitalism, it suffers just as much for the under-development of capitalism. So too, Whitman might have said, for democracy in America.

Democracy will never come to fruition until Americans shed their "prevailing delusion"

> that the establishment of free political institutions, and plentiful intellectual smartness, with general good order, physical plenty, industry, etc. (desirable and precious advantages as they all are), do, of themselves, determine and yield to our experiment of democracy the fruitage of success. With such advantages at present fully, or almost fully, possessed—the Union just issued, victorious, from the struggle with the only foe it need ever fear (namely, those within itself, the interior ones), and with unprecedented materialistic advancement—society, in these States, is canker'd, crude, superstitious and rotten. Political, or law-made society is, and private, or voluntary society is also. (*PW*, 369)

In other words, the problem worrying Whitman is not the politically rooted one of universal suffrage but the broader, social problem created by emerging mass conditions. Like Emerson in his essay "Fate," Whitman imagines himself to be a "physician diagnosing some deep disease."

> Never was there, perhaps, more hollowness at heart than at present, and here in the United States. Genuine belief seems to have left us. The underlying principles of the States are not honestly believ'd in (for all this hectic

glow, and these melodramatic screamings), nor is humanity itself believ'd in. What penetrating eye does not everywhere see through the mask? The spectacle is appaling [sic]. We live in an atmosphere of hypocrisy throughout. The men believe not in the women, nor the women in the men. A scornful superciliousness rules in literature. The aim of all the *littérateurs* is to find something to make fun of. A lot of churches, sects, etc., the most dismal phantasms I know, usurp the name of religion. Conversation is a mass of badinage. From deceit in the spirit, the mother of all false deeds, the offspring is already incalculable. . . . The depravity of the business classes in our country is not less than has been supposed, but infinitely greater. The official services of America, national, state, and municipal in all their branches and departments, except the judiciary, are saturated in corruption, bribery, falsehood, maladministration; and the judiciary is tainted. The great cities reek with respectable as much as non-respectable robbery and scoundrelism. In fashionable life, flippancy, tepid amours, weak infidelism, small aims, and no aims at all, only to kill time. In business (this all-devouring word, business), the one sole object is, by any means, pecuniary gain. The magician's serpent in the fable ate the other serpents; and money-making is our magician's serpent, remaining today sole master of the field. The best class we show, is but a mob of fashionably dress'd speculators and vulgarians. (*PW*, 369–70)

Blistering, impressionistic, righteously indignant, apocalyptic: Whitman's indictment of post–Civil War America would spare the democratic idea, as he understands it. But how to spare that idea when the reality with which the author himself identifies the sacred idea is so cankerous? Whitman obviously feels this dilemma, but he is unable to rise above it. It is this problem, originating in the attractive but politically premature linguistic union of "America" and "democratic" ("convertible terms"), that shadows *Democratic Vistas* and its nearly disillusioned author.

Whitman's positive political principle, or theory of democratic man, holds that "man, properly trained in sanest, highest freedom, may and must become a law, a series of laws, unto himself . . . " (*PW*, 375). The purpose of political association is to create democratic community by teaching men "to rule themselves" (*PW*, 380). Whitman calls this purpose the "ulterior object" of politics: "to open up to cultivation, to encourage the possibilities of all beneficent and manly out-croppage, and of that aspiration for independence, and the pride and self-respect latent in all characters" (*PW*, 379). Gay Wilson Allen has suggested that such statements in *Democratic Vistas* show Whitman's belief that democracy is not so much a political system as an ongoing experiment "for the development of individuals" (Allen 1955, 389). This is an accurate characterization of Whitman's observation of democracy in practice. "Political democracy, as it exists and practically works in America," he wrote, "with all its threatening evils, supplies a training school for making first-class men" (*PW*, 385). But Whitman had his eye on the future as well as on the present and was determined to prepare America for it by taking full account in his theory of the new mass social conditions. Thus in the last analysis he based his democratic precepts neither on a romantic glorification of the "People, the masses . . . nor [on] the ground of their rights; but [held] that good or bad, rights or no rights, the democratic formula is the only safe and preservative one for coming times" (*PW*, 380–81).

THEORY OF HISTORY

History, in Whitman's view, is thoroughly teleological. Its central purpose, however, has not always been known but has come to light only with the creation of America. All prior human experience and achievement await the outcome of the American experiment for their final valuation; world history fulfills itself in the triumph of American democracy. To Whitman, as to Hegel, Marx, Comte, Veblen, Turner, and others, historical development proceeds through stages. The central problem of history accordingly concerns the origins, mechanism, and meaning of each transition. History conceived in this way displays a process character, which in *Democratic Vistas* is conveyed through metaphors of gestation. The "present is but the legitimate birth of the past," says Whitman, and the future—which shall belong to America—is "a copious, sane, gigantic offspring" of the present (*PW*, 362). But the present—the American, democratic present—is utterly degenerate as well as "legitimate," and the future consequently could be still-born. Whitman's vehement critique identifies two alternatives: America will either "surmount the gorgeous history of feudalism, or else prove the most tremendous failure of time" (*PW*, 363).

Whitman's theory of history posits three stages: (a) the pre-American, feudal "ecclesiastical, dynastic world," encompassing ancient and medieval civilizations both east and west; (b) the American or modern and increasingly democratic, materialistic stage; and (c) the spiritualized democratic and imperial future stage (*PW*, 366, 363). Seen from the vantage of the self-fulfilling democratic principle, these three stages appear to Whitman to be linked together:

> I submit, therefore, that the fruition of democracy, on aught like a grand scale, resides altogether in the future. As, under any profound and comprehensive view of the gorgeous-composite feudal world, we see in it, through the long ages and cycles of ages, the results of a deep, integral, human and divine principle, or fountain, from which issued laws, ecclesia, manners, institutes, costumes, personalities, poems (hitherto unequall'd), faithfully partaking of their source, and indeed only arising either to betoken it, or to furnish parts of that varied-flowing display, whose centre was one and absolute—so, long ages hence, shall the due historian or critic make at least an equal retrospect, and equal history for the democratic principle. It too must be adorn'd, credited with its results—then, when it, with imperial power, through amplest time, has dominated mankind—has been the source and test of all the moral, aesthetic, social, political, and religious expressions and

institutes of the civilized world—has begotten them in spirit and in form, and has carried them to its own unprecedented heights—has had (it is possible) monastics and ascetics, more numerous, more devout than the monks and priests of all previous creeds—has sway'd the ages with a breadth and rectitude tallying Nature's own—has fashion'd, systematized, and triumphantly finish'd and carried out, in its own interest, and with unparallel'd success, a new earth and a new man. (*PW*, 390)

In other words, just as the pre-modern world was unified by the "divine principle," so the modern world shall one day be unified by the democratic principle. Democracy will seep into every part of life, reorganizing the whole and giving birth to "a new earth and a new man."

Given the unique role for America in Whitman's theory of history, it is appropriate that he scrutinize the American past. Here, too, he finds two historical stages and, projecting from them to the future, a third. The first stage is that of the Revolutionary and Constitutional generation and is wholly political in character.

The First stage was the planning and putting on record the political foundation rights of immense masses of people—indeed all people—in the organization of republican National, State, and municipal governments, all constructed with reference to each, and each to all. This is the American program, not for classes, but for universal man. . . . (*PW*, 409–10)

The second stage of American history "relates to material prosperity"—the great period of capital accumulation, distribution, investment, and economic expansion and achievement in the years stretching from 1789 to Whitman's own time (*PW*, 410). These first two stages are, of course, incomplete, merely the "grand stages of preparation-strata" which a new historical era will redeem and fulfill. The third stage, that of the future, will be characterized by the total extension and complete realization of the democratic idea. It will generate "a native expression spirit" and a "sublime and Religious Democracy" which together will transfigure American life, making it, as it were, truly American (*PW*, 410).

Underlying Whitman's remarks on American history is an intense fear that the Union will once again split into its component parts. The future redemption of the American past and present (and, by extension, of the world) stands as the obverse of what was probably the most deeply felt, formative experience of Whitman's life: the Civil War. Consider the following passage:

> The historians say of ancient Greece, with her ever-jealous autonomies, cities and states, that the only positive unity she ever own'd or receiv'd, was the sad unity of a common subjection, at the last, to foreign conquerors. Subjection, aggregation of that sort, is impossible to America; but the fear of conflicting and irreconcilable interiors, and the lack of a common skeleton, knitting all close, continually haunts me. Or, if it does not, nothing is plainer than the need, a long period to come, of a fusion of the States into the only reliable entity, the moral and artistic one. For, I say, the true nationality of the States, the genuine union, when we come to a mortal crisis, is, and is to be, after all, neither the written law, nor (as is generally supposed) either self-interest, or common pecuniary or material objects—but the fervid and tremendous IDEA, melting everything else with resistless heat, and solving all lesser and definite distinctions in vast, indefinite, spiritual, emotional power. (*PW*, 368)

As this passage shows, Whitman's fear of dissolution leads directly to the promise of a new, higher unity, a supra-political national entity, a *national character.* It would be hard to find a franker expression of the universalizing tendencies of the American literary mind, unless it be Whitman's own statement a little later praising the "liberalist of today" for precisely this ambition "not only to individualize but to universalize" (*PW*, 382).

What is needed are an agent and an agency for facilitating the triumph of "the fervid and tremendous IDEA," for ushering in the Age of Personalism. To this end Whitman's theory of history expresses a wish for historical transcendence. As he says toward the outset of *Democratic Vistas*, America must "surmount" the past or die; and because, in typically American fashion, "the past" is equated with Europe, or all that is not America, past and present, it follows that the fate of the world lies with America. His idealist theory of history leads him to define the problem of historical transcendence as a problem of surpassing the aristocratic-feudal cultural heritage. Citing "unknown Egyptians, graving hieroglyphs; Hindus, with hymn and apothegm and endless epic; Hebrew prophet, with spirituality, as in flashes of lightning, conscience like red-hot iron," Christ, Greek artist, and philosopher, Dante, Michaelangelo, Shakespeare, Kant, and Hegel, Whitman concludes:

> Ye powerful and resplendent ones! ye were, in your atmospheres, grown not for America, but rather for her foes, the feudal and the old—while our genius is democratic and modern. Yet could ye, indeed, but breathe your breath of life into our New World's nostrils—not to enslave us, as now, but, for our needs, to breed a spirit like your own—perhaps (dare we to say it?) to dominate, even destroy, what you yourselves have left! On your plane, and no less, but even higher and wider, must we mete and measure for to-day and here. I demand races of orbic bards, with unconditional, uncompromising sway. Come forth, sweet democratic despots of the west! (*PW*, 406–7)

In brief, the agency of transcendence is democratic literature, and the agent is a class of writers, "sweet democratic despots," who will promulgate Whitman's vision. Richard Poirier has argued that such notions, so common in our literature, "are an analogue of the effort by American fictional heroes to free themselves from the conventions of historically rooted environments" (Poirier 1966, 20–21). But in Whitman's case it was precisely the "conventions" of the present environment, everywhere rotten, which stimulated him to imagine an altogether new way of life centered on "the only reliable entity, the moral and artistic one" (*PW*, 368). This "world elsewhere," though for the present a literary wish, would fulfill itself through the "conventions" of a future real environment.

This exhilarating prospect, however, should not be misconstrued as a communist or socialist utopia. On the contrary, Whitman's historical speculations remain entirely within the framework of bourgeois capitalism and bourgeois liberalism; and *Democratic Vistas*, despite its trenchant attack upon the excesses of American capitalism, is an apology for capitalism. "The true gravitation-hold of liberalism in the United States will be a more universal ownership of property, general homesteads, general comfort—a vast, intertwining reticulation of wealth." Like Emerson, Whitman's faith in America and the future goes hand in hand with his reverence for "the safety and endurance of the aggregate of its middling property owners" (*PW*, 383). He acknowledges what he calls the "paradox" that

> democracy looks with suspicious, ill-satisfied eye upon the very poor, the ignorant, and on those out of business. She asks for men and women with occupations, well-off, owners of houses and acres, and with cash in the bank—and with some cravings for literature, too; and must have them, and hastens to make them. Luckily, the seed is already well-sown, and has taken ineradicable root. (*PW*, 384)

He adds, in the manner of an economic determinist, that material wealth forms the "sub-strata" on which is to be raised "the edifice designed in these Vistas" (*PW*, 384–85 n). The word "edifice" here reminds us that, for all its lightsome talk of the redeemed future, *Democratic Vistas* betrays an unequivocal and anachronistic belief in pre-monopoly capitalist institutions as the material basis of that redemption. Personalism was not as "generalized [an] anti-institutional creed for America" as some historians have presented it to be, among them George Fredrickson (Fredrickson 1968, 20). As in his best poetry, Whitman was capable of being quite specific.

LITERARY THEORY

I have saved consideration of the literary theory in *Democratic Vistas* until last because the logic of Whitman's essay, like the logic of his historical evolutionism, places it at the apex of his argument, making it the natural flowering of his political and historical theories. The literary theory would be incomprehensible apart from the political and historical theories; they in turn remain utterly pedestrian until seen as the foundation of Whitman's extraordinary claims for literature and for *littérateurs*. There are three main parts to Whitman's theory of literature: (1) a critique of all pre-modern literature; (2) a critique of prevailing notions of culture, along with a brief formulation of a new idea of culture; and (3) an elaboration of the hegemonic role of literature as the principal source of democratic archetypes suitable for the formation of democratic social character.

1. The Inadequacy of All Past Literature. All past literature is inadequate to modern—that is, American—conditions because it "never recognized the People." It has only tended "to make mostly critical and querulous men" (*PW*, 376). Past literature smells of aristocratic elitism and is contemptuous of democracy. "The great poems, Shakespeare included, are poisonous to the idea of the pride and dignity of the common people, the lifeblood of democracy . . . ; all smells of princes' favors" (*PW*, 388). But, as Whitman asserts in a passage I have already quoted, past literature is not to be discarded. Rather, its spirit is to be

absorbed into a democratic literature, at once preserved and superseded. The literary past is to be transcended, pressed into the service of democratic affirmation.

2. Culture Revised. Whitman's critique of the prevailing idea of culture rests on the same premises as his critique of past literature. The sponsors of culture—and Whitman mentions no names, but it is likely that he had in mind such figures as Emerson and Arnold—are the sponsors of a high-level effeteness, a version of culture as anti-democratic and unmanly as pre-modern literature. "As now taught, accepted and carried out, are not the processes of culture rapidly creating a class of supercilious infidels, who believe in nothing?" he asks (*PW*, 395). Nor is Whitman persuaded by the tone of benevolence and uplift he finds in exponents of "culture," or taken in by their demurral that, as he puts it, "culture only seeks to help, systematize, and put in attitude, the elements of fertility and power . . . " (*PW*, 396).

But Whitman does not reject the idea of culture, for he is attracted by its capacity for indoctrination. In a sense, his critique of culture amounts to saying that culture's sponsors have not gone far enough: they have stopped short of realizing the full democratic implications and uses of culture. They have only succeeded in devising a program "for a single class alone, . . . for the parlors or lecture rooms," rather than for the full range of "practical life." Culture "must have for its spinal meaning the formation of typical personality of character, eligible to the uses of the high average of men—and not restricted by conditions ineligible to the masses." If "culture" was "the word of ambition" to Emerson, it was all the more so to Whitman, for what he finally demands under his own banner of culture is what he calls "the democratic ethnology of the future" (*PW*, 396).

Native, individual *character* takes precedence over the claims of culture, particularly culture in its highly intellectualized versions. Whitmanesque culture would provide "a basic model or portrait of personality for general use for the manliness of the States (and doubtless that is most useful which is most simple and comprehensive for all, and toned low enough)"; therefore,

> we should prepare the canvas well beforehand. Parentage must consider itself in advance. (Will the time hasten when fatherhood and motherhood shall become a science—and the noblest science?) To our model, a clear-blooded, strong-fibered physique is indispensable; the questions of food, drink, air, exercise, assimilation, digestion, can never be intermitted. Out of these we descry a well-begotten selfhood—in youth, fresh, ardent, emotional aspiring, full of adventure; at maturity, brave, perceptive, under control, neither too talkative nor too reticent, neither flippant nor somber; of the bodily figure, the movements easy, the complexion showing the best blood, somewhat flushed, breast expanded, an erect attitude, a voice whose sound outvies music, eyes of calm and steady gaze, yet capable also of flashing—and a general presence that holds its own in the company of the highest. (For it is native personality, and that alone, that endows a man to stand before presidents or generals, or in any distinguished collection, with *aplomb*—and *not* culture, or any knowledge or intellect whatever.)

The intellectual development of Americans is already quite sufficient and "needs nothing from us here—except, indeed, a phrase of warning and restraint" (*PW*, 397). Whitman concludes his discussion of culture first with an apology—"Pardon us, venerable shade!"—and then with the assurance that what he wants above all is not to dismiss the idea of culture but to "supervise it, and promulgate along with it, as deep, perhaps a deeper, principle"—namely, the totalizing principle of democracy (*PW*, 403).

3. The Hegemony of Literature and Man of Letters. Whitman's is a pragmatic theory of literature; what most interests him is literature's function. Its function in America is to "furnish the materials and suggestions of personality for the women and men of that country, and enforce them in a thousand effective ways" (*PW*, 392). American liter-

ature is to promulgate "national, original archetypes" of the democratic social character outlined in his doctrine of culture (*PW*, 405). What Whitman calls "New World literature" will oversee and guide the development "of perfect characters among the people," instill in them a deep sense of individual identity, and, by giving imaginative expression to the doctrine of Personalism, "raise up and supply through the States a copious race of superb American men and women, cheerful, religious, ahead of any yet known" (*PW*, 405, 392–93, 295). At present, Americans are burdened by the contradiction between their dynamic, heroic, significant history, and their genteel and trivial literature (*PW*, 408–9). A New World literature will resolve this contradiction. Agreeing with the Librarian of Congress who in an address to a New York convention in 1869 declared that "the true question to ask respecting a book, is, *has it helped any human soul?*" Whitman adds that

> this is the hint, the statement, not only of the great literatus, his book, but of every great artist. It may be that all works of art are to be first tried by their art qualities, their image-forming talent, and their dramatic, pictorial, plot-constructing, euphonious and other talents. Then, whenever claiming to be first-class works, they are to be strictly and sternly tried by their foundation in, and radiation, in the highest sense and always indirectly, of, the ethic principles, and eligibility to free, arouse, dilate. (*PW*, 419–20)

Whitman's pragmatic theory of literature entails a pragmatic theory of literary criticism, one that will judge literature on its American merits, thus encouraging a literature sufficiently expansive to comport well with American historical reality, historical tendencies, and historical meaning. Literature becomes the agency for the spiritualization, and hence fulfillment, of American democracy and American material accomplishment. In short, the function of literature is to counterbalance "the force-infusion of intellect alone" (culture in the sense he rejects)

and of simple materialism with "an equally subtle and tremendous
force-infusion for purposes of spiritualization, for the pure conscience,
for genuine aesthetics, and for absolute and primal manliness and
womanliness. . . . " The tone of desperation running throughout *Democratic Vistas* becomes strident at this point, as Whitman once again
warns of the alternative: "our modern civilization, with all its im-
provements, is in vain, and we are on the road to a destiny, a status,
equivalent, in its real world, to that of the fabled damned" (*PW*, 424).

Literature is the agency that will guard against this catastrophe. The
matching agent is a literary elite,

> a little or a larger band—a band of brave and true, unprecedented yet [,] . . .
> a band, a class, at least as fit to cope with current years, our dangers, needs,
> as those who, for their times, so long, so well, in armour or in cowl, up-
> held and made illustrious, that far-back feudal, priestly world.

Whitman's dream of a literary elite, he confesses, "underlies these entire speculations . . . and the rest, the other parts, as superstructures,
are all founded upon it" (*PW*, 423–24). *Democratic Vistas* is at bottom a
rationalization and justification of a new literary elite whose role is to
formulate a national democratic character, which in turn, as the living
embodiment of the universalizing democratic principle, will take on
"imperial power" and prepare the people for world domination (*PW*,
390).

Life is to follow art. Literature will tell us not who we are but who
we are to become. The famous Whitmanesque love of the messy var-
iousness of experience is belied by this programmatic recommendation, and the yearning for a national literature produced by a race of
poets united by a common dogma contradicts democratic plurality
even as it presents itself in the guise of democratic principle. The affirmation of America withers into the affirmation of American literature
and the literati. Whitman was convinced that literature can and must

solve not just its own problems but the problems of the Republic. *Democratic Vistas* makes clear, if it was not clear from his previous writings, that Whitman imagines these two kinds of problems to be one and the same. His doctrine of Personalism, which as his version of Americanization underpins all his speculations, is not just a finely tuned expression of what Philip Rahv once called the "native bias"; it is in addition the fantasy of one influential man of letters which seeks fulfillment on an international scale.

Further, as though obedient to the main requirements of Whitman's theories of politics, history, and literature, contemporary literary historians carry on the Whitman vision unchanged. Thus Abraham Kaplan, in an otherwise superb account of American letters, identifies as one of his main assumptions the belief that "a democratic culture places high value on a consciousness which is expansive, resists constraint, and seeks restlessly for the boundaries of all commitments" (Kaplan 1972, ix). Like Whitman, Kaplan here unites the American and the democratic. I have tried to show that in *Democratic Vistas* Whitman's notion of the expansive consciousness becomes the literary talisman of an autocracy of letters. The idea of democracy in *Democratic Vistas* accordingly takes a sharp right-wing turn, toward a future empire inhabited by democrats fit for world domination. One wonders what the future would have looked like to Whitman had he relaxed his dogmatic belief that America and democracy are synonymous. The main argument of *Democratic Vistas* declares them "convertible terms." The tone of the prose suggests that a part of Whitman suspected that America and democracy just might form an oxymoron.

Was William James a Political Philosopher? "Vicious Intellectualism" Seen in a Political Light

★   ★   ★

Just what William James was—psychologist, philosopher, Philosopher, pragmatist, political philosopher—is, of course, a non-issue. *How* we ought, in various ways, to construe what he wrote and said is, however, a very important issue. Like Emerson, James is not the exclusive property of a particular academic discipline; how he is seen, therefore, is not wholly circumscribed by the methods and vocabularies of, say, the discipline of philosophy, which in any case are today undergoing substantial revision from within. In this chapter I focus on a familiar Jamesian theme—his critique of "vicious intellectualism"—by attempting to re-see it in the light of the philosophical history of the modern age, one inner dynamic of which consists of the permutations and vicissitudes of Emersonian privatism. Given that my theme is James on "vicious intellectualism," which to a large extent means James on Hegel (or what I will show to be "Hegel"), it will be useful to identify at the outset what I see as the central opposition in James's thought: that between "our passional nature," or the temperamental basis of thought, and the "vicious intellectualist" habit of mind which elaborates vast logical structures detached from, and in a peculiar sense antithetical to, concrete experience.[1] This opposition underlies much of the philosophical combat over the political significance of James's work.

Philosophical combat sometimes involves antagonists who might have been intellectual allies under public circumstances different from those which have conditioned twentieth-century politics and thought. Consider the radical critique of pragmatism offered by Max Hork-heimer. This critique is as deaf to the Hegelian side of William James as James was to the pragmatic side of Hegel, the philosophical progen-itor of this particular critic of pragmatism. To Horkheimer, pragma-tism is not merely mistaken or uncompelling as a philosophy; it is anti-philosophical in so far as it willingly forfeits (he says) philoso-phy's critical role in society. The price of the instrumentalization of reason, Horkheimer argues, is complicity in things as they are.

> Pragmatism, which assigns to anything and anybody the role of an instru-ment—not in the name of God or objective truth, but in the name of what-ever is practically achieved by it—asks scornfully what such expressions as "truth itself," or the good that Plato and his objectivist successors left un-defined, can really mean. It might be answered that they at least preserved the awareness of differences that pragmatism has been invented to deny—the difference between thinking in the laboratory and in philosophy, and consequently the difference between the destination of mankind and its present course. (Horkheimer 1974, 53)

Oddly, in his neo-Emersonian effort to rescue experience from mind, James discovered, as Emerson had in his defense of nature against cul-ture, the irrational tendencies inherent in abstraction. James even strongly suggested an inner connection between Enlightenment and domination, again echoing Emerson and prefiguring various twentieth-century attacks on abstraction, such as those by Whitehead, assorted philosophers of language, orthodox and revisionist phenomenologists, and, not least, the philosophers of the Frankfurt School, most notably Horkheimer himself.

That individual thinkers and whole schools of thought can rightly claim a common intellectual ancestry while upholding irreconcilable views is not at all unusual but on the contrary so common as to be scarcely worth mentioning. It is a fact of philosophical discursivity, however, that fundamental change in the way philosophical ideas are formulated, presented, and received is often initiated through efforts to re-see the commonplace. Richard Bernstein's synthetic work on philosophies of human activity is a pertinent case in point. Bernstein brings together, without homogenizing, thinkers as diverse as Arendt, Habermas, Rorty, Dewey, and Gadamer, and schools as hitherto widely separated from one another as phenomenology, analytical philosophy, the philosophy of science, and political theory. Thanks to Bernstein and others working to keep alive the contemporary recovery of philosophy, it may be possible to take a fresh look at William James as a political philosopher. Bernstein himself has prepared some of this ground in his treatment of pragmatism as a philosophy of action. Horkheimer, too, in his own way has prepared some of the ground by his challenge to the pragmatic conception of truth "as nothing but a scheme or plan of action," the implication of which, he thinks, is that "truth [to James] is nothing but the successfulness of the idea" (Horkheimer 1974, 42). Though I regard Horkheimer's paraphrase as at least half caricature, I do not focus on correcting it in the following pages; nor do I dwell on the pragmatic conception of truth. Rather, in the Jamesian belief that intellect follows and expresses passion, I examine the part of James's work in which I find the philosopher most passionately engaged. To my mind, that is his critique of "vicious intellectualism." In this critique, I argue, is to be found pragmatism in its least stable form. Jamesian pragmatism is really Janus-faced: the face we know is the breezy instrumentalism that is the darling of liberals and the blood enemy of radical Marxists. The face we can only barely see is a philosophy of freedom. The former thrives in the void left by the decline of the political in the modern age; it thrives, in other words, as a private vision, the brain-child of the social realm, which is the functionalization of privacy. The opposite face of pragmatism is an embryonic theory of political plurality. To make these claims clear requires a brief overview of what I have been calling, following Hannah Arendt, "the modern age."

ARENDT ON THE MODERN AGE

The era of heroic individualism in the west is bounded, on one end, by the loss of a common world beginning in the seventeenth century and, on the other, by the "annihilation of the individual" *in and through* his "glorification" in our own time, to recall Christopher Lasch's phrase (Lasch 1978, 70). But the Emersonian-Whitmanesque subject did not go exactly the way of the Foucauldian "I." The latter shrank to nothing, becoming an element in the microsystems of power. The former expanded, becoming a commodity in the new political economy of the self. Both, however, are gone. Their disappearance culminates what Hannah Arendt calls the flight from the world and into the self, a double movement which has steadily privatized political action and speech. This dual alienation—of self and world—describes the inner and outer dynamics of capital accumulation in the modern age. The modern age, according to Arendt, is inaugurated by "three great events": "the discovery of America and the ensuing exploration of the whole earth; the Reformation, which by expropriating ecclesiastical and monastic possessions started the twofold process of individual expropriation and the accumulation of social wealth; [and] the invention of the telescope and the development of a new science that considers the nature of the earth from the viewpoint of the universe" (Arendt 1958, 248). Each of these events is the beginning of a

long-term historical process, and taken together they dovetail to produce the dominant character of the modern age, defined by Arendt as
"world alienation." We need briefly to consider her analysis of world
alienation.

1. The discovery of new lands and the circumnavigation of the
globe led, ironically, not to a larger world but to a shrunken one.
This famous process continues, of course, into our own time, as space
is conquered by speed, distance by measurement. Thus Arendt sees
the airplane as "a symbol for the general phenomenon that any de-
crease of terrestrial distance can be won only at the price of putting a
decisive distance between man and earth, of alienating man from his
immediate earthly surroundings" (Arendt 1958, 250–51).

2. The tremendous shifts in property relations, commencing with
the Reformation, had a twofold effect. On the one hand, they unleashed the process of capital accumulation; on the other, they expro-
priated the feudal peasantry and transformed it into a new,
propertyless class. "The new laboring class, which literally lived from
hand to mouth, stood not only directly under the compelling urgency
of life's necessity but was at the same time alienated from all cares and
worries which did not immediately follow from the life process itself." This process, whose fantastic energy is the newly emancipated
"labor power," produces new property and redistributes wealth but
only on the condition that both property and wealth be "fed back into
the process to generate further expropriations, greater productivity,
and more appropriation" (Arendt 1958, 255).

Arendt holds that the loss of worldliness owing to these radical
changes in property relations occurred in two stages in the modern
age. In the first stage, ever greater numbers of "laboring poor" were
deprived of "the twofold protection of family and property, that is, of
a family-owned private share in the world. . . . " The "protection"
conferred by family and property refers to Arendt's contention that
prior to the modern age the laboring activity—the human life process

itself—had been housed in the family and was subject, therefore, to the family's necessities. Unleashed, the life process was obedient only to its own inner dynamic. As wealth was accumulated and individual ownership of property steadily declined, a new subject of the life process emerged: society. "Just as the family unit had been identified with a privately owned piece of the world, its property, society was identified with a tangible, albeit collectively owned, piece of property, the territory of the nation-state. . . . " With the appearance of society the second stage of world alienation was reached. The distinguishing feature of the modern age, considered in the light of these momentous changes, is not so much the cruelty, much less the irrationality, of life under capitalism as it is the loss of a common world. The eclipse of this world, Arendt insists, prepared the way for "the worldless mentality of modern ideological mass movements" (Arendt 1958, 255–56).

3. If the European discovery of America, followed by centuries of further exploration, was the most spectacular of the three events, and if the Reformation was the most disturbing, then perhaps the least noticed was Galileo's invention of the telescope (Arendt 1958, 249). The telescope made possible the "modern astrophysical world view." At the core of this world view lies a paradox. On one side, Galileo's invention clearly confirmed the ancient "fear that our senses, our very organs for the reception of reality, might betray us." That is, the telescope revealed to a human sense organ, the eye, things which had never before been seen or, what is more important, had always been presumed to lie beyond the limits of cognition via common sense and in the domain of mere speculation. On the other side, Galileo's startling revelations also seemed to revive the equally ancient "Archimedean wish for a point outside the earth from which to unhinge the world" (Arendt 1958, 261–62). It was as though, in the words of Kafka's paradox (which Arendt quotes), "He found the Archimedean point, but he used it against himself; it seems that he was permitted to find it only under this condition" (Arendt 1958, 248). Nature's laws,

as codified in the new celestial mechanics, were formulated from a perspective beyond not just the world—from whose "terrestrial prox-imity" and privately owned share men had been driven in flight—but the earth itself. Experimental science, oddly, dispensed with experi-ence itself in so far as "earth-bound experience" was transferred into the mind and comprehended from a "cosmic standpoint outside nature itself." Mathematics appropriately became "the leading science of the modern age" (Arendt 1958, 265). Privacy without property, political plurality unmediated by political community, the miracles of subjec-tivity displacing the facticity that is apprehended by common sense: these are some of the ever-shifting contours of the modern age. Swift-moving Jamesian pragmatism is another.

JAMES AND THE RELATIONS OF CONSCIOUSNESS

James did not want philosophy to search for truth, if by truth is meant "truth in itself " or "truth for itself." What he was after in his philosophizing was experience, and in this search for experience truth takes on significance only in so far as it is "founded on agreement with reality." Experience is primary in James's philosophy; truth is secondary. All rationalisms, he claims, err in reversing this priority. The rationalist, James explains in *The Meaning of Truth* (1909), defines reality as that which "agrees with truth," not the other way around, and this initial blunder accounts for "the bankruptcy of rationalism in dealing with this subject" (*W*, 443 n. 22). James was frequently at-tacked for allegedly holding that "purely theoretical knowledge of reality, and truth as such, are unattainable." Critics charged that his philosophy was crass, amounting to little more than a justification of mindlessness and action-worship. Radical critiques like Horkheimer's are indistinguishable from the others in this respect. But the critics, James retorted on many occasions, misrepresented his meaning and in-tention. Reduced to its simplest terms, his philosophy asserted that truth is above all relational: "whatever propositions or beliefs may, in point of fact, prove true, . . . the truth of them consists in certain definable *relations between them and the reality* of which they make report. . . ." Truth results from the interaction of mind and reality. It does not inhere in the mind but only originates there as the "mind's activities cooperate on equal terms with . . . reality." Thus "mind engenders truth upon reality . . . " (*W*, 448).

At first glance, the peculiar relationship James establishes between truth and experience might appear to denigrate theoretical knowledge of experience so severely, to "favor" experience so preponderantly, as to make the pursuit of theoretical knowledge seem a mere diversion, one, moreover, always on the verge of degenerating into "vicious intellectualism." But in fact James gives theoretical knowledge a high place in his philosophy. What, after all, is the purpose of our thinking? he asks. James answers that "in point of fact, the *use* of most of our thinking is to help us to *change* the world. We must for this know definitely what we have to change, and thus theoretic truth must at all times come before practical application." By "coming before" he means that in all cases theoretic truth must "fit the purpose at hand" (*W*, 448–49).

James's own theorizing over a lifetime he called by the name "radical empiricism." Whereas "rationalism tends to emphasize universals," James wrote in *Essays in Radical Empiricism* (1912), "and to make wholes prior to parts in the order of logic as well as that of being," empiricism in general "lays the explanatory stress upon the part, the element, the individual, and treats the whole as a collection and the universal as an abstraction." Radical empiricism, however, differs from the empiricism of Hume and his intellectual descendants by refusing to "admit into its constructions any element that is not directly experienced" and by admitting all those elements that are directly experienced. Radical empiricism defines as real *anything* capable of being experienced, whether a fact, a term, or a relation (*W*, 195).

Or, defined more systematically, "radical empiricism consists first of a postulate, next of a statement of fact, and finally of a generalized conclusion." James explains each of these in the following passage from *The Meaning of Truth*:

> The postulate is that the only things that shall be debatable among philoso-phers shall be things definable in terms drawn from experience. [Things of an unexperienceable nature may exist *ad libitum*, but they form no part of the material for philosophic debate.]
>
> The statement of fact is that the relations between things, conjunctive as well as disjunctive, are just as much matters of direct particular experience, neither more so nor less so, than the things themselves.
>
> The generalized conclusion is that therefore the parts of experience hold together from next to next by relations that are themselves parts of experi-ence. The directly apprehended universe needs, in short, no transempirical connective support, but possesses in its own right a concatenated or contin-uous structure. (*W*, 136)

The postulate, the statement of fact, and the generalized conclusion all come to bear on the question, "Does Consciousness Exist?" the problem James examines in the opening essay of *Essays in Radical Em-piricism*. He proposes in this essay to correct the mistaken view of con-sciousness held by neo-Kantians, whose concept of the transcendental ego threatens to destroy the relation between the knowing subject and the known object. For neo-Kantians, says James, the notion of con-sciousness implies "that experience is indefeasibly dualistic in struc-ture. It means that not subject, not object, but object–plus–subject is the minimum that can actually be." The trouble James finds with this view is that it contradicts his belief in "a world of pure experience." Experience, he holds, simply *is* "the primal stuff or material in the world, a stuff of which everything is composed. . . . " There are no dualisms with which philosophy should be concerned (*W*, 170).

Consciousness as an entity does not exist. To suppose that it does exist as an entity would be to affirm the existence of an *"inner duplicity"* (*W* ,172) in experience, a property which Emerson before him had similarly denied belonging to nature. On this view consciousness and its "contents" would be analogous to a container and its contents. Consciousness and ideas would then be radically different from, yet at the same time made from, material objects. Experience would be said to "have" a certain content which is apprehended, known, through consciousness. James finds this concept repugnant because logically it must deprive consciousness of "personal form and activity—these passing over to the content . . . " (*W*, 169).

In place of the neo-Kantian concept of consciousness as entity, under the ultimate tyranny of the transcendental ego, James substitutes the concept of consciousness as function. This latter concept James finds more congenial because it remains faithful to his belief in the primacy of experience. It enables him to explain the phenomenon of knowing as a purely functional relationship between parts of experience. What does it mean to know? James answers that knowing only signifies that one portion of pure experience has entered into a particular relation with another portion. That relation is called consciousness, and it consists of two terms, the knower and the known, either of which on other occasions may enter into relations not involving consciousness at all. Consciousness (as function) and content still exist in this way of looking at the problem of knowledge, but they are not conceived on the analogy of container and contents. Thus it is meaningless to say that consciousness remains when its content is subtracted from it. It is only meaningful to say that *knowledge comes into being* when certain portions of experience are related in particular ways to certain other portions of experience. In James's words:

Consciousness connotes a kind of external relation and does not denote a special stuff or way of being. *The peculiarity of our experiences, that they not*

only are, but are known, which their "conscious" quality is invoked to explain, is
better explained by their relations—these relations themselves being experiences—to
one another. (W, 178)

James's treatment of consciousness illustrates the anti-formalist and
anti-absolutist strain in his philosophy. Though primarily concerned
to demolish such idealist tenets as the neo-Kantian notion of the "Absolute Subject," from a broader point of view it can be seen that he
was most concerned with the "absolute" part of the "Absolute Subject." His constant foe in philosophy was absolutism. He warred tire-
lessly against all "transexperiential agents of unification, substances,
intellectual categories and powers, or Selves." The failure of philosophic rationalism is its abhorrence of the unruliness of experience, a
failure manifested (allegedly) in its incessant inventing of transexperiential agents to unify it.

The point of James's radical empiricism is simply that such absolutes are irrelevant. Relations between parts of experience are themselves susceptible of being experienced; any relation, disjunctive or
conjunctive, incapable of being directly experienced is not worth both-
ering about. James was equally severe with "ordinary empiricism,"
which from Berkeley to Hume and James Mill tended to stress the
lack of connections between things in experience and hence to pulver-
ize it. James contended that neither the supernal categories of rationalism nor the pulverization of experience by orthodox empiricism was
philosophically sound (W, 196).

James's discussion of how radical empiricism treats conjunctive relations illustrates his contention. How are we to understand, he asks,
the phenomenon of one experience passing into another "when both
belong to the same self"? This is the problem known in philosophy
as *"the co-conscious transition."* Are these utterly separate experiences?
Orthodox empiricism would presumably say yes. James implies, however, that the second question itself is misleading, for what is crucial is

the *fact* of transition or change. "*Change itself is one of the things immediately experienced*"; change "means continuous as opposed to discontinuous transition." Moreover, "continuous transition is one sort of conjunctive relation." Indeed, it is the most important conjunctive relation, for being in and of pure experience it makes unnecessary rationalism's absolutes while at the same time facing up to empiricism's task of accounting for conjunctive relations. Only by regarding continuous transition as a conjunctive relation capable of being experienced can philosophy free itself from "the corruptions of dialectics" and "metaphysical fictions." Thus, in answer to the original question of how we are to understand the phenomenon of one experience passing into another when both belong to the same self, James concludes that we do so not by conceiving of a metaphysical glue to bind the two experiences together, nor by denying that the two experiences have anything significant to do with one another, but only by conceiving of change itself as a conjunctive relation which is immediately experienced (*W*, 197–98).

"VICIOUS INTELLECTUALISM"

James elaborates his critique of rationalism in *Some Problems of Philosophy* (1911), in which he makes one of his several contributions to the long-standing dispute between rationalism and empiricism. He begins by inquiring into the nature and function of percepts and concepts. Where do our ideas come from and what is their value? Both rationalists and empiricists have asked this question, the former answering that concepts originate independently of sensory experience and the latter saying just the reverse. Siding with the empiricists, James nevertheless chides both traditions for missing the main question. Far more important than the origin of our ideas—whether inside or outside experience—is their "functional use and value;—is *that* tied down to perceptual experience, or out of all relation to it? Is conceptual knowledge self-sufficing and a revelation all by itself, quite apart from its uses in helping to a better understanding of the world of sense?" James addresses this second question by formulating a "mediating attitude" which recognizes, with the rationalist tradition, that conceptual knowledge is in fact self-sufficing, and affirms, with the empiricist tradition, that "the full *value* of such knowledge is got only by combining it with perceptual reality again." James's attempt to mediate the conflicting claims of the two schools leads him to point out both the import and abuses of concepts (*W*, 236–37).

Ideas come from experience, and their meaning and use must be conceived in terms of it. Ideas are useful because they help us sort out the chaos of experience. "We *harness* perceptual reality in concepts in order to drive it better to our ends" (*W*, 239). In helping us get command of perceptual reality, concepts perform three indispensable functions in human affairs:

1. They steer us practically everyday, and provide an immense map of relations among the elements of things, which, though not now, yet on some possible future occasion, may help to steer us practically;
2. They bring new values into our perceptual life, they reanimate our wills, and make our action turn upon new points of emphasis;
3. The map which the mind frames out of them is an object which possesses, when once it has been framed, an independent existence. It suffices all by itself for purposes of study. The "eternal" truths it contains would have to be acknowledged even were the world of sense annihilated. (*W*, 243)

To be useful, however, concepts must of course be meaningful, and to be meaningful they must be tied closely to perceptual reality. If they are not, they become vague and indistinct. James offers what he calls the "Pragmatic Rule," derived from his *Pragmatism* (1907), as the surest guide to determining the meaning and hence the usefulness of

ideas. "Test every concept," he advises, "by the question 'What sensible difference to anybody will its truth make?' " Only distinct ideas
will survive this test and reveal under examination whether they are
true or false. "If two concepts lead you to infer the same particular
consequence, then you may assume that they embody the same meaning under different names" (W, 238).

The pragmatic rule, or something like it, is precisely what in
James's view the rationalist tradition lacks, and its absence largely accounts for the inability of this tradition to view the world rationally.
This is the peculiar irony of philosophic rationalism. Rationalism since
Plato would exalt conceptual knowledge above the variegated, incoherent world of particulars, "would have it that to understand life,
without entering its turmoil, is the absolutely better part" (W, 224 n.
122). But James counters this prejudice of "the traditional intellectualist creed" with the claim that "the whole operation [of rationalist sys-
tems], so far from making things appear more rational, becomes the
source of quite gratuitous unintelligibilities." "Conceptual knowledge," he believes, "is forever inadequate to the fullness of the reality
to be known. Reality consists of existential particulars as well as of
essences and universals and class-names, and of existential particulars
we become aware only in the perceptual flux" (W, 244–45). Though
indispensable, concepts can easily be, and frequently have been,
abused.

The further we get from the perceptual flux, the greater the tendency to value knowledge of experience over experience itself. This
tendency ultimately produces what James calls "intellectualism in philosophy." Rationalists are easily enamored of the beauty and charm of
"conceptual form," but such love exacts a high price (W, 247). "Intellectualism," James writes, again restating the Emerson of *Nature*,
"draws the dynamic continuity out of nature as you draw the thread
out of a string of beads," mistakenly attributing the dynamic qualities
of experience to concepts themselves (W, 248). But to James concepts

are static, not dynamic, even when they designate dynamic things or relations in experience. Concepts remain "insufficient representatives" of and "thin extracts from perception." Intellectualism generates concepts which inhabit a lifeless void of "dialectic contradictions" in which philosophy witnesses its own self-defeat (*W*, 258).

Though intellectualism be doomed to defeat, philosophy cannot and need not tolerate such a loss. There must be a better way for philosophy to meet the needs of man's "sentiment of rationality." In an earlier book, *The Will to Believe* (1896), James had faced this challenge and formulated his basic philosophical position in response to it. *The Will to Believe*, like his later works, attempts to mediate conflicting philosophical claims, on the one hand, the "abstract monotony" of traditional rationalist systems (e.g., Spinoza's), and, on the other hand, the "concrete heterogeneity" of traditional empiricisms (e.g., Hume's). The one is barren of meaning; the other plunges us into an "empirical sand-heap world" (*W*, 319–20).

Traditional rationalism appeases the sentiment of rationality—defined by James as a "feeling of the sufficiency of the present moment, of its absoluteness, . . . [an] absence of all need to explain it, account for it, or justify it"—at best only imperfectly (*W*, 318). It is imperfect because all it has to offer are simple classifications of experience. These are satisfying in so far as man desires and needs the simplicity they afford. But, James observes, man is beset by other needs as well, which traditional rationalism is inadequate to satisfy. Indeed, its classifications fail to report "the fullness of the truth" about experience and in so failing constitute a "monstrous abridgment of life . . . " (*W*, 321).

Given the limitations of purely abstract rationality for making experience rational, it is necessary to "inquire what constitutes the feeling of rationality in its *practical* aspect" (*W*, 324). What philosophical conception, in other words, would elucidate our experience of "unimpeded mental function" and free us of "any feeling of irrationality"

(*W*, 324, 318)? James answers by giving rationality a radically pragmatic definition:

> Now, there is one particular relation of greater practical importance than all the rest,—I mean the relation of a thing to its future consequences. So long as an object is unusual, our expectations are baffled; they are fully determined as soon as it becomes familiar. I therefore propose this as the first practical requisite which a philosophical conception must satisfy: *It must, in a general way at least, banish uncertainty from the future.* (*W*, 326)

Later in "The Sentiment of Rationality," James adds a second requirement to this one, and together the two comprise the basic features of any philosophy capable of meeting human needs. The second requirement demands that philosophy "make a direct appeal to all those powers of our nature which we hold in highest esteem" (*W*, 345). James is particularly concerned with the power of faith, conceived broadly as being "synonymous with working hypothesis," and asks us to discredit any philosophy (e.g., materialism) that refuses to recognize the significance of faith in human affairs (*W*, 336).

James attempts to bolster his case for rational philosophy by criticizing two principal absolutisms: Hegelianism and what he calls scientific absolutism, both of which fall under the heading of "vicious intellectualism." His critique of Hegel appears as "Hegel and His Method" in *A Pluralistic Universe* (1909). This essay shows his preoccupation with the question of "the sentiment of rationality," first articulated in the essay by that title in *The Will to Believe*. Rephrased, it becomes: How much rationality can we expect to find in experience? James contends in this essay on Hegel that Hegel's grand system, by reducing experience to reason, is irrational through and through.

As his analysis of "Hegel and His Method" unfolds, one senses a sadness and even bitterness in James. For Hegel was a philosopher who had the right instincts, so to speak, who in his initial approach to a philosophy of experience came close to formulating a philosophical conception capable of mediating the rival claims of rationalism and empiricism, monism and pluralism. James admires Hegel's vision, or at least that part of it that asserts the dialectical and incessantly changing nature of concrete experience. For Hegel, James believes, was not "primarily a reasoner," as his followers were inclined to claim, but "in reality a naively observant man" with an "impressionistic" mind finely attuned to "the empirical flux of things . . . "(W, 512).

Hegel's error, James imagines, was that he did not remain faithful to his own temperament and propensities when he philosophized. Instead, he yielded to "the old rationalistic contempt for the immediately given world of sense and all its squalid particulars . . . " (W, 514). Hegel theorized, according to James, that taken by themselves particulars are unreal, are forever being negated by their "others." This view of reality, James argued, could never be developed into a pluralistic vision; empiricism could not hope to satisfy the author of such a concept. Hegel left the world of percepts altogether and devised a method for reconciling all the contradictions in experience by dealing with concepts by themselves. Once this method gets up a full head of steam, there is no stopping until the absolute Idea is reached, "the absolute whole of wholes, the all-inclusive reason . . . " (W, 516). Hegel's was a perfect example for James of that brand of philosophy which is founded on a profound fear of experience.

James suggested in *The Will to Believe* that we are all "absolutists by instinct," but he regarded this natural inclination as "a weakness of our nature from which we must free ourselves, if we can" (W, 724). We must struggle to control this instinct because, left uncontrolled, it sooner or later leads to irrationality, to vicious intellectualism. Far from trying to overcome his own personal inclination to absolutism, Hegel appears in James's view to have nurtured it carefully, producing a philosophical system justifying it on a world-historical scale. Hegel's method of double negation, which James thinks nullifies experience, "offers the vividest possible example of this vice of intellectualism" (*W*, 520). The method assumes "that a concept *ex*cludes from any reality conceived by its means everything not included in the concept's definition (*W*, 519). James's point here is precisely the same as his thesis about "the abuse of concepts" in *Some Problems of Philosophy*. Concepts are *of* finite things, and they retain meaning only so long as that relationship remains intact. Hegel's method ruptures that relationship by assuming that any concept, in not "being a concept of anything else," must entail as its "negative" or "other" "*the concept of anything else not being . . .* " (*W*, 520). This double negation robs the universe of empirical content, reducing it to concepts which, by means of the dialectical method, are further reduced to the one Idea or Absolute that has no negative.

However, despite the inadequacy of Hegel's method, James continues, its irrationality remains to be demonstrated. The Absolute itself, he says, must be examined as an open hypothesis (*W*, 521). Its adherents, particularly Hegel and his disciples, claim that it enables us to see the world as rational. But James contends that rationality has not one face but many, "intellectual, esthetical, moral, [and] practical." So far, he observes, philosophy has failed to find the world rational in all these respects; what is rational on one of these counts appears irrational on another. James concludes that therefore the most that philosophy can hope for is a philosophical "conception which will yield the largest balance of rationality rather than one which will yield perfect rationality of every description" (*W*, 522).

In the spirit of this restriction James concedes that the Hegelian Absolute offers a measure of "religious peace," but little more than that. And though to some minds it is satisfying aesthetically, it strikes James as less than satisfying *practically* because it necessarily remains aloof from immediate experience. It is most vulnerable, however, from a logical point of view. James's argument here is rather simple.

Hegelians assert that the Absolute consists of constituents on which the Absolute itself depends and which the Absolute in turn holds together in a single whole. But, James replies, this outlook presupposes nothing other than "the rankest empiricism"—an unacknowledged empiricism, at that. Furthermore and most importantly, if it is claimed that the Absolute is the perfect whole, it follows that the parts of which it is made are likewise perfect. In refusing to admit that the parts are perfect, absolutists are left with a "decidedly irrational" philosophy (*W*, 526).

It is an instructive irony of the history of philosophy that James "polemicized against Hegel again and again" without, however, having read him, and that, as the American philosopher closest to the spirit of Hegel, perhaps closer even than Josiah Royce, James's philosopher-colleague at Harvard and the leading American neo-Hegelian, James should have styled himself Hegel's arch American detractor. "James's attack against the block universe," Walter Kaufmann suggests, "though aimed at Hegel, would have found an enthusiastic ally in Hegel." Like James, Hegel insisted "that truth should make a difference in our lives, that philosophy is vision, and that the realm of faith and morals must not be severed from the realm of epistemology and metaphysics" (Kaufmann 1966a, 287).

Evidence in Hegel's Preface to *The Phenomenology* sheds further light on the similarity between James's and Hegel's respective assaults on the block universe. In the course of criticizing the "edifying" tendency current in philosophy in his own day, Hegel provides a succinct history of philosophy's emancipation from religion:

The eye of the spirit had to be directed forcibly to the things of this earth and kept there. Indeed, it took a long time to work that clarity which only the supernatural possessed into the must [i.e., mustiness] and confusion in which the sense of this world lay imprisoned; it took a long time to make attention to the present as such—what was called, in one word, *experience*—interesting and valid. (Kaufmann 1966b, 16; emphasis added)

But this new and successful philosophy of experience, the empiricism and scientific rationalism of the seventeenth and eighteenth centuries, had degenerated, in Hegel's opinion, in so far as it had lost by his time the precision of the Concept. The frozen rationalism of the Schoolmen had thawed and been supplanted for a brief time by a flourishing and promising philosophy of experience, but this philosophy in turn evolved into an equally frozen empiricism. Such are the perils of philosophy.

Hegel's response to this development was as rebellious as James's, and the object of his rebellion was very similar to James's. What Hegel set out to destroy was the block universe of bankrupt empiricism, on the one hand, and of the cult of feeling, on the other. Moreover, he saw these two philosophical developments as closely related to each other. He observed that "sense seems to be so firmly rooted in what is worldly that it takes an equal force to raise it higher."

> The spirit appears so poor that, like a wanderer in the desert who languishes for a simple drink of water, it seems to crave for its refreshment merely the bare feeling of the divine in general. By that which suffices the spirit one can measure the extent of its loss. (Kaufmann 1966b, 16)

Philosophy, in other words, is too modest; in fact, it is falsely modest in settling for "the *feeling* of the essence" in place of striving to become scientific.

> This modest contentment in accepting, or stinginess in giving, is, however, improper for science. Whoever seeks mere edification, whoever desires to shroud the worldly multiplicity of his existence and of thought in a

fog to attain the indeterminate enjoyment of this indeterminate divinity, may look out for himself where he can find this; he will easily find the means to impress himself with this enthusiasm and thus to puff himself up. Philosophy, however, must beware of wishing to be edifying. (Kaufmann 1966b, 16, 18)

Philosophy, Hegel seems to be saying, suffers as much from its victories as from its defeats.

Such, I intend to show, is the case with James's own philosophy, at the center of which is a relentless struggle to discredit the Absolutist hypothesis. The significance of James's effort is this: not only did he fail to comprehend Hegel's philosophical ambitions (so similar to his own), but he also grossly misrepresented Hegel's method. Hegel's innovation was not, contrary to James's claim, an attack on "experience" but a new logic for analyzing concepts. Hegel's innovation was the idea of thinking as critical or dialectical mental activity. This innovation represents Hegel's perfection of Aristotle's theory of the forms of being in his *Metaphysics* (Kaufmann 1966a, ch. 4). As Herbert Marcuse explains, Hegel's

dialectical thought starts with the experience that the world is unfree; that is to say, man and nature exist in conditions of alienation, exist as "other than they are." Any mode of thought which excludes this contradiction from its logic is a faulty logic. Thought "corresponds" to reality only as it transforms reality by comprehending its contradictory structure. (Marcuse 1960, ix)

Despite their similar philosophical aims, James and Hegel clearly part company on this score. Thinking, to James, remains positive, not critical; it is man's mode of affirming existence, the "unfinished universe." Still, the use of thinking, as the above discussion has pointed out, is "to help us change the world"—that is, change it practically.

The practical character of Jamesian change is not, however, predicated on the idea of alienation. Being and mind are not alienated from each other and from themselves but, to James's vision, co-exist in perfect harmony: hence the root difference between Jamesian change and Hegelian transformation. James missed this distinction largely because, instead of reading Hegel he read Hegelians, who by his time had succeeded in converting Hegel's dialectical logic into a species of theology.[2]

Jamesian affirmation occurs under the aegis of what Marcus Peter Ford characterizes as the technical flaw of assuming that "the same things may be both confluent and separate *at the same time*" (Ford 1982, 56). This assumption forms the cornerstone of James's pluralism. The key passage from *A Pluralistic Universe* is the following:

> In *principle*, then, the real units of our immediately-felt life are unlike the units that intellectualistic logic holds to and makes its calculations with. They are not separate from their own others, and you have to take them at widely separated dates to find any two of them that seem unblent. Then indeed they do appear separate even as their concepts are separate; a chasm yawns between them; but the chasm itself is but an intellectualist fiction, got by abstracting from the continuous sheet of experiences with which the intermediary time was filled. . . .
>
> What is true here of successive states must also be true of simultaneous characters. They also overlap each other with their being. (Qtd. in Ford 1982, 53)

This unearned conclusion is, however, more than technically interesting. It situates James on the side of the road that runs from Hegel to Dewey. The "continuous sheet of experiences" is itself an intellectualist fiction, which Wilfrid Sellars has called the "myth of the given" (Rorty 1979, 104ff.). Hegel distanced mind from the given and so exposed the unfinished condition of the given. It does not follow that, in being thus exposed, experience is violated. On the contrary, dialectical thought aids experience in so far as it articulates the contradictory structure of experience. Similarly, Dewey's distinction between experience, which occurs continuously, and *an* experience does not signify a flight into formalism. Instead, like the articulated antagonisms of man and nature, the Deweyan division represents exactly that piece which is *missing* in James's pluralism: in Ford's words, a "means of discriminating between the ways in which things are connected and the ways in which they are not" (Ford 1982, 56).

James's victory in his obsessive struggle against Hegelian absolutism was hollow. He won an even hollower victory through his critique of scientific absolutism, a critique that perfectly exemplifies the tendency in philosophy which Hegel called "edifying" and against which he warned. James's attack on scientific absolutism is part of *The Will to Believe*. In that book James seeks to reconcile the demands of religious faith and the logical intellect. He proposes to establish faith on experiential, logical, and rational grounds. His discussion of the experiential grounds of faith rests on his critique of the concept of pure reason, the reason assumed by scientists like the British mathematician William K. Clifford to be the sole arbiter of belief. " 'It is wrong always, everywhere, and for everyone,' " Clifford argued in a passage cited by James, " 'to believe anything upon insufficient evidence.' " The defect of this view, James argues, is that it grossly oversimplifies the process of belief. It altogether fails to account for the factor of will, for the varieties of human temperament, for "all such factors of belief as fear and hope, prejudice and passion, imitation and partisanship, the circumpressure of our caste and set," all of which take a place beside reason and insight in the determination of belief (*W*, 721).

Having suggested the complexity of belief and the experiential grounds of faith, James is prepared to state his thesis:

> *Our passional nature not only lawfully may, but must, decide an option between*
> *propositions, whenever it is a genuine option that cannot by its nature be decided on*
> *intellectual grounds; for to say, under such circumstances, "Do not decide, but leave*
> *the question open," is itself a passional decision,—just like deciding yes or no,—and*
> *is attended with the same risk of losing the truth. (W, 723)*

His defense of this thesis purports to be logical and rational and to
proceed from and reinforce his critique of the scientific absolutist's
concept of pure reason. There being "but one indefectibly certain
truth . . . [,] that the present phenomenon of consciousness exists,"
James charges scientists like Clifford (whom he calls "faith vetoers")
with corrupting true empiricism (W, 725, 732). Their exhortations in
the name of science and objective certitude against the religious hypothesis really have nothing to do with an alleged insufficiency of evidence in its support but merely reveal their preference for an anti-
religious belief. They "preach scepticism to us as a duty until 'sufficient evidence' for religion be found . . . " (W, 732). But this reasoning
"is tantamount therefore to telling us, when in the presence of the religious hypothesis, that to yield to our fear of its being in error is wiser
and better than to yield to our hope that it may be true" (W, 732).

James cleverly observes that such reasoning is fallacious because,
while claiming to set "intellect against all passions," in fact it amounts
only to "intellect with one passion laying down its law." James que-
ries: "Dupery for dupery, what proof is there that dupery through
hope is so much worse than dupery through fear?" (W, 732). In the
absence of proof, it would be sheer irrationality, James argues, to accept the scientific absolutist's "agnostic rules for truth-seeking . . . "
(W, 733). He concludes his defense of the will to believe with this ca-
veat for all scientific empiricists: *"a rule of thinking which would abso-*
lutely prevent me from acknowledging certain kinds of truth if those kinds of
truth were really there, would be an irrational rule" (W, 733).

One irony running through James's justification of belief is that, like the absolutist tendency he purports to be condemning, the idea of faith in an important sense contradicts experience. Thirty years before the appearance of *The Will to Believe*, Charles Sanders Peirce offered a cogent analysis of this very contradiction in his now-famous essay on "The Fixation of Belief" (1877).

> We are, doubtless, in the main logical animals, but we are not perfectly so. Most of us, for example, are naturally more sanguine and hopeful than logic would justify. We seem to be so constituted that in the absence of any facts to go upon we are happy and self-satisfied; so that the effect of experience is continually to counteract our hopes and aspirations. Yet a lifetime of the application of this corrective does not usually eradicate our sanguine disposition. Where hope is unchecked by any experience, it is likely that our optimism is extravagant. (Peirce 1955, 7–8)

Whereas James condemns vicious intellectualism as the despoiler of experience and defends the will to believe as an unassailable private entitlement, Peirce acknowledges the role of temperament in mental life but situates it in human community. Peirce's contextualism has little of the flavor of philosophical melodrama about it that pits heroic experience against the villain of intellectualism. In light of Peirce's analysis, the Jamesian will to believe comes down to an extravagant optimism, a habit which Peirce defines as the underpinnings of action in the world. Action thus originates, for Peirce, in the failure of experience to check our sanguine disposition.

Jamesian faith, like all purely private fixations of belief, operates according to what Peirce calls the "method of tenacity." Belief determines or leads to action. By contrast, not only does doubt not lead to action; it must be destroyed before action can occur. Thus belief tends to be a trait of character, whereas doubt is a feature of intellection. The method of tenacity would be harmless if men lived in isolation, where their opinions did not influence one another. But as social beings sooner or later they find that "other men think differently," that "another man's thought or sentiment may be equivalent to one's own," and their belief is consequently shattered (Peirce 1955, 12). The inference would appear to be—but Peirce does not draw it out—that action in the world is somehow affected by the collapse of the method of tenacity. Presumably men would become timid, or inactive, or possibly even reckless. However that might be, Peirce argues that, owing to the inevitable failure of the method of tenacity, the mass of men for ages have had to defer to authority in matters of belief. In this way the method of tenacity has been supplanted by the "method of authority"; whereas the former is anti-social, the latter, though intellectually its superior, is anti-liberal (Peirce 1955, 14).

More than anything else, James wanted to formulate a rational philosophy for "the strung-along unfinished world. . . ." He began by postulating that "reality MAY exist in distributive form, in the shape not of an all but of a set of eaches, just as it seems to—this is the anti-absolutist hypothesis" (*W*, 528).

> May not the flux of sensible experience itself contain a rationality that has been overlooked, so that the real remedy would consist in harking back to it more intelligently, and not in advancing in the opposite direction away from it and even away beyond the intellectualist criticism that disintegrates it, to—the pseudo-rationality of the supposed absolute point of view. I myself believe that this is the real way to keep rationality in the world, and that the traditional rationalism has always been facing in the wrong direction. (*W*, 508)

In *The Will to Believe*, as in his polemic against Hegel, James himself may have "advanced in the opposite direction away from . . . the flux of sensible experience." At the least, he seems to have jeopardized his own idea of an unfinished universe when he reduced rationality to a "sentiment" without providing a rational means of comprehending the unfinished character of that universe. Part of its unfinished character, no doubt, is the fact that, to recall Ford's analysis, things just are not "simultaneously connected and separate"; James's claim, his cornerstone assumption of *A Pluralistic Universe*, that "what is true of successive events must also be true of contemporary events," does not stand up to scrutiny (Ford 1982, 57, 56). James's radically anti-historicist notion diverts James from experience as his philosophical object and underpins his tendency to flirt with the abstract idea of the *possibilities* of experience as a substitute philosophical object. Thus he insisted, in a key passage I have already cited, that "the first practical requisite which a philosophical conception must satisfy . . . [is that] it must, in a general way at least, banish uncertainty from the future" (*W*, 326). Like Whitman and Emerson before him, James fled the past gleefully. But, unlike them, he was more guarded about the future, which he felt needed to be relieved of contingency in order for experience to remain the object of philosophical affirmation.

A PHILOSOPHER OF FREEDOM?

Any pluralism is a philosophy of freedom by definition. For pluralism says the universe is not necessarily as it must be. Novelty, newness are possible—or what Arendt calls natality, the ontological home of action, which is the pre-eminent political performance. Natality, she suggests, "may be the central category of political, as distinguished from metaphysical, thought" (Arendt 1958, 9). Jamesian pluralism, for all its flaws, is still the liveliest American attempt to philosophize in the name of novelty and openness. No doubt this lively quality comes, in part, from James's positioning of himself in the philosophical landscape in opposition to Josiah Royce: James the thoroughbred pluralist and Royce the monist. But, as Ford has shown, James failed to devise a minimally coherent philosophy of pluralism (or pluralistic

pantheism, as Ford labels it). He remained attracted to the very monism he assailed. Ford is only the latest in a line of philosophical critics
stretching back to James's German contemporary Julius Goldstein to
find substance in James's monist leanings (Ford 1982, 57).

I have concluded that James, like Emerson, was a political philosopher, not simply by dint of pluralism's being by definition a political
philosophy in some elementary sense, but *malgré lui*. The Jamesian
concepts of consciousness as function (rather than entity), indeterminacy, and pluralism all belong to the philosophical history of the modern age. The functionalization of consciousness, an indispensable
contribution to psychology and philosophy alike, is the outgrowth of
the journey into the interior which began in earnest in the seventeenth
century. Similarly, the pragmatic test of the truth of propositions—
there is no difference that does not make a difference—is a methodological principle without which the social realm, the realm of publicly functionalized privacy, could not exist. The invention of the
pragmatic test is accordingly a political event, no less so than the invention of the steam engine or the application and further development of the tenets of theoretical physics in the Manhattan project.
That each of these inventions was also a sub-political event is exactly
the point. The political issue raised by pragmatism is missed entirely
by critics like Horkheimer, whose analysis of pragmatism is nothing
more than an inversion of James's misguided critique of Hegel: loud
talk at cross-purposes.

The political issue, as I see it, is this: pragmatism, or instrumentalism, will continue as an expression of the infinitude of the private
man, as a feature of that cavernous interiority which turned outward
and found a home in liberal-capitalist America, so long as the public
world itself remains a sub-political world. A political renewal would
tame pragmatism. Without such a renewal, I see no other protection
against the social excesses of instrumental reason.

Literary "Ideas" in "An Age of True Pyrrhonism": Examples of R. P. Blackmur and Robinson Jeffers

They laid Jesse James in his grave and Dante Gabriel Rossetti died immediately. Then Charles Darwin was deplored and then, on April 27, 1882, Louisa May Alcott hurried to write in her journal: "Mr. Emerson died at 9 p.m. suddenly. Our best and greatest American gone. The nearest and dearest friend Father has ever had and the man who helped me most by his life, his books and his society. Illustrious and beloved friend, good-bye!" So she made a lyre of yellow jonquils for Ralph Waldo Emerson's preposterous funeral and somehow steered Bronson Alcott through the dreary business until he stood beside the coffin in the damp cemetery and mechanically drawled out the lines of a dire poem. Under the shock the tall old idler was a mere automaton with a bloodless face that startled watchers as he stepped back from the grave into which his one importance sank. Emerson was going from him! He was losing his apologist, his topic. His fingers fell on the shoulder of a little boy who had pressed forward to see and the grip became so cruel that Louisa saw and heard her hoarse voice rose [sic] in the hush, commanding: "Pa! Let go! You're hurting Georgie's arm!" But her father could hear nothing. She stooped and wrenched the child's arm free.

THOMAS BEER, *The Mauve Decade* (1926)

★   ★   ★

The infinitude of the private man finds its truth as rationalized senti-ment and will lose it, if ever, as political object. Herein may be the historical significance of James's definition of rationality as a senti-ment, at once the secret of pragmatism's success and the terms of whatever new political responsibility the future assigns to it as Ameri-ca's public philosophy. Emersonian privatism, the living ancestor of pragmatism, does not lack the resources for such self-development and self-criticism. Emerson's essay "Experience," arguably his best, is a work of just this genius. An inquiry into the interior, "Experience" paradoxically sidesteps the entire Kantian legacy. "Temperament," Emerson writes, "shuts us in a prison of glass which we cannot see." Life thus presents us many illusions. Yet within the glass prison we experience "a succession of moods or objects." "The secret of the illu-soriness [of life]," he says, "is in the necessity of a succession of moods or objects. Gladly we would anchor, but the anchorage is quicksand. This onward trick of nature is too strong for us: *Pero si muove* ['Still, it moves': Galileo, following his recantation]" (Emerson 1957, 258, 259). As Stanley Cavell says of this passage, "the fact that we are taken over by this succession, this onwardness, means that you can think of it as at once a succession of moods (inner matters) and a succession of objects (outer matters). This very evanescence of the world proves its existence to me; it *is* what vanishes from me." What-ever this philosophical view ought to be called, it is not solipsism; Emerson at his best is not a subjectivist, despite his tendency to en-courage that idea of himself (Cavell 1981, 127).

Those who were deeply influenced by Emerson typically were less able to avoid the pit of solipsism; it seemed to come *with* Emerso-nianism, if not *from* Emerson himself.[1] Melville was only the first to perceive the hazard, and *Pierre; or, The Ambiguities* (1852), the story of a young Emersonian seeker, probes every imaginable deadend of ide-alism. The hero, Pierre Glendinning, ends up lost in himself and, in

prison with his sister, kills himself. Melville points to the terror awaiting the soul *from inside itself*:

> But, as to the resolute traveler in Switzerland, the Alps do never in one
> wide and comprehensive sweep, instantaneously reveal their full awfulness
> of amplitude—their overawing extent of peak crowded on peak, and spur
> sloping on spur, and chain jammed behind chain, and all their wonderful
> battalionings of might; so hath heaven wisely ordained, that on first enter-
> ing into the Switzerland of his soul, man shall not at once perceive its tre-
> mendous immensity; lest illy prepared for such an encounter, his spirit
> should sink and perish in the lower-most snows. Only by judicious de-
> grees, appointed of God, does man come at last to gain his Mount Blanc
> and take an overtopping view of these Alps; and even then the tithe is not
> shown; and far over the invisible Atlantic, the Rocky Mountains and the
> Andes are yet unbeheld. Appalling is the soul of man! Better might one be
> pushed off into the material spaces beyond the uttermost orbit of our sun,
> than once feel himself fairly afloat in himself! (Melville 1964, 322)

An inversion of this fate awaited Bronson Alcott at Emerson's
graveside. If the "tall old idler was a mere automaton," as Thomas
Beer characterized him, it was because he had spent so much of his
life with Emerson-the-topic, the overlay of Emerson the man. But
now the topic was dead, and there were two topics, one of them an
automaton who was going to have to manage without his apologist.
Emersonian privatism is a stern discipline, and one of the penalties it
is always prepared to exact is radical deprivation, which bears little resemblance to the ordinary human experience of loss. The penalty
marks the limits, perhaps, of whatever critique we may wish to make
of Emersonian self-reliance.

Two twentieth-century literary lives—R. P. Blackmur's and Robinson Jeffers'—illustrate diametrically opposed styles for avoiding the
hazards of that radical inwardness which is the American literary-phil-

osophical heritage. Neither Blackmur nor Jeffers was a philosopher, and both paid their first allegiance to poetry, though only Jeffers made his mark as a poet, Blackmur leaving his as one of the best literary critics America has produced. Jeffers was one of the most popular American poets in the 1920s, and, though quickly canonized, he was never included in the first rank of modern poets with Eliot, Stevens, Rilke, Pound, and Yeats. Today Jeffers is read far less than he once was and seems to have been adopted as the patron saint of the Sierra Club, an honor that perhaps compensates for his diminishing representation in literary anthologies. Of Blackmur, Denis Donoghue has aptly said: "The criticism [he wrote], taken by itself, has always been in dispute but never in doubt. *Language as Gesture* [1952] and *The Lion and the Honeycomb* [1955] are discussed by nearly everyone who thinks that criticism matters" (Donoghue 1977, ix).

ROBINSON JEFFERS: "FOOLED IN A MIRROR"

Just as Walt Whitman's twentieth-century critics tend to accept and apply as evaluative criteria the terms of Whitman's self-stylization as a poet of democracy and sponsor of the beneficently expanding American consciousness, so Jeffers succeeded, for a time, in being regarded as a "poet of ideas." The roots of this minor episode in literary history reach into Jeffers' earliest years as a writer, 1905–1925, a period largely ignored by Jeffers scholars yet the source of all the ideas that showed up in a poetic career stretching from the 1920s to the 1960s.[2] Virtually unknown as a poet during these years, Jeffers later faced a frequently hostile audience in the 1920s and 1930s, an audience of influential critics whose penchant for moralizing about art tells us as much about literary taste as Jeffers' work tells us about philosophy. Harriet Monroe, reviewing Jeffers' *Roan Stallion* for *Poetry* in 1926, righteously announced that Jeffers' bloody, incest-ridden narratives were simply too revolting for modern taste (Monroe 1926, 161). A few years later, Morton D. Zabel dismissed Jeffers' poetry with the claim that "When recognizable moral principles are reduced to triviality, it is impossible for a poet to produce sound drama" (Zabel 1934, 229–30). And to Edmund Wilson, Jeffers was clearly a nihilist, a writer of "monstrous," "would-be elemental," "would-be barbaric tragedies" (Wilson 1962, 49). The remarkable thing about these expressions of outrage is that Jeffers never wrote a poem half as monstrous or revolting as even the mildest tragedy of Aeschylus or Shakespeare. Jeffers was not good enough to be a moral subversive.

Whether he was a "poet of ideas" depends, of course, on what one means by ideas and on how one thinks about what they do in literary works. What is clear is that Jeffers underwent his most significant development in the years 1905–1925. In these twenty years are the origins of his chief theme: what he called in the preface to *The Double Axe* (1948) the "rejection of human solipsism and [the] recognition of the transhuman magnificence" (Jeffers 1948, vii). Jeffers' career, as we shall see, begins and turns throughout on an effort to overcome what amounts to a version of the Emersonian past that is no less a caricature of Emerson's thought than Bronson Alcott was of Emerson the man.

A poem and a short sketch from the period 1905–1913 reveal the course of Jeffers' thought, which begins with an affirmation of man's harmony with the universe and culminates in a dead-end of solipsistic despair. To begin with, a typical early poem, titled "The Steadfast Sky" (1905):

> Hast thou seen the clouds at set of sun
>> Change color o'er the heaven's fair expanse,
> And with rich purple and fine gold enhance
>> The sober fashion of their vestments' dun?
> Ever they would change, ever the patterns run
>> In wonderful new glories that entrance

> The sense; but still thro' all this wildering dance
>   Always the sky remains the same, and one.
>
> Thus let they [sic] steadfast soul no whit abate
>   From firm continuance, but have withal
> New fancies still, new moods, new thoughts range,
>   At will and unafraid. So imitate
> The eternal sky that changes not at all
>   While ever the new splendors of it change.[3]

In the first stanza the speaker posits, through the metaphor of the changeful but unchanging sky, a familiar monistic view of experience. When he gazes on nature, he recognizes in its infinitely varied "patterns" a "wildering dance" of qualities. At the close of this stanza he concludes that nature is a grand unity. The second stanza embodies the moral lesson that the wise individual learns upon observing nature in this way. Observation should lead to imitation. From the steadfast sky one's soul learns to be steadfast. The speaker now feels confident to pursue "new fancies," to have "new moods" and thoughts, all of which will be authoritatively sanctioned by nature. "The One remains, the many change and pass."

The lukewarm Emersonian idea of man's ultimate harmony with the world stayed alive in Jeffers' poetic imagination throughout the period that ended with the publication of his first volume of poems, *Flagons and Apples*, in 1912. There it re-emerged in a new form that might easily be overlooked were it not for a suggestive inscription taken from Emerson's poem "Initial, Daemonic and Celestial Love":

> And ever the Daemonic love
> Is the ancestor of wars
> And the parents [sic] of remorse.

In Emerson's lyric, "Initial love," the poetic speaker austerely pronounces, is the love practiced by Cupid, who is "corrupted by the present toy / He follows joy and only joy." Cupid "Loves nature like a hornèd cow, / Bird, or deer, or caribou." Far more harmful is "Daemonic love":

> The Daemons are self-seeking:
> Their fierce and limitary will
> Draws men to their likeness still.
>
> . . . .
>
> The Daemon ever builds a wall
> Himself encloses and includes,
> Solitude in Solitudes:
> In like sort his love doth fall.
> (Emerson 1950, 398)

Daemonic love forces the individual back upon himself, inflating him with self-importance. This "Solitude in Solitudes" isolates the self from the rest of experience. The most noteworthy feature of *Flagons*, aside from its badness as poetry, is that the *a priori* harmony announced in "The Steadfast Sky" is conspicuously missing; in its place is a mood of aloneness mixed with intimacy. Trite versions of the "agony of love" turn up in poem after poem in which the speaker experiences the treacherous consequences of "Daemonic love." He is so anguished by the love affair that his capacity for "Celestial love," which once anchored him in the presence of the universal One, has disappeared. His repeated yearning in these poems for Peace, for a respite from constant loving, has replaced his earlier confidence that stemmed from Cosmic Peace.

By the following year, 1913, Jeffers' flirtation with solipsism is more noticeable and slightly more interesting. Whereas *Flagons* only hints at this problem through clumsy allusions to "Daemonic love," a strange sketch, titled "Mirrors," depicts a wholly solipsistic dilemma. This work, Jeffers' only published piece of fiction, is about a man named Adair who visits the narrator of the story to "unburden his soul, the night before he [Adair] smashed all his mirrors and sailed for Africa." Adair's experiences with his fiancée and another woman, an actress with whom he had had an affair two years earlier, somehow lead him to conclude that all human beings are merely " 'mirrors—senseless mirrors—blank spaces which reflect. If I do a thing, or say a thing, it is only because someone else has done it, said it. Nothing but mirrors.' " Nature and God are also "mirrors." When Adair looks at another person, or at the sky, he sees only one more image of his own face. In the end, cut off from everything but his own unhappy self, Adair clings to the fragile and seemingly futile notion that in Africa he may encounter something, anything at all, that does not "look like" himself (Alberts 1933, 129–31).

Jeffers' personal life in the period from 1905 to the end of the First World War suggests how he managed eventually to overcome the problem presented in the transparently autobiographical "Mirrors." One year after he wrote "The Steadfast Sky" he met and fell in love with Mrs. Una Call Kuster while they were students at the University of Southern California. The next six years were emotionally difficult ones for both of them, but Una made them easier by acting as a sympathetic and rigorous critic of the poet's work. Much of the poetry written after 1906 and virtually all of the poems in *Flagons* reflect the love affair. Just as the reference to "Daemonic love" suggests the author's steadily deteriorating belief in an organic universe, so also a second inscription to *Flagons* appropriately describes his emotional troubles: from the Song of Solomon, 2:5, the poet had remembered the lines: "Stay me with flagons, comfort me with apples: for I am sick of love." It is obvious that what Jeffers most needed at this time—both as man and as artist—was a strong measure of intellectual and emotional detachment. Like Adair, he was suffering from an acute preoccupation with himself, which was sapping his ability to write.

Although his marriage to Una in 1913, one year after her divorce from Kuster, eased his private life, Jeffers nevertheless published relatively few poems over the next ten years. The death of his father and of an infant daughter, Maeve, in 1914 probably tended to mitigate the emotional relief provided by his long-awaited marriage. If, as he gratefully admitted in his own Foreword to *The Selected Poetry* in 1938, Una "excited and focused" his "cold and undiscriminating" nature by giving it "eyes and nerves and sympathies," his poetry remained undistinguished until 1924, when *Tamar* marked a new beginning.

Jeffers' interest in several branches of science, together with the spectacle of the First World War, drew him out of himself. After taking a Bachelor's degree at Occidental College in 1905, he spent the next five years studying medicine and literature at the University of Southern California, medicine again at the University of Zurich and forestry at the University of Washington. Though he never received an advanced degree in any of these fields, he evidently was a very able student of science, indeed brilliant, according to his pathology professor at California (Bennett 1966, 41). The fact that he never settled into one specific field probably means that what interested him most was not a particular subject matter but scientific objectivity itself. Difficult though it is to determine exactly the literary significance of Jeffers' interest in science during these years, there was little question in his own mind as to the impact of the First World War upon his poetry. The Great War, as Henry May has shown, did not signify, much less cause, the end of American innocence for most American writers of the time; Modernism, moral and aesthetic, was fully evident in the work of T. S. Eliot, E. A. Robinson, and others before 1914 (May 1959). To Jeffers, however, the war was a liberating experience.

Speaking at the time in the third person, he summed up his opinion of the catastrophe in the following note (the exact date is uncertain): "He regards war with horror and disgust but believes it to be inevitable— and claims that he sees, at a certain level of contemplation, the tragic and the spectacular beauty of war, as of a storm or other natural disaster" (Bennett 1966, 86). At about the same time he confessed that the "conflict emotionally realized the external world for me and made much of the difference between my verses before the war and my verses since" (Bennett 1966, 86).

Jeffers' discovery of the external world inaugurated the poet's most creative period. Exactly what made it creative was his return to, rather than abandonment of, the problem of solipsism. In the light of his best work, this brittle issue turns out not to have been a merely adolescent pathos. For the metaphor of the mirror, he substituted the metaphor of incest, a device that he obviously believed held much richer possibilities when applied to narrative poetry. Tamar Cauldwell's incestuous relationship with her brother Lee in *Tamar* initiated a series of incest crimes that were to characterize Jeffers' narratives for more than three decades. The recurring incest motif, the source of the general sordidness of his work, became Jeffers' trademark in the literary economy. The conquest of solipsism became his explicitly avowed, animating interest as an artist. He explained his intentions in an undated letter to his friend, James Rorty. In reference to his ill-received narrative *The Women at Point Sur* (1927), he said that this poem was "an attempt to uncenter the human mind from itself. There is no health for the individual whose attention is taken up with his own mind and processes; equally there is no health for the society that is always introverted on its own members, as ours becomes more and more, the interest engaged inward in love and hatred, companionship and competition. These are necessary, of course, but as they absorb all the interest they become fatal" (rpt. in Alberts 1933, 38). In large measure, then, the importance of Jeffers' early writings rests on this

finally successful search for the appropriate form with which to drama-
tize the dangers inherent in what he came to believe was the essentially solipsistic human condition.

Unlike Adair, the new Jeffersean hero—the new Jeffers, as it were—
escapes from solipsism; and the drama of his escape clearly delineates
the author's final world-view: the doctrine of Inhumanism. Jeffers'
prose preface to *The Double Axe and Other Poems* provides the most
succinct exposition of this notion:

> A shifting of emphasis and significance from man to not-man; the rejection
> of human solipsism and recognition of the transhuman magnificence....
> This manner of thought and feeling is neither misanthropic nor pessimist
> [sic], though two or three people have said so and may again. It involves
> no falsehoods, and is a means of maintaining sanity in slippery times; it has
> objective truth and human value. It offers a reasonable detachment as rule
> of conduct, instead of love, hate and envy. It neutralizes fanaticism and
> wild hopes; but it provides magnificence for the religious instinct, and satis-
> fies our need to admire greatness and rejoice in beauty. (Jeffers 1948, vii)

Avoidance or rejection of Adair's predicament comes from upholding a stoical commitment to the "transhuman magnificence," now the
locus of *all* truth and beauty and greatness. Inhumanism reaffirms in
new guise the metaphysical passivity urged in "The Steadfast Sky."
Similarly, its ethic of reasonable detachment recalls another early
poem, "End of Summer." The Jeffersean protagonist in the poetry of
the 1920s and after embraces this ethic as he escapes from the slough
of solipsism through a mystical experience. Orestes in *The Tower Beyond Tragedy* and Gudrun in *At the Birth of an Age* follow the Inhumanist's creed and in death achieve a state of inhuman consciousness.
At the zenith of Orestes' experience he cries: "I was the stream /
Draining the mountain wood; and I the stag drinking; and I was the
stars / Boiling with light" (Jeffers 1938, 139). To Jeffers, "Organic

wholeness is the greatest beauty," as he says in "The Answer" (Jeffers 1938, 594).

Tamar (1924) and *Roan Stallion* (1925) brought to full fruition Jeffers' Inhumanism and prepared the way for all his later poetry. As *Tamar* introduced the single most important structural innovation in his poetry—the metaphor of incest—"The Truce and the Peace," a sequence of eleven sonnets published in the same year, firmly established his concept of the self. Throughout these poems the speaker wanders amid the ruin and chaos of the Great War in search of God. Unable to find him, he finally turns to the "essential me," which, he learns, has all along been the only "citadel where mastery remains"; within himself he discovers "The eternal living and untroubled God / Lying asleep upon a lily bed" (Jeffers 1938, 75–76). This divine essence is completely autonomous and inferior to no other deity, as Jeffers demonstrates in *Roan Stallion*. This poem, likely Jeffers' most famous, expands his concept of the self by investing it with a mystical capacity for transcendence. The heroine California's mystical-sexual union with the stallion-god transforms her into a "dark water, split by jets of lightning" (Jeffers 1938, 154). In an instant her single identity is fused with the divine being that lay behind all things; she has split the atom of her humanity by a monumental assertion of her own will. The ensuing release of energy enables her to glimpse Jeffers' "Steadfast Sky."

All of these themes converge in *The Tower Beyond Tragedy* (1925), the most complete dramatization of the Inhumanist-hero in conflict with himself, society, and nature. For this long narrative, Jeffers returned to "the feet of Aeschylus," as he remarked, to revive the Oresteia. If we bear in mind Jeffers' progress as a writer, his version of the story of Orestes' revenge becomes intelligible when considered as a mystical flight from an introverted, and therefore corrupt, society. After Orestes kills Clytemnestra, Electra proposes marriage to her brother—an incestuous relationship which she foolishly believes will perpetuate a glorious kingdom in Mycenae. By this time, however, her sensitive brother has already begun to have visions which lay open to him the horrible truth of their lives:

> I saw a vision of us [i.e., all humanity] move
> in the dark: all that we did or dreamed of
> Regarded each other, the man pursued the woman, the
> woman clung to the man, warriors and kings
> Strained at each other in the darkness, all loved or
> fought inward, each one of the lost people
> Sought the eyes of another that another should praise him;
> sought never his own but another's; the net of desire
> Had every nerve drawn to the center, so that they writhed
> like a full draught of fishes, all matted
> In the one mesh; when they look backward they see only
> a man standing at the beginning,
> Or forward, a man at the end; or if upward, men in the
> shining bitter sky striding and feasting,
> Whom you call Gods . . .
> It is all turned inward, all your desires incestuous, the
> woman the serpent, the man the rose-red cavern.
>
> (Jeffers 1938, 138)

Like the quaint protagonist of "Mirrors," the members of this society are all "regarding each other": they are not even aware of their own introversion, or what today would be called narcissism. These people regard each other compulsively, Orestes realizes, because of individual inner emptiness. In that void arise "incestuous desires."

Orestes, on the other hand, feels the same kind of despair and frustration that drove Adair to Africa. Orestes tries to explain to Electra that, when he lay on the hillside the day after he killed Clytemnestra and Aegisthus, feeling "sick with those visions" of an incestuous humanity, he suddenly fell "in love outward" and "entered the life of the brown forest" (Jeffers 1938, 138–39). Whereas to Adair the universe continuously mirrored to him images of his own face, to Orestes the universe is both distinct from the self and mystically accessible. At the end of *The Tower*, bewildered and disgusted by her brother's stubborn refusal to take the throne with her, Electra "entered the ancient house," her prison, while the Inhumanist Orestes "climbed the tower beyond time, consciously, and cast humanity, entered the earlier fountain" (Jeffers 1938, 140).

In his last poems Jeffers grew more bitter, and nowhere was his indictment of an introverted humanity more extreme than in *The Double Axe and Other Poems*, written during the Second World War. In the title narrative of that collection the Inhumanist-hero—called simply "The Inhumanist"—delivers a sermon to an imaginary audience of children that captures a great deal of the meaning of Jeffers' poetry when considered in light of the foregoing discussion:

> "O future children:
> Cruelty is dirt and ignorance, a muddy peasant
> Beating his horse. Ambition and powerlust
> Are for adolescents and defective persons. Moderate kindness
> Is oil on a crying wheel: use it. Mutual help
> Is necessary: use it when it is necessary.
> And as to love: make love when need drives.
> And as to love: love God. He is rock, earth and water, and
>   the beasts and stars; and the night that contains them.
> And as to love: whoever loves or hates man is fooled in a mirror...
>   love man in God."
>
> (Jeffers 1948, 106)

Here once again are Emerson's three kinds of love which caught Jeffers' attention as he was writing *Flagons and Apples*: "Initial love"

(" 'make love when need drives' "); "Celestial love" (" 'love God' ");
and the ever-present "Daemonic love," which deceives individuals and
societies alike. Haunted throughout his life by the same fear that
prompted him to write "Mirrors," Jeffers struggled to overcome the
solipsistic tendencies in his own mind by presenting in art a satisfying
paradox: through absolute self-abasement the self discovers its own divine nature and is then, like Orestes, prepared to know God.

★

Diluted, Emersonianism becomes a tedious recitation of neo-romantic
oddities. Jeffers' work spans the full range of them. The mere positing
of organic harmony in the early poems is as unconvincing as the bizarre posture of detachment found in the mature work. Such specious
harmony caricatures Emerson's *Nature* and "Self-Reliance," while Jeffersean detachment is a self-parody alongside Emerson's treatment of
moods and objects in "Experience." Mysticism becomes the sole and
predictable solution to solipsism, but both problem and solution per-
vert the Emersonian terms on which Jeffers' entire body of work depends. The only falsehood denoted by Inhumanism is one to which it
is indifferent: the falsehood that accompanies idea-mongering when
the latter becomes more interesting to the poet than poetry.

R. P. BLACKMUR: AGAINST THE CONTROL OF FALSE NAMES

Often, indirect influences stimulate the best creations. Just to grow up
in what his biographer, Russell Fraser, calls the "moralized landscape
of . . . Cambridge" (Fraser 1981, 5) in the tens and teens of this century
ensured that R. P. Blackmur would inherit the Emersonian legacy.
William James was a "near neighbor," as were others from the intellectual culture of Harvard—Royce, Santayana, Charles Eliot Norton:
"near neighbors" all, but in spirit only, for Blackmur's family was
genteel poor, and Richard Palmer Blackmur grew up in his mother's

boarding house, living there to age twenty-six. Blackmur was his mother's favorite all his life, and, though he never had a steady income until he began teaching at Princeton in 1940, he would often send her five or ten dollars during the depression years. Blackmur hated his father, who was a poor provider. In 1930 Blackmur married Helen Dickson, a painter; they were divorced after twenty-one mostly unhappy years in 1951 (Fraser 1981, 16, 248). In a brilliantly revealing passage Fraser points directly to Blackmur's literary ambition: "The damage of a lifetime cannot be repaired in the act of composition. It can be translated, though" (Fraser 1981, 91).

Translation entailed above all linguistic control. When he was only twenty, Blackmur wrote in his notebook: "What you control only under the form of false names, *you* do not control at all" (qtd. in Fraser 1981, 78). The control Blackmur values here, as Fraser remarks, means "taxonomy, not the 'vital control' of the [neo-]Humanists but the preternatural eye" (Fraser 1981, 78–79). Blackmur had a preternatural eye for poetry, and he became, if anyone has ever become, a poet-critic, as Robert Boyers has said. The taxonomy that is meant by control in Blackmur's work is always twofold: just as the act of writing requires one to draw the taxonomy exhibited in one's own composition, so the act of reading requires one to re-draw the taxonomy one discovers through careful study of another's work.

Though Blackmur did not take a college degree and attended only a few Harvard classes, he knew at this early age that his life would be a life of words; and he knew what it *meant* for a life to be such. He began, early, to "create a language for his sensations and feelings" as a writer and reader "in order that he might better know them," as Fraser observes (Fraser 1981, 78–79). In the creation of that language Blackmur wrote as though obedient to Emerson's directive, "Build, therefore, your own world." There is virtually no evidence of direct influence, however, not even the commonplace literary-historical evidence one finds in, say, Jeffers' formative years. What matters in

Blackmur's case, it seems to me, is that his life-long analysis of Modernism should have begun in the way that it did, with the above notebook entry, should have begun in that distinctively Emersonian mood of disciplined observation of his feelings and of words, a mood Blackmur sustained in his critical work for forty years. To say, as many have said, that Blackmur is the foremost critic of Modernism, is, I would say, to count him a true American Scholar. Language is the gesture of our uncreated selves, he once said, a remark that in the light of American literary-philosophical history conjures Emersonian monsters as well as cheerful Whitmanesque democrats, and recalls Emerson's demand that the writer take the whole society in an act of re-envisioning the broken social whole, with its strutting human figures of specialization.

Blackmur's critical achievement re-envisioned the whole, which has never been more broken than in the twentieth century. By the time he wrote, "Build, therefore, your own world" had been transformed by three or four neo-romantic generations into, in part, "What I say is both myself in truth and creates a new world," an aphorism Blackmur coined in his *Anni Mirabiles, 1921–1925: Reason in the Madness of Letters*, the Library of Congress Lectures for 1956.[4] But Blackmur asks of this cultural project: *Is* what I say in truth said in truth? What kind of new world does it create? What does truthful reporting on one's own self have to do with the making of worlds? Blackmur's critical work, from his first book, *The Double Agent* (1935), to his last, *A Primer of Ignorance* (posthumously published in 1967), turns on the manifold ambiguities of this aphorism, as the following discussion is meant to show. That it also describes his own divided mind only attests to the integrity with which Blackmur dedicated himself to replacing the control of false names with true names for both literature and criticism in the modern age.[5]

Though usually identified exclusively with the school of New Criticism, Blackmur developed his literary and other opinions not in the

Fugitive-Agrarian movements of the teens and twenties but in the more catholic and liberal ethos of the northeast. His subjects were almost wholly drawn from the literature and social thought of the post-Romantic period; and though, like virtually all twentieth-century critics, he owed a large intellectual debt to T. S. Eliot, he never showed in his work a consuming or even significant interest in the seventeenth-century Metaphysical poets from whom Eliot derived some of his critical principles as well as the essential tenor of his Anglo-Catholicism. Blackmur paid more attention to the modern novel than did any other New Critic, developing many of his ideas about fiction, as well as about the modern condition, through his studies of Henry James, Henry Adams, Flaubert, Dostoevsky, Mann, and Joyce. Blackmur's early work examined English and American poetry since Tennyson and Dickinson, but in his last books he was wholly preoccupied with the self-imposed task of restoring the lost prestige of bourgeois humanism, the principal vehicle of which, he believed, is modern literature. Though Blackmur did not use the term "bourgeois humanism" until the mid-forties, a decade after his reputation as a literary critic had been established, its meaning runs through all his work. In a late essay, Blackmur gave this concise definition:

> Bourgeois humanism (the treasure of residual reason in live relation to the madness of the senses) is the only conscious art of the mind designed to deal with our megalopolitan mass society: it alone knows what to do with momentum in its new guise; and it alone knows it must be more than itself without losing itself in order to succeed. (P, 13)

Much of my purpose in the following account of Blackmur's work is to elucidate this statement. Bourgeois humanism, I suggest, originates as a vigorous critique of such ideas as Emerson's dream of "the infinitude of the private man," Whitman's fantasy of democracy fulfilling itself in noble poems, and William James's belief in the temperamental basis of philosophical thought. Nowhere in his work, to be sure, does Blackmur directly confront Emerson, Whitman, and James as his intellectual forebears. Rather, he shaped his concept of bourgeois humanism as a critical response to other, contemporary writers' various assumptions about literature, criticism, and morals in mass society—assumptions that I cannot imagine coming into existence and seeming significant to an American literary intellectual in the early twentieth century had Emerson, Whitman, and James not contributed as decisively as they did to the formation of the *zeitgeist* current at that time.

Blackmur synthesized both American and European cultural legacies as a man of feeling well versed in the names and predicates through which emotion appears in public form. Denis Donoghue is right when he says that Blackmur "loved thought, but he felt that it was nearly always premature." "It was not that he despised ideas," Donoghue adds, "though indeed he was more concerned with feeling at a stage somewhat earlier than that in which it settles into the ripe old age . . . of ideas," a quality of mind Blackmur shares with Emerson (Donoghue 1977, xvi, xxvii–xxix). Blackmur's criticism—practical and theoretical, literary and social—occupies the intermediate stage that comes between feeling and the old age of positive doctrine. When Blackmur took up this issue itself and attempted to chart the ground between feeling and form, he produced his most comprehensive and difficult piece of work: "Between the *Numen* and the *Moha*: Notes Toward a Theory of Literature" (1954). By taking this essay as my starting point for the following account of his thought, I mean to highlight that facet of Blackmur's complex sensibility to which Donoghue alludes and which is only crudely formalized under the conventional heading of art in its manifold relations to life.

In "Between the *Numen* and the *Moha*: Notes Toward a Theory of Literature" (1954), Blackmur defines literature as the exemplary mediation between morals and behavior. As a moralist Blackmur offers "one way of seeing how it is that morals get into literature and what happens to them when they get there." "Morals" he defines as "what we think about in our quarrel with behavior." Because behavior also "gets into literature," Blackmur is equally interested in showing "what it does to morals when it gets there." This dialectical interplay of art and life, he warns, should not be viewed as a problem belonging to the upper reaches of aesthetic theory or ethics. It is both more elusive and more immediate, he claims. "We can begin, right up to the minute, at the threshold of our own consciousness, the point where what we do first declares itself, which is also the point where what we have thought mires itself in action. This is the point where dreams indeed become responsibility and thought a nightmare." In other words, morals get into literature because of certain ascertainable qualities of human action and thought. Action, he says, has the capacity to "declare itself," that is, to present itself at the threshold of consciousness with a name. As action takes on a name at the threshold of consciousness, so too thought "mire[s] itself in action." That is, the action that thought leads to is always a disappointment: it is never an adequate, or satisfying, version of its mental image. Thought takes on the appearance of "nightmare" when it turns into action (L, 289–90).

This perplexity is the basis of Blackmur's definition of literature as "a confrontation with behavior." Literature formally mediates thought and action, morals and behavior. "The arts and especially the arts of literature give theoretic form," he writes, drawing on Croce's terminology, to our passionate involvement with other people, whose behavior we fail to see because we either "minutely scrutinize" it or "refuse to recognize" it (L, 290). As we shall see, this claim for the uniqueness of literary apprehension, along with the implied critique of common sense and other non-literary modes of thought, is a recurring theme in Blackmur's vision of bourgeois humanism.

Human existence as pure behavior ensures the recurring "downfall of morals," which in turn "must always be remade, always on the old

grounds." The activity of remaking or re-invigorating morals is one
principal enterprise of what Blackmur calls "rational art." Together,
"rational art and morals . . . stand within the terms" *Numen* and *Moha*
in that they give form to the formlessness of human experience. In the
following passage Blackmur defines *Numen*:

> The *Numen* or *numinosus* is that power within us, greater than and other
> than ourselves, that moves us, sometimes carrying us away, in the end
> moving us forward unless we drop out, always overwhelming us. So far as
> it may be felt in literature it resembles the force of the sublime described by
> Longinus—the blow that transports us. It is a force sometimes cultivated as
> magic, as superstition, as mystery: it is related to the rhythm which gives
> meaning to action. Religion has always cultivated this force with the piety
> of excruciated sense, and religion has always taken it as the spring of Incar-
> nation or the Crucifixion. Thus the *Numen* enters, though it is not itself,
> behavior. It is the reality that presses into behavior but never reaches whole
> incarnation there. (*L*, 293)

The reason the *Numen* never remains itself upon "entering" behavior
is that it is immediately transformed by the *Moha*: "transformed, . . .
deflected, . . . or degraded into . . . the uncontrollable behavior which
tends to absorb and defile both the chill and the fire of spirit." *Moha*,
the Sanskrit word for cow, denotes "the basic, irremediable, irreplaceable, characteristic, and contemptuous stupidity of man confronted
with choice or purpose: the stupidity because of which he goes
wrong, without which he could not survive." Between transcendent
numinosus (*Numen*) and blind but "irreplaceable" and tenacious "will"
(*Moha*) lies reason (*L*, 293–94). Reason makes its explicit appearance in
the world "either as art or as the reflective faculty." This means that
reason is "the whole mind, the residual form of all we have been, and
the conceiving matrix of all that we may become." Art serves reason
by "reawakening" it "to its perennial vital task to see things together,

to be the subject not the agent of refreshment, to be the adjudicator not the master of the permanent but changing turbulence of the union of the *Numen* and the *Moha*" (L, 302).

As art and as reflective faculty, reason is the criterion Blackmur uses in his analyses of modern poetry and criticism in *The Double Agent*. In the name of reason, he explores in this book the poetry of Cummings, Pound, Stevens, Lawrence, Crane, Moore, and Eliot, as well as Henry James's Prefaces and assorted topics in criticism. These are essays on what writers do in their struggle over the inevitable asymmetry between language and its object, a struggle originating in the enduring incongruity between the individual writer's intentions and the shifting relationships between the *Numen* and the *Moha*. *The Double Agent* identifies two kinds of art: public, rational art, and private, irrational art.

Wallace Stevens is doubtless Blackmur's best example of a public artist. Stevens transforms his words into knowledge "by combining the insides of those words he found fit to his feelings" (D, 69).

> [Stevens'] great labor has been to allow the reality of what he felt personally to pass into the superior impersonal reality of words. Such a transformation amounts to an access of knowledge, as it raises to a condition where it may be rehearsed and understood in permanent form that body of emotional and sensational experience which in its natural condition makes life a torment and confusion. (D, 94)

The transformation of private experience into public art entails, in Stevens, the perfection of the *rhetoric* of his craft.

> Mr. Stevens is a genuine poet in that he attempts constantly to transform what is felt with the senses and what is thought in the mind—if we can still distinguish the two—into the realm of being, which we call poetry, where what is thought is felt and what is felt has the strict point of thought. And I

call his mode of achieving that transformation rhetorical because it is not lyric or dramatic or epic, because it does not transcend its substance, but is a reflection upon a hard surface, a shining mirror of rhetoric. (*D*, 100)

The unification in the poem of sensory experience and intellection makes Stevens' work the preserve of "a new sensibility" which thrives on the tension between the facticity of raw experience and the aesthetic harmony of the forms of expression. "Mr. Stevens," Blackmur claims,

has created a surface, a texture, a rhetoric in which his feelings and thoughts are preserved in what amounts to a new sensibility. The contrast between his subjects—the apprehension of all the sensual aspects of nature as instances of fate,—and the form in which the subjects are expressed is what makes his poetry valuable. Nature becomes nothing but words and to a poet words are everything. (*D*, 101–2)

To a poet words are "everything" only if what Blackmur calls their "insides" are connected to the private sensibility. The connection produces in the poem "an access of knowledge," a transformation which places the poem in public view. The error of connecting what he calls the "outsides" of words to the private sensibility produces at best a formalist rationality, at worst irrationality: the "baby talk" and the "violent inner confusion" of E. E. Cummings, whose poetry, in Blackmur's estimation, fails not because of insufficient intellectual force but rather because it represents the felt experience of the poet in mere supersensible abstractions, remaining a private vision and private vocabulary (*D*, 28).

This distinction between the "insides" and the "outsides" of words establishes in Blackmur's essays on modern poetry his theory of poetic language. Poetic language exploits the "insides" of words for the purposes of producing as much meaning or rationality as possible. "When a word is used in a poem," he declares, "it should be the sum of all its appropriate history made concrete and particular in the individual context; and in poetry all words act as if they were so used, because the only kind of meaning poetry can have requires that all its words resume their full life; the full life being modified and made unique by the qualifications the words perform one upon the other in the poem" (D, 8). Poetic meaning thus comes from the *action* of words upon each other. Words can act upon each other only if the poet knows their "insides" thoroughly; in the essay on Stevens he explains that

> If a poet knows precisely what his words represent, what he writes is much more likely to seem new and strange—and even difficult to understand—, than if he uses words ignorantly and at random. That is because when each word has definite character the combinations cannot avoid uniqueness. Even if a text is wholly quotation, the condition of quotation itself qualifies the text and makes it so far unique. Thus a quotation made from Marvell by Eliot has a force slightly different from what it had when Marvell wrote it [sic]. Though the combination of words is unique it is read, if the reader knows his words either by usage or dictionary, with a shock like that of recognition. The recognition is not limited, however, to what was already known in the words; there is a perception of something previously unknown, something new which is literally an access of knowledge. Upon the poet's skill in combining words as much as upon his private feelings, depends the importance or the value of the knowledge. (D, 69)

On the other hand, the poet who is ignorant of the "insides" of words is compelled to use them randomly, the randomness of his usage standing as the prominent sign of his own inner turmoil.

It is a mark of the irrationality of our time, Blackmur seems to be saying, that the "discursive relationships" of ordinary communication are made of words "commonly spoken and written with the least possible meaning preserved, instead of the most. History is taken for granted, ignored, or denied. Only the outsides of words, so to speak, are used: and doubtless the outsides of words are all that the discursive intelligence needs" (D, 8). The perfection of the "outsides" of words in the language of public discourse is one of the precondi- tions in the domain of culture for fascism. The alternative, so far as the domain of culture is concerned, is "rational art," with its simul- taneous sublimation of private experience and production of publicly accessible knowledge. "No time could have greater need than our own for rational art," Blackmur wrote in his essay on Crane in 1935, for "no time could surrender more than ours does daily, with drums beating, to fanatic politics and despotically construed emo- tions" (D, 121).

Public art, a major medium of human mutual recognition, is not an unreachable ideal beyond human artistic capacities. Nonetheless, it is a rarity in modern literature, as the essays in *The Double Agent* demon- strate. Between the opposite poles of, on the one end, private irration- ality and, on the other, publicly accessible knowledge, Blackmur displays the works of these writers, judging each of them by the crite- ria summarized above while raising further issues. Chief among these issues is the "demon of enthusiastic inspiration," examined in the es- say on Lawrence's verse, "D. H. Lawrence and Expressive Form." "Expressive form" is a fallacy because it spells the end of what Black- mur calls "education," as well as the end of form itself. "If you become content, even tormentedly," he wryly declares, "with self- expression, the process of education no less than that of taste ceases, and anything may come to stand, and interchangeably, for anything else" (D, 107). This means that expressive form willy-nilly gives rise to a democratic anonymity of words and is therefore one of the tendencies in the democratic age that needs to be resisted. Put differently, expressive form is the literary correlate of radical individualism, an individualism so extreme that ironically it leads the artist to subvert his own work. How? "When you depend entirely upon the demon of inspiration, the inner voice, the inner light, you deprive yourself of any external criterion to show whether the demon is working or not. Because he is yours and you willfully depend upon him, he will seem to be operating with equal intensity at every level of imagination" (*D*, 106). It is precisely this tendency which Blackmur claims is "the plague afflicting the poetry of the last hundred and fifty years," of which Lawrence was only "the extreme victim" (*D*, 105).

It is not by any means, however, an inevitable tendency in modernist culture, and there are significant countervailing tendencies that Blackmur was equally interested in examining, such as those in Stevens' work. In "The Method of Marianne Moore" Blackmur presents an especially instructive example of the "attack upon the formless in life and art" (*D*, 145). He agrees with Moore that "we cannot have poetry until poets can be 'literalists of the imagination' " (*D*, 148). To be a "literalist of the imagination" is to employ poetic method as the "agent of growth and the recording instrument of" sensibility: method as the source of limits, not "formula" (*D*, 169). The "intellectual base of all her work," her "practical aesthetic," Blackmur says, is to be found in the last lines of her poem "The Past is the Present" (*D*, 160).

> Ecstasy/affords the occasion and expediency/determines the form.

Moore's poetic method enables her to make this jump from occasion to form because her method is entirely consistent with her peculiar sensibility. Her method is both "pervasive" in her work and "integral" to it, "integral to the degree that, with her sensibility being what it is, it imposes limits more profoundly than it liberates poetic energy." The consequence of Moore's application of her poetic method is "the astonishing fact that none of . . . [her] poems attempt to be major poetry[;] . . . she is content with smallness in fact so long as it suggests the great by implication" (D, 168–69).

Eliot is as strict as Moore in his observance of limits in poetic composition but tends rather toward a philosophical realism than a philosophical nominalism. In "T. S. Eliot: From Ash Wednesday to Murder in the Cathedral," Blackmur considers the implications of a statement in Eliot's *After Strange Gods*, later to be well known: "I should say that in one's prose reflexions one may be legitimately occupied with ideals, whereas in the writing of verse one can only deal with actuality" (D, 184). The actual, for Blackmur as for Eliot, is the formless—whether in life or in art. It is, in Eliot's words, "the deeper, unnamed feelings which form the substratum of our being, to which we rarely penetrate" (D, 185). Named, feelings become emotions, and the process by which they are named, according to Blackmur, is the process of art: "poetry is the concrete . . . presentation of experience as emotion." Blackmur claims that in Western culture there have been but three sources of names with which to apprehend actuality: the Church; the rationalist tradition as carried in the philosophy of Plato, Montaigne, and Spinoza; and "that nameless tradition of the supernatural in daily life which includes folk-magic and extra-Christian religion." All three of these cultural superstructures, he notes, are today either ignored or regarded as "modes of escape" (D, 185). Yet they remain the only avenues along which actuality can be reached and in terms of which it may be represented in poetry. Eliot has elected a variant of the first of these three: Anglo-Catholicism. Blackmur's task in this essay is to explain precisely how Eliot has fused religious belief and poetic imagination, and more generally to suggest how the reader of modern poetry might regard it as an elaborate play of ideas and systems of belief, more or less useful for giving names to what we actually feel. In the case of Eliot, "no fact requires so much emphasis as the fact that . . . Mr. Eliot's poetry is not religion," a point that was lost to many of Eliot's readers. Religion is the "background"; the "actual" is the "foreground"; and, standing between the two, Eliot "in the light of the one operates upon the other" (*D*, 188).

It follows from this reconstruction by Blackmur of the relation of the poet to his work that the problem for criticism is that of "the moral and technical validity of Mr. Eliot's Christianity as it labors to seize the actual for representation in his poetry" (*D*, 187). In other words, Blackmur defines Eliot's poetry not as religious statement in poetic garb but as a "dramatised projection of experience," with Eliot's Anglo-Catholicism serving as the means of dramatic projection (*D*, 191). Once achieved, the dramatic projection—the poem—reaches inside the shell of the once dominant Christian culture which, to modern readers, exists only as "stereotypes of spiritual manners." "These stereotypes form our natural nexus with the impetus or drive of his poetry; and it is as we see them filled out, refreshed, reembodied, that his poems become actual for us" (*D*, 195). But it would be a gross error to imagine that such an effect in the reader is tantamount to a religious experience for which we should prayerfully thank the poet. If anything, Blackmur's analysis of Eliot only reaffirms the secularism of both Blackmur and the age. By subjecting Eliot's poetry to the test of how much and how well it dramatically projects experience—provides names for the hitherto nameless—Blackmur leaves Eliot's religious commitments to Eliot, while at the same time placing Eliot's work within the purview of rational art. For a reader—other than Eliot himself, perhaps—to regard the "religious bias" in his poetry as anything more than incidental to it is to invite theological argument from the religious and arrogant dismissal of Eliot's work from the irreligious. The latent mechanistic aesthetic common to both such responses to Eliot's religiosity fails to grasp the major contradiction in his work: on one side, its aesthetic modernism; on the other, his otherworldliness, and, in between, the transformation through art of personal religious

piety into concrete enactment. The upshot of this analysis is that
Eliot's piety, an embarrassment to most of his readers, disappears into
his poetry, where it exists not as content, not as form, but as sheer
heuristic. Thus Eliot's poems, like thought itself, are "beacons," ways
of seeing.

Blackmur's pivotal essay "The Critical Prefaces of Henry James," a
concise summary of James's criticism of the novel, may serve as an
apposite statement of Blackmur's theory of the relation of art to life.
For James,

> the subject of art was life, or more particularly someone's apprehension of
> the experience of it, and in striving truly to represent it art removed the
> waste and muddlement and bewilderment in which it is lived and gave it a
> lucid, intelligible form. By insisting on intelligence and lucidity something
> like an ideal vision was secured; not an ideal in the air but an ideal in the
> informed imagination, an ideal, in fact, actually of life, limited only by the
> depth of the artist's sensibility of it. Thus art was the viable representation
> of moral value; in the degree that the report was intelligent and intense the
> morals were sound. (D, 242)

In other words, what art does is to construct moral value from the
materials of amoral and formless experience. This construction of
moral value is what Blackmur (and James) mean by "representation";
that is, art does not give a mimetic presentation of experience but
something like a moral account of it, perhaps a moral victory over it.

Blackmur, following James, locates the mainsprings of art in the
artist's conflict with society.

> [James] wanted the truth about the important aspects of life as it was expe-
> rienced, and he wanted to represent that truth with the greatest possible lu-
> cidity, beauty, and fineness, not abstractly or in mere statement, but
> vividly, imposing on it the form of the imagination, the acutest relevant

sensibility, which felt it. Life itself—the subject of art—was formless and likely to be a waste with its situations leading to endless bewilderment; while art, the imaginative representation of life, selected, formed, made lucid and intelligent, gave value and meaning to, the contrasts and oppositions and processions of the society that confronted the artist. The emphases were on intelligence—James was avowedly the novelist of the free spirit, the liberated intelligence—on feeling, and on form. (D, 267)

The subject of art is life—meaning that contradictory, inchoate, incoherent, mystifying social reality which the artist feels bearing down upon him. As the second passage points out, society is thought to *confront* the artist. The artist gets his revenge by creating a work which in turn confronts life. Literature is a confrontation with behavior. The act of producing the literary work involves a transmutation of the artist's own peculiar social situation into an aesthetic comprehension of it, which is embodied in the work. There is, therefore, a sense in which the real subject of all modern art is the artist himself, or more precisely the felt tension between the artist and society. In James's case, this aesthetic rationalized his preoccupation with the so-called "liberated intelligence," that is, rationalized his wish for a world freed from its intrinsic irrationality and dominated by intelligence and sensitivity.

The most comprehensive yet succinct statement of Blackmur's critical thought in *The Double Agent* is his well-known "A Critic's Job of Work," the concluding essay. Blackmur calls this piece an exercise in "theory and apologetics" employing the "implicit" statement almost exclusively. The chief premise of his argument could be said to be this: no critical approach to literature can be truly definitive, for all approaches are invariably incomplete. Blackmur considers the incompleteness of every possible approach not a regrettable failing but a highly desirable quality. Even more desirable is the attitude of the critic who acknowledges the partialness of his particular approach; Blackmur regards such candor as a sign that the critic is capable of observing intellectual limits. The worst criticism is that which attempts to substitute its distinctive partialness for wholeness, thereby risking the loss of whatever strength it may possess in its incompleteness alone. Granville Hicks's *The Great Tradition* (1933) typifies criticism that presumes to substitute the part for the whole—a reductionist economism that is almost beyond salvaging (*D*, 283). Less obnoxious to Blackmur is the work of I. A. Richards, but Blackmur vigorously disagrees with Richards' claim that literary criticism can, much less ought to, be made into a science of linguistics, or into any science. Blackmur holds that "literary criticism is not a science—though it may be the object of one; and to try to make it one is to turn it upside down" (*D*, 290–91).

The purpose of "A Critic's Job of Work" is to provide a definition of literary criticism. If literary criticism is not a science, what is it? It is "the formal discourse of an amateur," Blackmur says. Just as literature consists in an elaborate naming of human experience, criticism consists in an elaborate naming of literature.

> When there is enough love and enough knowledge represented in the discourse [of the amateur] it is a self-sufficient but by no means an isolated art. It witnesses constantly in its own life its interdependence with the other arts. It lays out the terms and parallels of appreciation from the outside in order to convict itself of internal intimacy; it names and arranges what it knows and loves, and searches endlessly with every fresh impulse or impression for better names and more orderly arrangements. (*D*, 269)

Criticism and art are analogous cultural activities, united symbiotically as in the Jamesian vision examined earlier, but in the following comments given an Arnoldian twist:

> It is only in this sense [Blackmur continues in the same passage] that poetry (or some other art) is a criticism of life; poetry names and arranges, and thus arrests and transfixes its subject in a form which has a life of its own

forever separate but springing from *the life which confronts it*. Poetry is life at the remove of form and meaning; not life lived but life framed and identified. So the criticism of poetry is bound to be occupied at once with the terms and modes by which the remove was made and with the relation between—in the ambiguous stock phrase—content and form; which is to say with the establishment and appreciation of human or moral value. (*D*, 269; emphasis added)

At its best, criticism draws on the resources of "unindoctrinated thinking," of which the two leading exemplars are, in Blackmur's view, the dramatic irony of the early Plato and the imaginative skepticism of Montaigne. The *Dialogues* and the *Essays* are marked by "the absence of positive doctrine," i.e., the absence of a fixed idea or ideas. In the place of positive doctrine Plato and Montaigne offer the spectacle of conflicting ideas held in "shifting balance" and discourse informed with a "provisional, adjudicating irony." What is important is the play of ideas, the dynamics of the mind, as opposed to either the proffering or the seizing of doctrinal truth. When criticism is infused with unindoctrinated thinking, it can effectively carry out its naming and appreciatory functions (*D*, 274–75). Criticism is first of all, then, a wide-ranging intellectual activity, not a professional technique, much less an assortment of methods. Blackmur takes pains to show that criticism rightly includes the work of such diverse thinkers as George Santayana (*Three Philosophical Poets* [1910]), Van Wyck Brooks (*The Pilgrimage of Henry James* [1925]), Granville Hicks (*The Great Tradition* [1933]), I. A. Richards (*Science and Poetry* [1926]), Kenneth Burke (*Permanence and Change* [1935]), S. Foster Damon (*William Blake* [1924]), and others.

In general, "any rational approach is valid to literature and may properly be called critical which fastens at any point upon the work itself " (*D*, 277–78). This is a more useful assertion than it might at first appear to be. It enables Blackmur to endorse Richards' concept of poetry as "the chief source of meaning and value for the life we live," because Richards' concept forces close attention to the poetic text, while at the same time discarding his scientific pretensions. Blackmur's flexible definition of valid literary approaches prepares him also to credit Santayana's skillful disclosure of the philosophical import of Lucretius' *De Rerum Natura*, because the poem actually has significant philosophical import, while at the same time insisting that it is not the philosophy but the idiom which makes Lucretius' poem a poem. No matter how close Richards gets to the poem—even to the point of reducing it to its linguistic components—or how distant Santayana remains from the poem—to the point of missing its idiom nearly altogether—both approaches to literature are rational because each in its own way is at least tangentially attached to the text.

Blackmur defines as "invalid" any approach to literature which is "confused," i.e., lacking internal limits because whatever limits may be possible for it "tend to cancel each other out," yielding a discourse characterized by "the evil of stultification and the malice of controversy." Invalid criticism is by definition irrational criticism. The work of Irving Babbitt, for example, is invalid because it is "governed by an *idée fixe*" (namely, the inner check and the higher will), a self-serving concept which effectively purges Babbitt's criticism of its potential rational content, leaving behind pure emotionalism, at times even fanaticism (D, 278).

Blackmur is circumspect and metaphorical in describing the main features of his own approach to criticism.

> It is, I suppose, an approach to literary criticism—to the discourse of an amateur—primarily through the technique, in the widest sense of that word, of the examples handled; technique on the plane of words but also technique on the plane of intellectual and emotional patterns in Mr. Burke's sense, and technique, too, in that there is a technique of securing and arranging and representing a fundamental view of life. (D, 299)

Technique as defined here means: language, intellectual and emotional patterns, and the presentation of a view of life. Technique is all.

> The advantage of the technical approach is I think double. It readily admits other approaches and is anxious to be complemented by them. Furthermore, in a sense, it is able to incorporate the technical aspect, which always exists, of what is secured by other approaches—as I have argued elsewhere that so unpromising a matter as T. S. Eliot's religious convictions may be profitably considered as a dominant element in his technique of revealing the actual.

That is, technique is, in Blackmur's definition, a category so all-encompassing as to rise above any conventional distinction between literature and literary criticism. Blackmur in fact sees an affinity between his own technical literary criticism and Eliot's approach to poetic composition; both are preeminently technical.

> The second advantage of the technical approach is a consequence of the first; it treats of nothing in literature except in its capacity of reduction to literary fact, which is where it resembles scholarship, only passing beyond it in that its facts are usually further into the heart of literature than the facts of most scholarship. Aristotle, curiously, is here the type and master; as the *Poetics* is nothing but a collection and explanation of the facts of Greek poetry, it is the factual aspect that is invariably produced. (*D*, 299)

In other words, the advantage of the technical approach is first of all that it is empirical. The assumption here is that there is such a thing as literary factuality, and, further, that one can and should observe literary facts. This assumption raises the question of what a literary fact is, a question that necessitates a dialectical shift from the empirical to the rational plane.

The rest of the labour is in the effort to find understandable terms to fit the composition of the facts. After all, it is only the facts about a poem, a play, a novel, that can be reduced to tractable form, talked about, and examined; the rest is the product of the facts, from the technical point of view, and not a product but the thing itself from its own point of view. The rest, whatever it is, can only be known, not talked about. (*D*, 299–300)

The disclosure of literary facts and the invention of names to fit them: these are the two activities comprising the critic's "job of work." So defined, does not the critic's task call for sheer pedestrian effort? The answer is no, for literary factuality is problematic and the invention of names to fit the facts of literature is a process that calls into question, at every turn, the nature of literature and even of reason itself.

Blackmur cautiously admits that there may be "principles that cover both the direct apprehension and the labour of providing modes for the understanding of the expressive arts. If so, they are Socratic and found within, and subject to the fundamental skepticism as in Montaigne." As if this were not enough to deter the search for such principles, he adds the following comment, which in effect places skepticism and irony at the heart of literature and literary criticism alike:

There must be seeds, let us say—seeds, germs, beginning forms upon which I can rely and to which I resort. When I use a word, an image, a notion, there must be in its small nodular apparent form, as in the peas I am testing on my desk, at least prophetically, the whole future growth, the whole harvested life; and not rhetorically nor in formula, but stubbornly, pervasively, heart-hidden, materially, in both the anterior and the eventual prospect as well as in the small handled form of the nub. What is it, what are they, these seeds of understanding? And if I know, are they logical? Do they take the processional form of the words I use? Or do they take a form like that of the silver backing the glass, a dark enholding all brightness? *Is*

> *every metaphor—and the assertion of understanding is our great metaphor—mixed*
> *by the necessity of its intention? What is the mixture of a word, an image, a no-*
> *tion?* (D, 300)

Understanding is the supreme end to be achieved, yet is never
achieved: not because it is an unreachable ideal but because the very
assertion of understanding is itself only an exercise in "the persistent
reformulation of the myth of reason" (D, 272). Reason exists, therefore, not pure but only in its infinitude of reformulations, which we
call with inevitable overconfidence "understanding." Inhering in the
choice of a word, an image, a notion are what Blackmur calls the
"seeds" or "germs" of understanding. "Every metaphor" may thus be
a mixed metaphor, made so by virtue of its having arisen from the
complex intentions of its creator. There is no understanding, only attempts to understand. Some of these attempts are logical and "take the
processional [i.e., linear] form of words." Other attempts at understanding are pre-logical, a-logical, or non-logical, and assume a form
"like that of the silver backing a glass, a dark enholding all brightness." Clearly, the dichotomies here are those of reason and imagination, mechanism ("procession") and organism ("seeds"), consciousness
and the pre-conscious.

Art originates in the tension between these analogous dichotomies.
Blackmur's answer to his own question, "What is the mixture of a
word, an image, a notion?" makes this point clear by asserting an epistemology of literature:

> The mixture . . . even in the fresh use of an old word, is made in the pre-
> conscious, and is by hypothesis unascertainable. . . . By intuition we adven-
> ture in the pre-conscious; and there, where the adventure is, there is no
> need or suspicion of certainty or meaning; there is the living, expanding,
> prescient substance without the tags and handles of conscious form. Art is
> the looking-glass of the pre-conscious, and when it is deepest seems to par-

ticipate in it sensibly. Or, better, for the purposes of criticism, our sensibility resumes the division of the senses and faculties at the same time that it preens itself into conscious form. Criticism may have as an object the establishment and evaluation (comparison and analysis) of the modes of making the pre-conscious consciously available. (*D*, 301)

The epistemology stated here and throughout Blackmur's literary criticism in *The Double Agent* may be said in summary to consist of the following premises: (a) the region of the pre-conscious, or pure sensibility, is the seed-bed of words, images, and ideas, all of which go by the term "prescient substance"; the pre-conscious can be entered only by intuition since it is by definition formless, form being the hallmark of consciousness; (b) the pre-conscious, however, is neither autonomous nor static; rather, it has the capacity to "preen itself" into conscious form, which it does through various modes; these modes are the modes of art; (c) as the "looking-glass of the pre-conscious," art is therefore the reflection of the prescient substance of sensibility and its mixtures of words, images, and ideas; (d) one purpose of criticism is to analyze these artistic reflections, to discover what the prescient substance has made of itself.

From "Between the *Numen* and the *Moha*" we may recall the following interwoven themes: (a) the idea of literature as the exemplary mediation between morals and behavior; (b) the double complexity of mind and language, which produces an ever-present disparity between language and its object; (c) the dialectic of public and private, rational and irrational, art. The essays on poetry in *The Double Agent* all start with considerations of language (b) and in the course of exploring the craft of modern poetry take up allied considerations of the public-private dialectic (c). The James essay reveals that the idea of literature as a confrontation with behavior (a) undergirds the essays on poetry; this essay also explains the sense in which Blackmur thinks any use of language or manipulation of form is a moral act. Finally, the essay on criticism establishes the link between rational art and rational criticism and articulates the epistemology of literature on which Blackmur bases his practical criticism.

In his provocative book, *The Post-Modern Aura: The Act of Fiction in an Age of Inflation*, Charles Newman has traced the post-modern mentality to two twentieth-century revolutions: the first, "that remarkable explosion of artistic talent and high skepticism, so broadly based yet chronologically concentrated, which wrenched us forever from 19th Century Positivism and whose accomplishments were in place by the First World War"; the second, "the revolution in pedagogy and criticism which interpreted, canonized and capitalized the Modernist industry" (Newman 1985, 27). Neither post-Modernism nor Modernism foresaw "the possibility that Bourgeois culture may have escaped Bourgeois control, or that any critique of Bourgeois consciousness must be to some extent self-criticism" (Newman 1985, 30). Blackmur contributed significantly to both revolutions, but it is because of those contributions, not in spite of them, that he stands as an instructive partial exception to Newman's generalizations. Though Blackmur's literary thought did not significantly change after *The Double Agent*, his essays in social criticism of the 1940s and 1950s were entirely devoted to exploring the prospects for bourgeois humanism. It was exactly Blackmur's thesis in these essays that bourgeois culture—or bourgeois humanism—had escaped bourgeois control. Just as important, he insisted that mass society was thereby left rudderless. For Blackmur, in these late essays, the fate of modern society was intertwined with the fate of literature and of the man of letters. There is a recurring tension, common to all these essays of his later phase, between the abstract content of bourgeois humanism and its entrustment by Blackmur to the custodial care of an intellectual elite, a tension that influences the content of bourgeois humanism itself and partly accounts for the peculiar sense of urgency characteristic of Blackmur's last work.

Blackmur defined this problem for the first time in "A Featherbed for Critics," the concluding essay of *The Expense of Greatness* (1940). The writer, Blackmur suggested, is a person without a profession in American life. That is, the writer lacks a public role and public support. The institutions of "capitalist democracy" are at fault: the priest "requires the church, . . . the lawyer requires the courts, . . . the doctor requires the hospital and the school. . . . " "Serious writers," Blackmur continues, "are no different; for them it would seem to-day that the university is the only available institution . . . " (*E*, 287). And the university is inadequate because, like American society itself, it does not take the writer seriously, or not seriously enough, in that it does not as a rule bring him into its midst to teach what he knows (the profession of writing) but to teach a variety of other subjects (*E*, 284). Were this institutional problem to be rectified, Blackmur says, there might be generated a renewed "respect . . . for men of letters," even a new "race" of such men. But the problem has deep roots; the entire history of the American writer, as compared with the history of his European counterpart, offers no reason to think it can be solved: "The difference between Zola and Dreiser, Rousseau (of *The Confessions*) and Wolfe, is not only a difference of talent; it is a difference, too, in the quality of the operative force of the whole social institutions which they willy-nilly represent" (*E*, 281).

As a group lacking professional status, writers often trap themselves by their own obsession with technique; they are inclined to presume that "if you know *how* to do, *what* you do will take care of itself" (*E*, 299). This presumption leads—or cannot be prevented from leading—to "fanaticism," which to Blackmur is an expression of the absence of authoritativeness (*E*, 300). Opposite of "fanaticism" is what Blackmur calls "conviction," the tone and character he prefers in the professional writer. "Conviction" means "inward mastery of the outward materials of experience" (*E*, 301). That is, the "convicted" writer is not just technically adept; he is also virtuous, and in a double sense. First,

he recognizes that his material is morals. Second, he possesses sufficient moral courage to remain faithful to his vision of experience.

> The material of the writer is morals; as the de Goncourts said, ethics in
> action; inescapably: not creative morals, not ideal morals, but actual morals
> of behaviour, whether projected or real. The writer cannot help taking soci-
> ety as he finds it; his difficulty and his obligation as a writer consist in the
> attempt to see what he finds as actual, remembering always that the fantas-
> tic and the illusionary may be as good witnesses to the actual, if seen in the
> buff, as the quotidian and the undeluded; and very likely better. His diffi-
> culty as a man and his obligation toward society consist in the attempt to
> be honest in distinguishing the actual—never failing to separate what can be
> felt from the mere wilful imperative of what ought to be felt and never
> using an imperative at all except in a subordinate position outside the focal
> interest. To combine conceptual honesty and the act of vision is the con-
> stant athletic feat of the artist, requires all the poor talent he can muster,
> and of course most often stops short at failure—showing mere honesty or
> mere vision or mere mechanism. The test of success is enduring interest;
> and there, in enduring interest, lies the writer's whole authority and his sole
> moral strength. It is perfidy to the actual that weakens a writer and disinte-
> grates his writing, and it is fidelity to the actual that strengthens him and
> gives his writing its only effect on society. (E, 293)

To have such an effect on society, however, the writer needs the support of his own profession, which in turn needs the support of society. "Without the profession of writing behind him, the individual
writer is reduced to small arms; without society behind it, the profession is impotent and bound to betray itself " (E, 303).
Blackmur proposes that one sector of professional American writers—professional critics—undertake the rehabilitation of the profession
of writing. Their task will be to create among writers a professional
consciousness and appropriate social support for it. Critics should be

conscious that what they are doing in carrying out this task is prepar-
ing the way for a new historical era when, once again, as in the Christian Middle Ages, there will be a unified culture whose values,
according to Blackmur, the writer articulates, conserves, modifies, and
sometimes re-creates. The new class of writers, to be brought into
being with the aid of professional critics, will create the "next moment of mastery" in society by disclosing society's "convictions." The
rehabilitation of the profession of writing is thus a pre-condition of a
new social order, when, as a matter of course, rather than (as now)
out of near desperation, the writer will know and will act on his true
responsibility. "To the responsible writer," Blackmur concludes,
"conviction turns everything to strength"—meaning, creates moral
value out of the writer's fidelity to the actual.

"The Economy of the American Writer," published five years after
"A Featherbed for Critics," extends the analysis of the profession of
writing into American history in order to refute the common notion
of the "cultural market" as the mechanism believed to guarantee the
survival and prosperity of serious writing. Blackmur argues that the
free market in literature in fact only guarantees the decline of literary
standards and may even spell the ruination of literature. In other
words, the free market in literature produces the same effects as the
free market in society generally:

> it dissolves all but the lowest values and preserves only the cheapest values:
> those which can be satisfactorily translated into money; for it is only the
> cheapest sort of life, of thought, of art that can throw its values into the
> competition of the open market as the market developed in the nineteenth
> and early twentieth century without loss of values themselves. (L, 56)

The universalizing and leveling tendencies of the market are especially
reckless in the mass society. Unlike more obviously class-structured
societies, the mass society is diffuse in every department of life where

diffuseness can be fatal—that is, in intellectual pursuits and in the arts. Pragmatic economic activity and radical population expansion, on the other hand, seemingly thrive on this very randomness. In the following passage, Blackmur adapts Henry Adams' "scientific" vocabulary to account for the evils of the free market in American literature and thought:

> The breaking of a continental wilderness and the explosion of population from five to a hundred millions within a century built up over what it used an enormous dispersed, unorganized reserve of human energy—intellectual and artistic as well as mechanical and economical. It did not begin to concentrate the intellectual energy until about 1900 and has not yet effectively concentrated the artistic energy; and until energy is concentrated—or organized in some way—it can have only a low degree of availability. Thus intellect and art in the United States tended to operate on a kind of average or low level of potential though in relatively great quantity. That is, the mass was great but the intensity was almost non-existent. Thus our society has been administered more by the forward drive of its inertia in the mass, which happened to be accelerating and therefore kept ahead of its problems, than it was administered by direct intelligence and imagination. (*L*, 53–54)

Blackmur's aim—the aim he sets for himself and other critics and by extension for the profession of letters—is to find ways of reversing this historical development. By 1945, when this essay was published, he had already noted one new trend: some writers and artists (himself included) had begun to affiliate themselves with universities, whether with good or with ill effect for either artists or universities, he could not say. He observed, though, that universities themselves were increasingly pressured by mass social conditions, and as a result were being drawn into "the orbit of the market system." They were becoming as a result "social and technical service stations" (*L*, 60).

As these two early exercises in social criticism suggest, Blackmur would substitute elite leadership for the prevailing and bankrupt cultural market. "A Burden for Critics" (1948) and "The Lion and the Honeycomb" (1950) reiterate his recommendation that professional critics assume their proper duties as the cultural vanguard. The critique of the New Criticism, for which these two essays are well known, is subsumed under this larger issue of the social role of the literary elite and, in my view, cannot adequately be understood apart from the overall development of Blackmur's elitist thought.

"A Burden for Critics" opens on the theme of ignorance, a theme to which Blackmur would return many times in the course of his social thought. "Poetry," he writes, "is one of the things we do to our ignorance"(L, 198). The mass society has thrown up its own new form of ignorance—labeled by Blackmur the "new illiteracy" for the first time in "The Economy of the American Writer"—which transforms the task of poet and critic alike (L, 56).

> In our own time . . . almost everything is required of the arts and particularly of literature. Almost the whole job of culture, as it has formerly been understood, has been dumped into the hands of the writer. Possibly a new form of culture, appropriate to a massive urban society, is emerging: at any rate there are writers who write with a new ignorance and a new collective illiteracy: I mean the Luce papers and Hollywood. But the old drives persist. Those who seem to be the chief writers of our time have found their subjects in attempting to dramatize at once both the culture and turbulence it was meant to control, and in doing so they have had practically to create—as it happens, to re-create—the terms, the very symbolic substance, of the culture as they went along. (L, 201)

Literature, of all the intellectual and aesthetic activities of modern life, alone possesses sufficient comprehensiveness and insight to re-make the inchoate symbolic substance of modern culture into an expression of morals and mind.

These same historical conditions require that criticism explain what poetry has done to our ignorance—by teaching us to read and by explicating poetry's innumerable concrete enactments of moral value. To carry out the job of criticism, the modern critic must become a cultural midwife, mediating between literature and the audience. As the general mind of society is narrowed to the literary, as "the whole job of culture" falls to writers, there is a corresponding degradation of the audience's capacity for response. That is, at precisely the historical moment when literature assumes (by default, Blackmur later explains) the heaviest cultural burden and is most needed, the audience "is able to bring less to the work of art than under the conditions of the old culture. . . . " The "burden of criticism in our time . . . is to make bridges between the society and the arts: to prepare the audience for its art and to prepare the arts for their artists." What the "audience needs" is "instruction in the lost skill of symbolic thinking" (L, 206).

The instability and formlessness of the mass society produce a larger and debilitated audience. Its incompetence is ensured by two interrelated consequences of mass social conditions. The first is "the disappearance or at least the submergence of tradition"

in the sense that it is no longer available at either an instinctive or a critical level but must be looked for, dug out, and largely re-created as if it were a new thing and not traditional at all. We have also a decay of the power of conviction or mastery; we permit ourselves everywhere to be overwhelmed by the accidents of our massive ignorance and by the apparent subjectivity of our individual purposes. Thus we have lost the field of our common reference, we have dwindled in our ability to think symbolically, and as we look about us we see all our old unconscious skills at life disappearing without any apparent means of developing new unconscious skills. (L, 203)

The loss of a common world, once presided over and given a measure of continuity by folk knowledge no less than by intellectual tradition, is accompanied by the emergence of the highly atomized yet
highly coordinated mass society whose "mind" reflects the radical division and fragmentation of labor (*L*, 202). In the mass society all aspects of life submit to a peculiarly intellectualistic appropriation. In
place of the old skills of life, we have

> instead a whole series of highly conscious, but deeply dubious and precar-
> ious skills which have been lodged in the sciences of psychology, anthro-
> pology, and sociology, together with the whole confusion of practices
> which go with urbanization. Consider how all these techniques have been
> developed along lines that discover trouble, undermine purpose, blight con-
> sciousness, and prevent decision; how they promote uncertainty, insecurity,
> anxiety, and incoherence; how above all they provide barriers between us
> and access to our common enterprise. (*L*, 203)

Blackmur's animadversions on mass society clearly imply, as these
passages show, some kind of political or public solution. What he is
most worried by is the collapse of "our common enterprise," the loss
of "the field of common reference," the prevention of "decision," the
prevalence of "uncertainty, insecurity, and anxiety." This aspect of his
social thought signifies a political awakening, an embryonic recognition of the distinctively political nature of the predicament of modern
society as it has been disclosed to him through his analysis of the
profession of letters and of the place of literature itself in mass society.
   "The Lion and the Honeycomb" (1950) makes slightly more explicit
Blackmur's political understanding. In this essay he draws a contrast
between the "Greece of Plato and Aristotle and the contemporary
mass society with respect to each society's use of the mind" (*L*, 180).
He sees in this period of ancient Greek civilization full interplay of the
three modes of the mind: poetic, dialectic, and rhetoric. Poetic means

"the creative action of the mind which has an eye to truth in the objects it makes." Dialectic means "the reasonable conversation of the mind which has an eye to the truth in ideas" (Blackmur adds that dialectic "has nothing to do with Hegel"). And by rhetoric he means "the art of persuasion, properly, in the service of dialectic or poetic; improperly, in the service of argument on the pleading of a 'cause' . . ." (*L*, 176–77). This trichotomy has long since broken down, Blackmur admits, and in contemporary literary criticism rhetoric has risen to a position of dominance, encompassing poetic and dialectic. His fellow New Critics (Ransom, Brooks, Empson, et al.), their leading adversaries (e.g., R. S. Crane), and others harder to classify by school (e.g., Burke) all share a common commitment to rhetoric and have developed a highly rhetorical criticism of poetry, a partial criticism that threatens to "harden" the mind "into a set of unrelated methodologies without the controlling advantage of a fixed body of knowledge, a fixed faith, or a fixed purpose" (*L*, 178). As he said in a "Critic's Job of Work," what is needed is not that such partial approaches be rejected out of hand because they are partial but that they be "compensated" and "reduced." Blackmur proposes that critics undertake to develop a new, more complete theory based on a synthesis of Coleridge and Aristotle, since Coleridge offers the most fertile ground on which to apprehend the nature of the behavior of words and Aristotle the most fertile ground on which to discover the nature of things designated by words.

What is faintly political about this suggestive proposal to overhaul literary theory at the time is that it proceeds from a recognition of the perils of "a rhetoric-sodden world," a world that is itself "partial" in that it has come to be dominated by one mode of the mind, rhetoric, which in the mass society tends to be omnivorous and low-grade. As Blackmur tries to show in *A Primer of Ignorance*, Expressionism in art conforms perfectly to the general character of the "rhetoric-sodden age" in not seeking "truth in the objects it makes," which is the aim of poetic. Rather, Expressionism inverts and thereby nearly corrupts this mode of the mind by claiming to find truth in the *subjects* it makes and endlessly re-makes: "what I say is both myself in truth and creates a new world" is the central principle of what he called private, irrational art in *The Double Agent* (P, 16). Similarly, the aim of dialectic—the mind's conversation as it seeks truth in ideas—is undercut by the general anti-intellectualism endemic to mass society.

This latter issue forms the central theme of "Toward a Modus Vivendi" (1954), Blackmur's most comprehensive examination of mass society and his most earnest plea for elite leadership. Blackmur was consciously ambivalent about the nature and role of elites. To recall his somewhat nostalgic description of American society in the late eighteenth and early nineteenth centuries, influenced by Henry Adams, he yearned for an American social order "administered by direct intelligence and imagination" (L, 54). But the reluctant democrat in him rejected such fantasies, as the opening sentences of "Toward a Modus Vivendi" make clear:

How do we go about converting energy and momentum into intellect? I take it that the power of intellect is at work when the whole mind is engaged in the whole field of its interests.

This has nothing to do with intellectualism: where the intellectual arrogates the mere interests of his class as they clash with others.

It has nothing to do with that intellectual power which converts itself into pure energy, sometimes called ambition or the struggle for personal power.

It has a great deal to do with the idea of a modus vivendi as the first and continuing and ever-necessary act of the mind. A modus vivendi brings out agreements and disagreements. It encourages discernment of the consequences of our own action and should determine whether or not we undertake it. Only under a modus vivendi do we see the cost of action, because it is only in the condition of a modus vivendi that we feel the actual clash of adverse wills. (*L*, 3–4)

The second and third paragraphs here state Blackmur's unequivocal rejection of mandarinism, in both its personal and its class forms of expression. But the remaining portion of this passage contains a covert theoretical endorsement of exactly the mandarin position. Blackmur appears to be oblivious of the contradiction here and throughout his later thought between, on one side, his social critique of mandarinism, and, on the other, his theoretical endorsement of it. He professes to be opposed to dictatorship by intellectuals even as he prepares the theoretical groundwork for it. This contradiction is all the more highlighted by Newman's sharp advice on the same matter a generation later. "It is about time," Newman writes, "the American writer ceased confusing his peripherality with freedom of expression, and began to find out where he fits into productive and social relations of the world which most affects him." "If the literary community is to survive it must reconstitute itself, not in terms of a stylized adversary but by recovering its own structural integrity" (Newman 1985, 167, 169). In other words, the literary community needs to assume a new institutional form and to give up its compensatory political vision.

Blackmur, too, sensed in these late essays that what was at stake was not well defined as the predicament of the man of letters and that the very survival of literature was in doubt. The core of this issue was the transformation under mass social conditions of the content of literacy and illiteracy and the ensuing new relations of the one to the other. In "Toward a Modus Vivendi" he presents the following three-part taxonomy of American intellectual and political life.

The New Illiteracy. The old illiteracy was inability to read; as the old literacy involved the habit of reading. The new illiteracy represents those who have been given the tool of reading (something less than the old primary school education) without being given either the means or skill to read well or the material that ought to be read. The habit of reading in the new illiteracy is not limited to, but is everywhere supplied by a press almost as illiterate as itself. It is in this way that opinion, instead of knowledge, has come to determine action: the inflammable opinion of the new illiterate is mistaken for the will of the people, so that arson becomes a chief political instrument. . . .

New Intellectual Proletariat. All those in all parts of the world who as a result of their own initial talents (not necessarily great) and the better routines of higher education find themselves in a society where they are alienated because there is nothing serious for them to do with their training. . . . Call it what you like, the double apparition of mass society and universal education is producing a larger and larger class of intellectually trained men and women the world over who cannot make a living in terms of their training and who cannot, because of their training, make a living otherwise with any satisfaction. . . .

Distrust of the Ability of the Audience. We deliberately take the quality out of our thought precisely when it is most valuable: when we wish to persuade others of the truth or desirability of what we believe. . . . Instead of telling our audience what we believe, we tell it what we suppose in our own more futile moments they already believe. . . . We believe our audience is not up to what we really have to say, and so we end up inferior to the potential response of the audience, and there is no more good in our talking at all. (*L*, 6–9)

There is a peculiar circularity in Blackmur's late essays. For if the above-mentioned undeniably real social ills proceed in part from the decline in the prestige and influence of bourgeois humanism, how is it that bourgeois humanism should be taken seriously as the only possible remedy? History does not stand still, as it would have to for this recommendation to make sense.

Blackmur's reasoning represents a twentieth-century version of the belief, first identified by Poirier, that only language or mind, and not politics and historical experience, can create the "liberated place." Blackmur shares this assumption with other American writers, most notably Emerson and Whitman, but he also expresses its negation in his attempts to resolve the dilemmas facing literary intellectuals in mass society. Lacking Emerson's attachment to nature or Whitman's democratic idealism, Blackmur imagines that the historical and political crises of the twentieth century can be solved only through the application of bourgeois humanist vision. In Joyce, Mann, Eliot, Yeats, Kafka, and a few others, Blackmur sees the superior intelligence of our time—superior to other literary intelligences and superior, too, to virtually all non-literary intellectual activity, from social science to philosophy. But what, we should ask, ought to be the institutional basis or medium of this vision (never mind for the moment the fact that it is not a unitary outlook)? Blackmur himself credits the artist—properly, I believe—as the one

> above all who *realizes* that revolutions—however fresh, violent and destructive, however aspiring, or groping, or contagious—have always *already* taken place; as private murder represents a relation already at crisis or already sundered. Revolution and murder are only the gross cost, assessed too late: the usury of dead institutions. (*P*, 13)

Bourgeois humanism and its artists also see the humanist enterprise in peril. The blind spot of bourgeois humanism is hardly its failure to imagine itself in crisis—writers and artists have been doing that compulsively since the era of Emerson and Baudelaire—but rather an inability to discern its own social basis crumbling under foot. Blackmur saw instead the mass society itself coming apart for lack of bourgeois humanist influence and guidance. The truth may be that mass society *just is* that social order which not only can get along without bourgeois humanism but is positively bent on eliminating it, along with literature itself. If so, the question which Blackmur, with Newman's help, leaves on the table is: "Is literature as an institution worth fighting for? If so, why?"

AN AGE OF TRUE PYRRHONISM

The cost of the journey inward, into the infinitude of private, subpolitical man, can look like a benefit. Such is the real cost. Wittgenstein, in his own struggle against the false names that are available courtesy of solipsistic deprivation, said in the *Tractatus*:

> We cannot think what we cannot think; so what we cannot think we cannot *say* either. (5.61)
> This remark provides the key to the problem, how much truth there is in solipsism.
> For what the solipsist *means* is quite correct; only it cannot be *said*, but makes itself manifest.
> The world is *my* world: this is manifest in the fact that the limits of *language* (of that language which alone I understand) mean the limits of *my* world. (5.62)

If the solipsist cannot say what he means, what *is* it that he says? What is this meaningless saying?

Wittgenstein did not ask these last two questions. Blackmur asked them repeatedly. What Wittgenstein concluded was the proper amount of truth in solipsism—namely, that *my* world is delimited by *my* language—Blackmur saw as the ambiguous mainspring of modernist culture. What *is* it that the solipsist says? In an "age of true Pyrrhonism"—its truth or completeness coming from the age being "self-conscious of its own fictions," hence given to "doubting the value as well as the fact" (*P*, 11)—Blackmur's answer to this question appears to be: No one knows what it is the solipsist says, only that there seems to be much of it. Some of it, I would add, holds only academic interest, such as Jeffers' poetry, that odd re-writing of "Build, therefore, your own world" as a low-fare ticket to Cosmic Oneness. Other examples belong to current ideological wars.

Blackmur's brief for bourgeois humanism, while unconvincing and tedious, has the merit of sharply identifying what he took to be the chief ideological enemy: all those "techniques of trouble," from sociology to psychoanalysis, which he believed prevent us from experiencing life morally. New knowledge, he said, comes in the form of "techniques for finding trouble in ourselves and in the world" (P, 21). Hannah Arendt, a tougher fighter on this theme, put essentially the same issue better when she alluded to the social or institutional basis of technical rationality. She wondered whether today "knowledge [as know-how] and thought have parted company for good." Instrumental reason this advanced would make citizens into "the helpless slaves, not so much of our machines as of our know-how, thoughtless creatures at the mercy of every gadget which is technically possible, no matter how murderous it is" (Arendt 1958, 3). In other words, techniques of trouble, or, in the institutional form some of them assume, modern technology, have the capacity to dissolve the moral character of experience. They are not mere means in a tidy, ahistorical means-ends calculus but powerful institutional barriers to the conduct of politics. Hence the political question is not whether technology can be mastered at last, as though it were truly characterized under the innocuous label of "applied science," and as though its would-be masters had not already been transformed by it.

A recent study of the "social history of engineering" in the United States lends weight both to Blackmur's complaint against manipulative social science and to Arendt's speculation about the political meaning of ever-expanding know-how. According to David F. Noble, the American history of technology refutes popular myths of runaway technocracy devoid of human purpose. For since the 1880s technology and corporate capitalism have been closely allied, mutually benefiting each other as they have shaped the modern economy and society. This alliance simultaneously describes both the human content of technology and the true identity of the dominant class (Noble 1977, xviii, 321). Domination by this class carries a heavy penalty, however, which is suffered by all and is most clearly apparent in the continuing absence of a common—political—world. Modern America may well be a designed society, as Noble has suggested. But design undertaken in sub-political circumstances only produces a citizenry of what Arendt calls "thoughtless creatures," who, in turn, eventually become, in Heidegger's words, "standing-reserve," so much well-ordered inventory and so many appendages to intricate apparatus (Heidegger 1977, 27). Blackmur's category, "techniques of trouble," accurately describes the uniform of the repressive semiotic he called the New Illiteracy while remaining indifferent to the powerful institutional body inside.

Nonetheless, Blackmur had a clear eye for the false security that comes from false names. In the end, he composed a rather anachronistic justification for bourgeois humanism which attributes the most significant set of false names to fragmented sub-specialties of knowledge which rationalize modern modes of social control. The anachronistic feature of Blackmur's bourgeois humanism is the blindness, which he sees as vision, to its own limitations—to its own shifting social basis. If the mass society is that society which not only does not need bourgeois humanism but disposes of it, then bourgeois humanism perhaps should be known as the cultural tradition which can only name but cannot offer an attractive alternative to the proposition, "What I say is both myself in truth and creates a new world." This Expressionist dictum licenses the entire underside of modern culture and politics in so far as it sanctifies as a noble achievement the loss of the public—the loss of the arena in which we recognize ourselves and others as human. Not bourgeois humanists but twentieth-century monsters, heirs

to those Emerson identified, rule social life. Blackmur suspected that
as a civilizing force bourgeois humanism was now a desideratum,
though he scarcely believed it to be merely his personal dream. What
he apparently did not see was the possibility that *as* a desideratum,
bourgeois humanism comprises an increasingly marginalized world of
thought and feeling whose marginality is ensured by the disappearance
of its traditional social basis, on the one hand, and, on the other, the
continuing absence of new institutions of culture in which its legacy
might sustain and transform itself within (or against) the main structures of the political economy of advanced capitalism. Bourgeois humanism ironically constitutes just another privatized world,
functionally indistinguishable from that of the solipsistic neo-romantic
and the sub-political theaters of technological reason. The civilizing
power of bourgeois humanism in these American worlds is, at best,
homeopathic.

CHAPTER FIVE

Shadows of Democracy

★   ★   ★

If it is a truism that symbol-making is one agency of civilization, it is far from obvious whether civilization in our time, the symbolic product, has taken the side of human existence or stands against it as the ultimate threat. This question—namely, whether faith in symbol-making, or worldmaking, ensures a modus vivendi in the future—is the shared message of philosophers, critics, theologians, writers, and ordinary citizens who otherwise have very little in common. "Post-Modernism" in fiction, for example, according to Charles Newman, "harbors the deep suspicion that we have only unpleasant choices; that we have seen the best civilization has to offer" (Newman 1985, 51). The future may well be a world whose dominant trait is what Stanley Cavell calls "soul-blindness." In such a world "nothing that happens [would] any longer strike . . . us as the objectification of subjectivity, as the act of an answerable agent, as the expression and satisfaction of human freedom, of human intention and desire": a world, in short, in which humanity assumes the forms of automatonity (Cavell 1979, 468). The existence of the human species would demonstrate the absence of humanity. Opposite yet strangely similar possibilities perpetuate the Emersonian faith in self-culture. More precisely, in the case of Ralph Ellison, they transform that faith by shedding its anti-politicism and inverting the Emersonian flight from the past into a ra-

tionale for self-consciously fashioning a personal identity with the materials of the Emersonian tradition itself.

These two opposed tendencies in contemporary literary culture have
little to do with what Newman calls "the phony dualism between Formalism and Realism, and the tortuous idolatries of style it inspires"
(Newman 1985, 179). Nor do they describe (or re-describe) the main
outlines, respectively, of such radically different authors as William Gass
and Saul Bellow, who, Newman argues, represent the antipodes of
Post-Modern fiction. Rather, considered in the light of the foregoing
chapters, the question whether indeed it is good for us to believe that
"the best civilization has to offer" lies in the past is the same as the question whether only self-destruction remains as the tradition of the infinitude of the private man. In other words, our ideas of the future depend
upon our readings of the past. The conservative adjustment by Post-
Modernism to the past as the historical site of "the best civilization has
to offer" perhaps overlooks two facts: first, the contributions of the
American tradition of anti-politicism to Post-Modernism's own escha-
tology; and, second, vestigial capacities in the American tradition of radical interiority for envisioning a future whose dominant feature is not
"soul-blindness." These issues come to life through a comparison of Joseph Heller's investigation of language games in the bureaucratic state in
Catch-22 and Ralph Ellison's autobiographical reflections on citizenship
in the republic of letters. Heller and Ellison each trouble us with soul-
blind worlds in which reification is so total as to erase the human ability
to recognize the humanness of agents and agencies.

Catch-22: THE END OF THE LIBERATED PLACE

The American literary tradition of believing that only language and
not history or politics can create the liberated place comes to an end—
at least in the sense of reaching its absurd outer limit—in Heller's
Catch-22. Catch-22 is in part an exposé of the function of language in

the modern bureaucratic state. The linguistic world in which the novel's characters live functions as though in no way connected to human purpose and rationality. Yet it is far from being purposeless or irrational. Rather, the manifold uses of words—clarification of thought, communication, socialization, aesthetic creation, playfulness, and the like—are radically narrowed to coincide with the requirements of the bureaucratic state itself, in particular those of the war machine. Words and their uses are bureaucratic conveniences, indispensable instruments of bureaucratic rationality, modes of weaponry, propaganda. In *Catch-22* words not only ensure social control; they are nothing but social control. By a weird Heideggerian logic, language speaks through the mouths and the being of characters, supervising individuals by addling their minds.

The function of language is endlessly mysterious to the characters in *Catch-22*. The act of naming, for example, seemingly leads nowhere. Here is how Major Major is told of his promotion: " 'You're the new squadron commander,' Colonel Cathcart had shouted rudely across the railroad ditch to him. 'But don't think it means anything, because it doesn't. All it means is that you're the new squadron commander.' "¹ The label "new squadron commander," or more precisely the affixing of this label, seems to be a meaningless gesture, pointing to nothing but the act of conferring itself, the title "new squadron commander" doubling back on itself purely gratuitously. The apparent meaninglessness of this utterance yields two different effects: bewilderment for the already bewildered Major Major, and humor born of verbal irony for the reader. But the meaninglessness of this verbal gesture is only apparent, for in an important sense the gesture is quite meaningful. Here, as elsewhere in the novel, the function of naming things is to strengthen the structure of domination. Colonel Cathcart appears merely to be informing Major Major of his new position; actually, he is giving a command. He is doing something *in* saying something, in J. L. Austin's formulation (Austin 1962). The ostensible substance of his speech is not its real substance, and the informational content of his words is virtually insignificant compared to their social effects. Indeed, the informational content *is* their social effects. The real substance of Cathcart's speech resides in its function, which is to affirm in a small way his own authority while simultaneously diminishing that of the recently promoted Major Major. Far from leading nowhere, the act of naming places on center stage a shadow of the structure of domination, the hidden but ever-present sub-political authority, looming like Hamlet's ghost, in the name of which the act is taken and to which actor, act, and object are yoked in common allegiance. Major Major himself is instantly transformed by this contradictory elevation in status into a component of that structure: the men with whom he has been playing basketball and who have heard Colonel Cathcart's announcement become, to his perception, "a reef of curious, reflective faces all gazing at him woodenly with morose and inscrutable animosity," and henceforth "almost on cue, everyone in the squadron stopped talking to him and started staring at him" (C-22, 91). He has become a leader but in name only. (Major —— de Coverly, by contrast, is a leader in slightly less than name only.)

Official communication in the catch-22 world employs a bizarre species of synecdoche, wherein, as in this instance, the part ("new squadron commander") comes to stand for the whole (the bureaucratic structure and its imperatives). Communication is surreal: words are ripped from their familiar referential contexts and reinserted into new, inappropriate contexts, whereupon there ensues a frantic search on the part of one or more of the participants for a meaning. The model of this use of language is ex-PFC Wintergreen's muttering of "T. S. Eliot" over the telephone—a response not to the caller, Colonel Cargill, but to a query contained in one of Colonel Cargill's numerous "homiletic memoranda," which Wintergreen reads while sorting memos in the mailroom of headquarters. Cargill's memo challenges the reader to name "one poet who makes money." The unexpected, anonymous response, "T. S. Eliot," ignites a string of exchanges between Colonel Cargill and General Peckham, on one end, and Colonel Moodus and General Dreedle, on the other, each side rushing to find the meaning of this cryptic utterance. Though the meaning eludes them, it does not elude sly Wintergreen, who retains a tight grip on the connection between the word and its meaning. That it does not elude him means only that he was in the right place at the right time, or in other words that bureaucratic rationality depends on, rather than merely tolerates (say, as a joke), such individual initiative. This is the secret to Wintergreen's rise to power in the army bureaucracy (*C-22*, 37–38).

Private conversations between individuals, especially those between Yossarian and Orr, conform to the Wintergreen–T. S. Eliot model. The conversation between Yossarian and Orr on the subject of crab apples, horse chestnuts, rubber balls, and big cheeks is one of the more intricate examples. Upon entering his tent after being released from the hospital, Yossarian finds Orr fixing a valve on his homemade stove. As in the "T. S. Eliot" episode, there is a series of questions and answers initiated by a cryptic remark: Orr's declaration, wholly inappropriate to Yossarian's complaint about his tinkering, that as a kid he "used to walk around all day with crab apples in my cheeks. One in each cheek" (*C-22*, 23). Of course Yossarian cannot resist asking "Why?" but as soon as he does he is trapped, Orr's method of irony and equivocation reducing Yossarian to a condition of intellectual impotence. Yossarian's failure to grasp Orr's meaning arises from his inveterate literalism: he naively expects straight answers to straight questions. What he gets is the handiwork of a supreme ironist, Orr, whose story about crab apples constitutes not only a parody of communication but a parable of survival. It is the first of two parables Yossarian is to hear from Orr, both of which he fails to understand until the end.

The second parable that Yossarian fails to grasp is Orr's convoluted account of why the girl was hitting him on the head (C-22, 323–26). Each detail in these two parables parallels a detail in the situation shared by Orr and Yossarian. In the one about crab apples Orr himself (and not crab apples, etc.) is the key detail: Orr whose ingenuity conceals and protects his ironical outlook, his precious survival mechanism, making him a source of amusing confusion to his friends when he was young and to Yossarian now. The parable of the girl hitting Orr on the head contains numerous details more familiar to Yossarian, but here, too, Yossarian fails to see the parallels, and therefore the point is lost on him. Orr even tells Yossarian when he is on the right track and when he is going astray. " 'That wasn't the question,' Orr informed him with victorious delight. 'That was just conversation' " (C-22, 323). Later, when Yossarian is completely exasperated and incapable of following Orr's direct guidance through the maze of words: " 'Why don't you ever fly with me?' Orr asked suddenly and looked straight into Yossarian's face for the first time. 'There, that's the question I want you to answer' " (C-22, 324). Yossarian's inability to see the correspondences between the details of these parables and the details of the desperate situation he shares in common with Orr reflects his overall inability to manipulate language to his ends.

The Bologna bombing mission, a *tour de force* of ironical juxtapositions in a novel replete with them, dramatizes more forcefully than perhaps any other episode the oppressive and mystifying function of abstractions in the catch-22 world while with equal force displaying Yossarian's incompetence to deal with them. "Incompetence" is the apt word here, for the Bologna mission is a revealing test of Yossarian's capacity to manipulate abstractions in the interests of self-preservation. The abstraction he manipulates at the outset of this episode is not a word but the dread non-verbal symbol of the upwardly spiraling number of missions—the scarlet ribbon, the "bomb line" pinned to the map of Italy in headquarters. Yossarian's maneuver—placing the ribbon over Bologna to indicate that the city has already been taken and therefore need not be bombed—is immediately absorbed and muffled within the bureaucratic structure, as General Peckham is awarded a medal for valor, and as new plans for a bombing run are laid, once it is discovered that the Bologna ammunition dumps are still intact.

This desperate effort by Yossarian to play by what he imagines to be the rules of the game—endeavoring to counter perceived bureaucratic arbitrariness with his own arbitrariness—only precipitates ludicrous misinterpretations of reality, followed by assorted terrors in the sky. When the planes return from the first run, from which he and his crew have turned back half-way to the target, Yossarian is dozing on the beach:

> He woke up blinking with a slight pain in his head and opened his eyes upon a world boiling in chaos in which everything was in proper order. He gasped in utter amazement at the fantastic sight of the twelve flights of planes organized calmly into exact formation. The scene was too unexpected to be true. There were no planes spurting ahead with wounded, none lagging behind with damage. No distress flares smoked in the sky. No ship was missing but his own. For an instant he was paralyzed with a sensation of madness. Then he understood, and almost wept at the irony. The explanation was simple: clouds had covered the target before the planes could bomb it, and the mission to Bologna was still to be flown.
>
> He was wrong. There had been no clouds. Bologna had been bombed. Bologna was a milk run. There had been no flak there at all.
> (*C-22*, 148)

But Bologna was no milk run the second time. Designated lead bombardier and flying with McWatt in the first formation, Yossarian "came in on the target like a Havermeyer, confidently taking no evasive action at all, and suddenly they were shooting the living shit out of him!" (*C-22*, 149–50).

The Bologna mission begins and ends with superstitious gestures by Yossarian, gestures reversing cause and effect, as Clevinger points out. More daring than the other men, who held "macabre vigil at the bomb line in brooding entreaty as though hoping to move the ribbon up by the collective weight of their sullen prayers," Yossarian is willing to try anything once, and moves the ribbon (*C-22*, 122). When the mission is over, he resorts to superstition again, this time in an effort to account for the fantastic experience: "Yossarian bounded up with a one-syllable cry that crackled with anxiety and provided the only rational explanation for the whole mysterious phenomenon of the flak at Bologna: *Orr!*" Didn't Orr draw "flak like a magnet?" he reasons (*C-22*, 155). But of course "*Orr!*" possesses no cabalistic qualities, and Yossarian's explanation is anything but rational. He is so disoriented by events that he loses capacity to interpret experience realistically and to conclude, as in this instance, that the flak at Bologna was "caused by" German anti-aircraft batteries put there to fortify vital ammunition dumps. Yossarian is not merely desperate and blind to reality; the *quality* of his desperation and blindness issues directly from the tyrannical abstractions of the ruling authority, of which his consciousness is an almost perfect replica.

Yossarian not only fails to manipulate symbols in order to comprehend reality and shape it to his ends; he also, and for precisely the same reason, fails even to penetrate the fortress of ruling authority for the purposes of simple communication. Over Bologna, the ruling authority is embodied in the person of Aarfy:

> The plane was slammed again with another loud, jarring explosion that almost rocked it over on its back, and the nose filled immediately with sweet clouds of blue smoke. *Something was on fire!* Yossarian whirled to escape and smacked into Aarfy, who had struck a match and was placidly

lighting his pipe. Yossarian gaped at his grinning, moon-faced navigator in utter shock and confusion. It occurred to him that one of them was mad.

"Jesus Christ!" he screamed at Aarfy in tortured amazement. "Get the hell out of the nose! Are you crazy? Get out!"

"What?" said Aarfy.

"Get out!" Yossarian yelled hysterically, and began clubbing Aarfy backhanded with both fists to drive him away. "Get out!"

Several futile attempts later:

Down they sank once more into the crunching, thudding, voluminous barrage of bursting anti-aircraft shells as Aarfy came creeping back behind Yossarian and jabbed him [with the stem of his pipe] sharply in the ribs again. Yossarian shied upward with another whinnying gasp.

"I still couldn't hear you," Aarfy said.

"I said get *out of here!*" Yossarian shouted, and broke into tears. He began punching Aarfy in the body with both hands as hard as he could. "Get *away* from me! Get *away!*"

Punching Aarfy was like sinking his fists into a limp sack of inflated rubber. There was no resistance, no response at all from the soft, insensitive mass, and after a while Yossarian's spirit died and his arms dropped helplessly with exhaustion. He was overcome with a humiliating feeling of impotence and was ready to weep in self-pity.

"What did you say?" Aarfy asked.

"Get *away* from me," Yossarian answered, pleading with him now. "Go back in the plane."

"I still can't hear you."

"Never mind," wailed Yossarian, "never mind. Just leave me alone."

"Never mind what?" (*C-22*, 152–53)

Just as Yossarian, the naive literalist and comic straight man, finds Orr's parables of survival inscrutable, so too does he founder here in the presence of bureaucratic arrogance and obtuseness. In the former instances, Yossarian attempts but fails to understand. Here, he faces apparently sheer meaninglessness. The traps laid for him by Orr have a way out, as we discover at the end of *Catch-22*, when Yossarian, at last learning from Orr's example, rows to Sweden, using a dixie-cup spoon while fishing for cod off the back of his life raft in waters (the Mediterranean) in which there are no cod. The trap closing on him in this scene, however, in which Aarfy serves as the voice of the war machine's inner logic, offers no way out. Yossarian's literalist intelligence is unequal to the task of comprehension, not because the meaning of this experience is obscure, but because in this situation a literalist intelligence only mirrors the very obstacle confronting it.

Aarfy's speeches constitute another example of synecdoche: as verbal fragments, they function in the name of the whole, the abstract tyranny of catch-22. Yossarian is unable even to glimpse, much less re-envision à la Emerson's American Scholar, the whole which tightens its grip on him: Aarfy cannot hear Yossarian, or *refuses* to hear him, as the final line, "Never mind what?" suggests. Yossarian's ineffectual literalism is the impress left by the bureaucratic state, the token of its total authority over his consciousness. In the linguistic madness shared with Aarfy over Bologna, Yossarian is not a would-be interpreter of parables but a character in a parable—one whose theme is the grotesque and destructive irony of consciousness in the catch-22 world.

Human experience in *Catch-22* has been reduced to a single word: "catch-22." As the chapter called "The Eternal City" reveals, "catch-22" denotes brute force. It means they can do whatever they want, Yossarian learns; and, to complete the circular logic, whatever they do is done in the name of catch-22. "Catch-22" thus serves as the talismanic word for the deadly and mystifying telos of the modern bureaucratic state. The war machine has appropriated unto itself all language and therefore all mind. There seems to be no point outside this totalitarian universe from which to hurl a name at it and in that way bring it into the purview of rational understanding. Because it is a world that cannot be talked about, action is impossible and political possibility is negated. The catch-22 world constitutes a monolith, a truly common world in that no one and no experience lie outside it (except for "Sweden"), but it is as though the pre-condition of this human association is the banishment of common sense. A common world without common sense is governable only through tyranny, the novelty of which in this instance is its utterly abstract character. Physical violence terrifies Yossarian, but it is the irrationality of the whole which controls him. Because language and thought have been assimilated to the bureaucratic intelligence, Yossarian is powerless to think his way out of the cage of reifications. Perhaps the most poignant evidence of catch-22's power, as well as the most stultifying irony of all, lies in the banishment of the comic view of life. Characters wander humorlessly in a bureaucratic junkyard where there is no space for either laughter or freedom.

Catch-22's treatment of words in their relation to worlds fictionalizes—but only in order to shatter—the philosophical problem of other minds. Heller's book posits a fictive world in which the problematic other is not only monstrous; it is also unknowable, yet thoroughly believable. Literature and song since Homer have thrived on the problematic other, without which, obviously, narrative and drama would hardly be conceivable. Indeed, one way to think about periodizing the history that these forms have made since classical antiquity is to notice the changing character of the other as a problem. In this tradition, others are knowable in two (shifting) senses simultaneously: they are knowable for *who* they are, and they are knowable *that* they are.[2] Thus when Euryclea glimpses the scar on Odysseus' leg, she affirms *his* existence in her own mind in an act of *recognition* (Auerbach 1953, 3ff.).

This moment of recognition further heightens the drama of the poem, and this heightening of dramatic interest sustains the problem of the other. The other in this way paradoxically retains its status as a problem each time it is "solved." Problem and solution are alike ineradicable. Philosophical skepticism questions the existence of the other, but skepticism is entrapped by the irreducibility of belief, at whose core is the phenomenon of recognition. "Believing in other persons," J. L. Austin concluded in his paper on "Other Minds" (1946), is "as much an irreducible part of our experience as, say, giving promises, or playing competitive games, or even sensing coloured patches." Each reaffirmation of this belief is a performance, an "essential part of the act of communicating," as Austin put it (Austin 1961, 83). For some of these acts, we can invent rules "for their 'rational conduct,' " as in the law, or in the study of the past, or in psychological analysis. But rules are not the same as justifications, and in an important sense we are simply unable to justify those performances of ours which find us contending with and affirming the existence of knowable others. Austin's point is that in such cases the inability to justify designates no weakness but only a condition of our humanness.

Philip Rahv may have been looking for just such an unavailable justification when, somewhat exasperated, he said, "It seems as if in the modern world there is no having done with Romanticism—no having done with it because of its enormous resourcefulness in accommodating the neo-primitivistic urge that pervades our culture, in providing it with objects of nostalgia upon which to fasten and haunting forms of the past that it can fill with its own content" (Rahv 1969, 204). Rahv's polemic here (written in 1953) was directed at 1950s myth critics, whose examination of myth in literature comported perfectly with the requirements of then fashionable neo-orthodox Christianity. "Back to myth if you want to be saved!" (Rahv 1969, 204). But Romanticism, as Cavell suggests, does not come down to this, even though it is open to being distorted to fit the face of the clever critic.

It is that distorted practice which needs justification; as Rahv says, it fails to do so. Romanticism itself, in so far as it installs the encounter with the other as a self-ramifying activity in all departments of culture, has no end, and thus can neither be justified nor not justified.

Catch-22 says nothing about this problem, just as it says nothing about "the modern bureaucratic state." The philosophical appearance it creates, moreover, is not an appearance *of* the problem of other minds—whether there are any, whether or how we may know them, etc.—but a dramatic projection of the near elimination of this problem from the course outline of philosophy. For in *Catch-22* the line between self and other, at least as concerns the role of intelligence and the function of consciousness, defines zaniness as the socio-linguistic norm. This definition, moreover, only shows that Yossarian's mind and the "mind" of the war machine are close to being identical; in the case of Aarfy the identity is complete. The marvel of the book consists, in my view, in Heller's producing so much from so little, in fashioning a profound narrative out of that tiny gap which separates the mind of his protagonist from the protagonist's environment of unfreedom. If the rediscovery of the problematic other designates the starting point of European Romanticism, as Cavell has suggested (Cavell 1979, 467), then perhaps the significance of *Catch-22* for American literary-philosophical history is that it re-presents the problem of other minds as the problem of *my* mind, in other words as a variation on the familiar Emersonian theme of idealized privatism. If so, then Heller's book belongs also to that long conversation about "the substitution of privacy for rationality" which began, as Anthony Kenny has shown, with "Descartes' innovation in philosophy of mind" (qtd. in Cavell 1979, 470). It belongs, then, to the political history of the modern age.

RALPH ELLISON

The contribution of Romanticism to the political history of the modern age, in particular to the pre-history of democracy, takes on a meaning quite different from that of the familiar historical stories recounting the march of individualism and heroic struggles for equality, if we take seriously Cavell's thesis concerning the analogous and interpenetrating narratives of literature and philosophy. The other's becoming a problem is a political event of the first importance and not merely the philosophical topic scrutinized by Rousseau in *The Confessions* or the object of Emerson's attention in a journal entry—such as the one for April 1846: "I like man, but not men" (Emerson 1957, 304). In America, the recurring sign of the nineteenth century's discovery of the other is the Afro-American. The conflict between the abstract claims of enlightenment humanism, bodied forth in the *Declaration of Independence*, and the fact of chattel slavery yielded race as principle and as motive in American politics and thought.[3] The Afro-American, Ralph Ellison wrote in 1976, became in the age of Emerson the "keeper of the nation's sense of democratic achievement" (G, 335). Not only is the other discovered to be a problem in the sense that selfhood and identity now loomed as interesting, vexing issues in the romantic sensibility. As soon as the public problem of the other in America appears, it assumes a radically privatized form. The Afro-American emerged as the keeper of the democratic bad conscience *and* as an invisible being. As a private figure bearing a prefabricated public meaning, the Afro-American, Ellison suggests, has been the living "symbol of guilt and redemption" from the Founding period to the present (G, 335). The cost of this status is well known: the being of the Afro-American in this historical symbology is secretly yet publicly allied with his "thinghood." And as Cavell remarks, the difference between a being and a thing may be *the* central distinction in philosophy (Cavell 1979, 468)—and, I would add, in the theory and practice of political democracy.

Historically, the other becomes problematic when, in Europe, the
defense of bourgeois privacy receives its most perverse and absolute
expression: in the writings of the Marquis de Sade and, later,
Nietzsche. The progressive critique of this philosophical radicalism
was "fired," according to Horkheimer and Adorno, by its "trum-
pet[ing] far and wide the impossibility of deriving from reason any
fundamental argument against murder."

> Inasmuch as the merciless doctrines [of Sade and Nietzsche] proclaim the
> identity of domination and reason, they are more merciful than those of the
> moralistic lackeys of the bourgeoisie. "Where do your greatest dangers lie?"
> was the question Nietzsche once posed himself [*Die Fröhliche Wissenschaft*,
> vol. 5, 205], and answered thus: "In compassion." With his denial he re-
> deemed the unshakable confidence in man that is constantly betrayed by
> every form of assurance that seeks only to console. (Horkheimer and
> Adorno 1972, 119)

Consolation there was in abundance in mid-nineteenth-century America, the heyday of what George Fredrickson calls "romantic racialism." The most extreme version of romantic racialism depicted Afro-
Americans as " 'the choice blood of America,' " in the words of the
Methodist Bishop Gilbert Haven, a race distinguished, in the Bishop's
view, by a docility so absolute as to constitute "the ultimate in Christian virtue" (Fredrickson 1971, 102).

Given such sentiments, it is perhaps not surprising that the ruling
theme in American discourse about race and ethnicity is the issue of
identity. Talk about race—regardless of the racial self-identification (if
any) of the person speaking—is talk about who is who. "Who am I?"
W. E. B. Du Bois (1868–1963) implicitly asks throughout *The Souls of
Black Folk* (1903). He answers in words that since have become
famous:

After the Egyptian and Indian, the Greek and the Roman, the Teuton and Mongolian, the Negro is a sort of seventh son, born with a veil, and gifted with second sight in this American world—a world which yields him no true self-consciousness, but only lets him see himself through the revelation of the other world. It is a peculiar sensation, this double-consciousness, this sense of always looking at one's self through the eyes of others, of measuring one's soul by the tape of a world that looks on in amused contempt and pity. One ever feels his twoness,—an American, a Negro; two souls, two thoughts, two unreconciled strivings; two warring ideals in one dark body, whose dogged strength alone keeps it from being torn asunder. (Franklin 1975, 214–15)

Du Bois's emphasis in this passage on the impoverished inner life should not be misconstrued as an implied yearning after a purely inner, or mentalistic, remedy. On the contrary, the "true self-consciousness" to which he aspires can be achieved only in and through the transformation of the outer world. Attaining "true self-consciousness," Du Bois says, stressing his own experience, depends upon a courageous acceptance of the doubleness of being black and American. He must not deny his Americanness, he cannot deny his African origins, and he cannot escape the complex interplay of the two in his experience. For to pretend that he is not really an American would be to repudiate both his familial heritage and traditional enlightenment ideals of liberty and equality (Jordan 1968). And to pretend that his African origins are of no significance would be to deny the undeniable: as he later put it, "The problem of the Twentieth Century is the problem of the color-line" (Franklin 1975, 239). So, in answer to the ancient question, "Who am I?" Du Bois would say: "I am that man who abides with the complexity that comes from acknowledging the warfare between these two souls."

In other words, Du Bois holds that the Afro-American's personal identity is an affair of some choice; if truly seen, the peculiar circumstances of his existence force him, paradoxically, to choose who he shall be. The free acknowledgment of complexity is itself the result of struggle and occurs on contested ground. Personal identity just *is* what comes of remaining in the fray. No one, Du Bois implies, can be *forced* to acknowledge the complexity he identifies, or any complexity, for that matter. Indeed, it is far easier not to acknowledge it and to cultivate one or the other side of the racial illusion: the belief that all value is racially determined, that every human experience *is* human by virtue of a preferred, specifiable racial determinant. However, not to acknowledge the warfare of these two contending souls in no way removes one from the battle. On the contrary, it only assures that one will be a casualty.[4]

Ralph Ellison, born in 1914, fifty-six years after Du Bois, has similarly been preoccupied with issues of identity. He, too, defines these issues as a warfare of two souls, and seeks to reconcile the rival claims of his blackness and his Americanness. More so, perhaps, than any other American writer, Ellison conceives the American racial predicament in the terms the subject deserves. For he has always written from a perspective in which questions of race, of personal and group identity, and of black-white relations in general are embraced by the larger demands and the still unfulfilled promises of democracy. It is in democratic terms that he conceives of the duality of his own condition and that of Afro-Americans generally. Thus he does not so much resist the nationalist or separatist idea of earlier Afro-American writers like Marcus Garvey as he transforms it, assimilating it to his own vision of American ethnic and racial pluralism. In somewhat the same way, he regards his Americanness not as an abstract fact but as a historical condition whose full meaning can be realized only through the development of a collective understanding of the ways in which politics and culture have shaped each other over time.

Ellison came to maturity after the Harlem Renaissance of the 1920s, and in an important sense he signaled a more mature, hard-hitting brand of authorship than any Harlem writer practiced, save, perhaps, that of Jean Toomer or Zora Neale Hurston. Alain Locke had complained that there were "too many prophets and preachers" at work among the Harlem artists and writers, whose relentless "propaganda perpetuates . . . group inferiority" (qtd. in Huggins 1971, 202). As though in answer to Du Bois, who had claimed there was no "true self-consciousness" as yet among Afro-Americans, and in reply to Locke's analysis of the irony of pro-black propaganda, Ellison introduces a new self-understanding, one characterized by, in Nathan Huggins' words, a transformation of his dual soul "into the very instrument that could slice through the boundaries that defined it" (Huggins 1971, 201). The instrument was Ellison's prose.

Ellison's thoroughgoing democratic commitment accounts for much of the distinctive character of his writing. The reader of Ellison's work needs to have an ear for polemical irony and to be as free as possible from racial sentimentalism, of either the black or the white variety, in order to hear the voice of the author in the following interview:

> INTERVIEWER: What do you think of the present level of Negro sculpture? What future do you see for it?
>
> ELLISON: I know little of current work in sculpture by Africans, but that which I have seen appears to possess little of that high artistic excellence characteristic of ancient African art. American Negro sculpture is, of course, simply American sculpture done by Negroes. Some is good, some bad.[5]

Ellison's essays, collected in *Shadow and Act* (1964) and *Going to the Territory* (1986), investigate the issue he points to in passages like this one. That Ellison, an American with no particular interest in "Negro sculpture" and no particular knowledge of African art, ancient or modern, would be expected to have opinions on these subjects worth reporting in a national magazine—the assumptions manifested in such discourse, such talk about race, were themselves a major target at which Ellison's essays were aimed. What gives these essays their urgency, in my view, is the author's steadfast refusal to be type-cast as a "Negro spokesman," a moral refusal calling for courage, betokening independence, and both leading to and proceeding from vigorous self-study. By rejecting the role of "Negro spokesman," Ellison was able to eschew cant and nonsense in the treatment of public themes like identity, race, and the place of art in a democracy.

All of Ellison's work centers on one complexity: the ways in which members of a racially diverse polity, founded on the enlightenment values of freedom and equality and burdened by the legacy of slavery, see themselves and one another. What George Eliot said of lovers' relationships in *Middlemarch* (1871–1872) also describes the grounds of human confusion and folly Ellison examines: "For surely all must admit that a man may be puffed and belauded, envied, ridiculed, counted upon as a tool and fallen in love with, or at least selected as a future husband, and yet remain virtually unknown—known merely as a cluster of signs for his neighbors' false suppositions" (Eliot 1956, 105). Ellison's novel, *Invisible Man* (1952), tells the story of a man who learns to move around in the shadowy world constituted by such a social psychology. In Ellison's essays—on American writing, on Jimmy Rushing, on Minton's in New York, on his running controversies with influential New York literary critics, on American movies, on Twain and Melville, on Richard Wright, on Negro laughter, and on his own struggle to abide the ambiguities of his identity as an American who *happened* to be black but who *decided* to be a writer—we hear in these essays a voice quite different from the narrator's in *Invisible Man*, yet one speaking to themes similar to those in the novel: personal identity and artistic work in an unfinished society.

Ellison's early essays were composed at a time (late 1930s–1960s) when public discussion of the place of racial identity in the world of literature and culture sometimes turned on the question of whether white writers should attempt to "define Negro humanity" in their work, what the merit of any such writing is, whether the lack of such efforts signified irresponsibility, and so on. Ellison replied to such questions by saying, first, that he would never wish for "white writers to define Negro humanity"; instead, they should learn to "recognize the broader aspects of their own" humanity. Black writers, for their part, should assume responsibility for "depicting the experience of their own groups" he argued in "Twentieth-Century Fiction and the Black Mask of Humanity" (1946, 1953). Underlying this advice was Ellison's democratic belief that the American people are a "still forming" people and that their image is accordingly a composite one (S, 59–60).

"Depicting the experience of their own groups" may have struck a reformist note in 1946, the year this essay was written, a bland if necessary corrective to the rather feckless question of whether white writers should attempt to portray black experience. However, Ellison himself soon found that his own efforts to depict black experience—*Invisible Man*—were to be measured by a different criterion by such influential black publicists as John O. Killens. Writing in *Freedom* in 1952, Killens welcomed *Invisible Man* with the following review:

> How does Ellison present the Negro people? The thousands of exploited farmers in the South are represented by a sharecropper who has made both wife and daughter pregnant. The main character of the book is a young Uncle Tom who is obsessed with getting to the "top" by pleasing the Big, Rich White Folks. A million Negro veterans who fought against fascism in World War II are rewarded with a maddening chapter [of] crazy Vets running hogwild in a down home tavern. The Negro ministry is depicted by an Ellison character who is a Harlem pastor and at the same time a pimp and a numbers racketeer.

> The Negro people need Ralph Ellison's *Invisible Man* like we need a hole
> in the head or a stab in the back.
>   It is a vicious distortion of Negro life. (Qtd. in Cruse 1967, 235)

Of which commentary Harold Cruse aptly remarks: "Well, there you
have it! The socially restrictive covenant of radical Left socialist realism, establishing the inviolable range of social theme for the Negro
writer, was never better stated" (Cruse 1967, 235). Cruse's point, of
course, is that it is as a writer, and as neither a leftist nor a black apologist, that Ellison demands to be seen. Ellison's subtle understanding
of his vocation comes through all the essays in *Shadow and Act* and
Going to the Territory and stands in direct contrast to the doctrinaire
views of men like Killens. Assessing the lessons he learned from other
twentieth-century authors, for example, Ellison remarks: "I use folk-
lore in my work not because I am Negro, but because writers like
Eliot and Joyce made me conscious of the literary value of my folk
inheritance. My cultural background, like that of most Americans, is
dual (my middle name, sadly enough, is Waldo)" (*S*, 72).
   Recognizing the duality of his cultural background no doubt con-
tributes to Ellison's preoccupation with the mutual impoverishment
arising from color prejudice. Unlike Jeffersonian liberals, Ellison is
concerned with the effects of prejudice not just on white people—a
point of view that lies behind the question of whether white authors
should write about black experience—but on all people. Indeed, *mutual*
impoverishment is the refrain that exactly identifies his work. The
color-line does not so much divide black from white as it designates
their subtle interrelationships, inquiry into which is the purpose of Ellison's social psychology. It is as though Ellison envisions an altogether new type of hyphenated American: Black-White– or White-
Black–Americans. Conventional hyphenations are all too inadequate.
For black Americans are just that: black and Americans. In the twentieth century, if not before, they are only misleadingly identified, by

themselves or by others, through the reductionist category of "displaced Africans": too much history, so to speak, has happened to them in conjunction with whites to warrant such a sentimental veneration along purely racial lines. White American immigrants, similarly, regardless of which side of the Mason-Dixon line they call home, acquire their respective social characters, not outside the orbit of interracial social relations, but in part through the mediations afforded by them. As Ellison says in "On Initiation Rites and Power" (1969, 1974), while writing *Invisible Man* he

> began to realize that even before we were a nation, people of African background had been influencing the nature of the American language, that amalgam of English English, of French and German and Dutch and American Indian dialects, and so on. All of this, long before we were a nation, had already begun to form; American culture began to evolve before we were a nation. And some of the people contributing to it were my own people. (G, 48)

This process of Americanization, however, while potentially a democratizing process, has always conflicted with the non-democratic social and political institutions dominant since the colonial period (G, 142). Afro-Americans, European immigrants, and other peoples of color are united in uneasy tension by the enlightenment ideal of freedom and equality—a political-ethical principle daily contradicted in practice throughout American history.

In his essays, Ellison did not restrict himself to the task of exposing, over and over, this obvious, albeit profound, contradiction in American historical experience. He was a good polemicist, when aroused, but for Ellison polemic was never an end in itself but instead was inspired by his larger purposes as a writer and a democrat. Ellison was fascinated, for example, by the failure of American literature and art to achieve tragic proportions, an issue on which nearly every American literary intellectual and a good many European observers have commented in the last century and a half. Ellison argued that the absence of tragedy in American art was directly traceable, at least in part, to racial prejudice:

> By excluding our largest minority from the democratic process, the United States weakened all national symbols and rendered sweeping public rituals which would dramatize the American dream impossible; it robbed the artist of a body of unassailable public beliefs upon which he could base his art; it deprived him of a personal faith in the ideals upon which society supposedly rested; and it provided him with no tragic mood indigenous to his society upon which he could erect a tragic art. (S, 53)

The tone of this passage is obviously polemical, but the purpose is far more serious than that of routine polemic on the topic of white racism. Ellison suggests that the Afro-American *as public but invisible symbol* ensures the loss of the public world itself: "all national symbols," all "public rituals," indeed, the entire "body of unassailable public beliefs," all is gone. The relation of American politics to American artistic production is thus a symbiotic one, analogous to the social relations of blacks and whites themselves. American justice and American art have a common history as well as separate ones. Ellison would have us try to understand the complexities woven by the tangled threads of politics and culture in American history.

Yet public discourse in America, when it centers on a topic in any way concerned with race relations, often amounts to little more than a trafficking in clichés and contraband political weaponry. Recall the vogue of Maoism among Black Nationalists in the 1960s. Or consider the recent moralistic diatribe against reading *Adventures of Huckleberry Finn* in the schools. To John H. Wallace, leader of a "nationwide campaign against Mark Twain's greatest work," *Huckleberry Finn* is "the most grotesque example of racist trash ever written"; Wallace believes it is irresponsible to require young students, especially young black students, to read it. Any skilled reader, however, knows that *Huckleberry Finn* is a superb piece of fictive irony, and that to read it and miss the irony is to miss the book Twain wrote—and, in effect, to make a bad joke out of a comic masterpiece. Writing in *The Nation*, Leo Marx forces this issue when he asks, "How much do we know, actually, about the ability of teachers, or of children of various ages and social backgrounds, to make sense of ironic discourse?" Though his question implies we know very little of this ability, Marx nonetheless rather illogically recommends that "educators could take a large step towards resolving the current controversy simply by eliminating the requirement . . . and allow[ing] each teacher to decide whether his or her students should be asked to read *Huckleberry Finn*." This recommendation, far from being the "ideal solution" that Marx believes it to be, begs an important question. For there are many teachers whose confidence in their ability to "make sense of ironic discourse" is not well founded. Indeed, it may be that the Wallace campaign, wrongheaded as it is, in part comes from a desire to combat the evil effects arising from inept teaching. The even more egregious moral error of the Wallace campaign itself lies in mistaking the cause of the evil it would eradicate (Marx 1985, 150–52).

Whereas the Wallace-inspired controversy over *Huckleberry Finn* simply confuses issues of literacy with issues of racial justice, the book itself, Ellison argues in "Twentieth-Century Fiction and the Black Mask of Humanity," forms them into a morally and aesthetically coherent whole. Ellison argues that Huck's finest moment—" 'Alright, then, I'll *go* to hell' "—signifies a new and distinctively democratic "definition of necessity" in American experience. Huck's action embodies Twain's insight into the nature of social institutions: though they appear to be natural and therefore beyond human control, they are in fact artificial and therefore malleable.

> Huck Finn has struggled with the problem poised [sic] by the clash between
> property rights and human rights, between what the community considered
> to be the proper attitude toward an escaped slave and his knowledge of
> Jim's humanity, gained through their adventures as fugitives together. He
> has made his decision on the side of humanity. (S, 48)

By being true to his immediate experience with Jim, Huck not only
violates the established moral norm; like Prometheus, with whom Ellison compares him, Huck "embraces the evil implicit in his act in order to affirm his belief in humanity." The implied new conception of
"necessity" thus dramatized is accordingly a social ideal which places
all humanity on an equal footing.

> In this passage Twain has stated the basic moral issue centering around Ne-
> groes and the white American's democratic ethics. It dramatizes as well the
> highest point of tension generated by the clash between the direct human
> relationships of the frontier and the abstract, inhuman, market-dominated
> relationships fostered by the rising middle class—which in Twain's day was
> already compromising dangerously with the most inhuman aspects of the
> defeated slave system. And just as politically these forces reached their
> sharpest tension in the outbreak of the Civil War, in *Huckleberry Finn* (both
> the boy and the novel) their human implications come to sharpest focus
> around the figure of the Negro.
>   Huckleberry Finn knew, as did Mark Twain, that Jim was not only a
> slave but a human being, a man who in some ways was to be envied, and
> who expressed his essential humanity in his desire for freedom, his will to
> possess his own labor, in his loyalty and capacity for friendship and in his
> love for his wife and child. Yet Twain, though guilty of the sentimentality
> common to humorists, does not idealize the slave. Jim is drawn in all his
> ignorance and superstition, with his good traits and his bad. He, like all
> men, is ambiguous, limited in circumstance but not in possibility. . . . Jim,
> therefore, is not simply a slave, he is a symbol of humanity, and in freeing

Jim, Huck makes a bid to free himself of the conventionalized evil [i.e., the ruling definition of necessity] taken for civilization by the town. (*S*, 48–49)

When read in the context of the recent dispute over *Huckleberry Finn*, Ellison's analysis points up the shamelessness of Twain's detractors and the timidity of his defenders. In so far as the "debate" between them is not informed by a common agreement as to the primacy of teaching students *and* teachers to attend to *both* Twain's narrative method and the facts of American race relations, past and present, the followers of Wallace, along with their adversaries within the professoriat, only perpetuate the problems they would solve. To be a good reader, to be a disciplined observer of the human scene like Ellison: these are the capacities that our educational institutions ought to be cultivating. Instead, if the furor over *Huckleberry Finn* may be taken as a fair sample of public discourse about literacy and racial justice, then it is clear that our schools and colleges only deepen the longest shadow of democracy.

★

In our society it is not unusual for a Negro to experience a sensation that he does not exist in the real world at all. He seems rather to exist in the nightmarish fantasy of the white American mind as a phantom that the white mind seeks, unceasingly, by means both crude and subtle, to lay. (*S*, 290)

In "Hidden Name and Complex Fate," an address delivered at the Library of Congress in 1964, Ellison remarks that for him and for others with whom he grew up in Oklahoma City being black was much more than a burden. It was a discipline. Discipline took several principal forms in Ellison's youth, but it was the discipline of music to which he later traced the beginnings of his education: the endless musical rehearsals in public school, presided over by the enterprising Mrs. Zelia N. Breaux, through whose initiative young people had the opportunity to take part in band, orchestra, a brass quartet, an operetta, chorus, glee club, and European folk dances, which "were taught throughout the Negro school system" (S, 157). When Ellison began to play jazz with local jazzmen, he found that their standards of excellence were, if anything, even more rigorous, the preparation they exemplified and demanded more arduous than Mrs. Breaux's regimen.

In addition, and as an illustration of what Ellison called the "Ironies and Uses of Segregation," there was the discipline afforded by reading. "No law, only custom," forbade blacks from using the public library in Oklahoma City. When a prominent black minister discovered this fact, he quickly set about the job of putting together a library in a rented office building, hired a "Negro librarian," built shelves and stocked them "with any and every book possible." Ironies of segregation aside, "how fortunate," Ellison declared fifty years later, "for a boy who loved to read!" Ellison read everything, it seems, he could get hold of: Shaw, Maupassant, the Harvard Classics, the Haldeman Julius Blue Books, *Vanity Fair* and the *Literary Digest*, and, under the tutelage of Mrs. L. C. McFarland, the work of the Harlem writers Langston Hughes, Countee Cullen, Claude McKay, and James Weldon Johnson, among others.

Looking back on his youth, Ellison recognized a common thread in his moral education connecting his decision to be a writer and his general democratic beliefs. The passage from his review of Gunnar Myrdal's *An American Dilemma* (1944), which I quote above, provides a perfect starting point for understanding his line of reasoning. Like Du Bois before him, Ellison observes that the touchstone of his "complex fate" as a black American is the peculiar doubleness of his identity. White fantasy would have him be thus and so: a "phantom that the white mind" is driven "to lay." It is as though white society grants the Afro-American personal identity on the paradoxical condition that it be a ghostly identity—that is, no identity. What is lost through the operation of this social psychology is not only selfhood but a sense of reality itself. Knowledge of such paradoxes shaped Ellison's distinctive literary career, which he called "my . . . search to relate myself to American life through literature" (S, xviii).

But Ellison's subtle comprehension of American race relations did not stop with this personal literary ambition. For he saw in the "American dilemma" a political meaning that escaped even Myrdal himself and those who quickly lionized him. "There is a danger," Ellison argued, "in [Myrdal's] demonstration of how the mechanism of prejudice operates. . . . "

> For the solution to the problem of the American Negro and democracy lies only partially in the white man's free will [as Myrdal had claimed]. Its full solution will lie in the creation of a democracy in which the Negro will be free to define himself for what he is and, within the large framework of that democracy, for what he desires to be. Let this not be misunderstood. For one is apt, in welcoming *An American Dilemma*'s democratic contribution, to forget that all great democratic documents—and there is a certain greatness here—contain a strong charge of antidemocratic elements. Perhaps the wisest attitude for democrats is not to deplore the ambiguous element of democratic writings but to seek to understand them. For it is by making use of the positive contributions of such documents and rejecting their negative elements that democracy can be kept dynamic. (S, 290–91)

Keeping democracy dynamic requires disciplined attention to what is real; in Hannah Arendt's terms, it requires the acknowledgment, individual and collective, of the primacy of appearances (Arendt 1978), if only, as we shall see in Ellison's treatment of the joke, to be alive to what happens when they are turned upside down. Literature, Ellison believes, shows us what is real, provided, that is, that the writer heed some version of Heraclitus' dictum, "Geography is fate" (G, 198). Social science at best still prefers the type to the concrete enactment. And it is finally the concrete enactment of literature, and not the analytical

conclusions of social science, which he thinks confronts most decisively the Afro-American illusion residing in white fantasy. In reified
form this illusion walks and talks, the Everyman "darky entertainer"
(S, 62)—and his many ghostly imitations and replicas haunting the
social-psychological hall of mirrors of American racial experience.

To illustrate this perilous interplay of fantasy and reality, Ellison
tells the following story:

> "A small brown bowlegged Negro with the name 'Franklin D. Roosevelt
> Jones' might sound like a clown to someone who looks at him from the
> outside," said my friend Albert Murray, "but on the other hand he just
> might turn out to be a hell of a fireside operator. He might just lie back in
> all of that comic juxtaposition of names and manipulate you deaf, dumb
> and blind—and you not even suspecting it, because you're thrown out of
> stance by his name! There you are, so dazzled by the F. D. R. image—
> which you *know* you can't see—and so delighted with your own superior
> position that you don't realize that it's *Jones* who must be confronted."
> (S, 153)

The observer who "looks at [F. D. R. Jones] from the outside" and
concludes he is "a clown" is, of course, a poor observer: he has not
really seen Jones at all (though he is about to). He has failed to apprehend the appearance called *Jones*, and is unconsciously (and smugly)
content merely to decode his name. But his decoding goes awry.
("What you control only under the form of false names, *you* do not
control at all," we remember from Blackmur.) The observer's superior position turns out to be an inferior position. His representation
explodes before him into so many bits and pieces, objective correla-
tives of his own racial fantasies, inept powers of observation, false
suppositions.

Ellison tells a similar story in *Going to the Territory*:

Recently we had a woman from the South who helped my wife with the house but who goofed off so frequently that she was fired. We liked her and really wanted her to stay, but she simply wouldn't do her work. My friend Albert Murray told me I shouldn't be puzzled over the outcome. "You know how we can be sometimes," Al said. "She saw the books and the furniture and the paintings, so she knew you were some kind of white man. You couldn't possibly be a Negro. And so she figured she could get away with a little boondoggling on general principles, because she'd probably been getting away with a lot of stuff with Northern whites. But what she didn't stop to notice was that you're a *Southern* white man. . . ." (G, 304)

If *Catch-22* points to a solution to the problem of other minds by evoking a world in which it makes no sense to know, then these two stories by Ellison remind us that there is much yet to be learned from our facing up to the exclusion of the other. Ellison thus keeps alive the problem of other minds, and in so doing he recapitulates what I believe, with Cavell, may be seen as the opening gesture in Romanticism. For Ellison, as for Wittgenstein, the point at issue is the simple question, "What don't I see when everything is in front of my eyes?" (Cavell 1979, 370)—as, for instance, when I look at a painting or a face (like Jones's). Everything there is to be seen is there. The painting, like Jones, is, "as it stands, already everything it can be, unless it changes." But then I notice something I had overlooked. What I see has not changed: yet I "see it differently." On the other hand, "if what I fail to see is a possibility, then since it can have no metaphysical status other than the aspect I, as it were, succeed in seeing, what I do see is also a possibility" (Cavell 1979, 370)—the brute possibility that Jones is who he is and not someone (something) else. The joke comes—the joke is "gotten"—when the tension that comes from not seeing everything *there* can no longer be sustained, and Jones turns out to enjoy the superior position. This reversal in position radically alters the observer's experience of what is real, hence alters the reality the observer acknowledges. Apprehension of the actual other thus begins in the observer's failure to see a possibility. It ends in the observer's seeing a *possibility*: namely, the sudden appearance of a being out of the void constituted by the use of a mere name to the exclusion of seeing what is there.

Ellison's conception of the joke, including his treatment of the phenomenon of laughter, subtly explores the question of personal identity, which comprises a large part of the American version of the problem of the other. Laughter is crucial both to Ellison's self-conception and to his vision of art in democracy. In *Going to the Territory*, for example, he tells the story of a black student from Tuskegee named Whyte who was shaken down and beaten by sheriff's deputies somewhere in Alabama for refusing, upon being challenged by these officers, to deny his name. Back at the dormitory, the students told and re-told the story of this terrifying experience, each rendition evoking more laughter than the last, "cruel but homeopathic laughter . . . [which] transcended the violence" of the incident (G, 168–71). In another essay, called "An Extravagance of Laughter," Ellison's examination of laughter illustrates what Cavell calls "the touchstone of the unnatural" (Cavell 1979, 415). In this apology to Erskine Caldwell, Ellison narrates the events in the theater one night when he broke into uncontrollable laughter at the sight of Caldwell's "Ellie May's and Lov's 'horsing' all over the stage of *Tobacco Road*." To Ellison this spectacle was an absurd display of libidinous frolicking that transformed Ellison himself into a spectacle, as the theater audience and even the actors on stage turned and glared at the black man heaving with laughter, out of control.

The scene with Ellie May and Lov was not, however, what Ellison was laughing about. He was laughing at the recollection, provoked by the scene on stage, of a story he had grown up with in which the officials of a small southern town decreed that any black moved to laughter in a public place had to do his or her laughing in the nearest laughing barrel. This preposterous scheme quickly fell apart. Whites soon discovered that

> in addition to reacting to whatever ignorant, harebrained notion had set him off in the first place, the Negro was apt to double up with a second gale of laughter—and that triggered, apparently, by his own mental image of himself laughing at himself laughing upside down. It was all, whites agreed, another of the many Negro mysteries with which it was their lot to contend; and *whatever* its true cause, it was most disturbing to a white observer. (G, 190)

In short, it became clear that "somehow the Negro in the barrel had them *over* a barrel," and the decree was revoked (G, 192–93). What was intolerable to the whites was "the *unnatural* and corrupting blackness of Negro laughter" (G, 191).

For Ellison as for Cavell laughter is something like "the reverse of amazement"—the amazement we experience, for example, in the presence of an automaton that we had thought was human (Cavell 1979, 412ff.). One is amazed upon recognizing that this *being* is really a *thing*. One had thought it was human, but it is not: hence amazement. Conversely, one laughs upon recognizing that a *thing* is really a *being*. One had thought it was a thing, but it is not: hence laughter. In the laughing-barrels anecdote, the absence of laughter by whites in the face of coerced, feigned automatonity indicates that they do not recognize such automatonity for what it is. This obtuseness is the same as not recognizing the blacks' humanness. By the same token, the enforced concealment—privatization—of the blacks' laughter testifies to the blacks' own belief in their humanness. "It would follow from the absence of our laughter in the face of . . . automatonity," Cavell explains, "that we do not know others to be human" (Cavell 1979, 415).

So too it follows that laughter is the natural response to automatonity when we *know* the other to be human: when we know, for example, that the automatic behavior enforced by the town's prohibition on public laughter—the sticking of heads into barrels and of hind ends into the air—is proof of the humanness of the blacks. Such proof is, literally, re-cognition. Laughter is the "touchstone of the unnatural" (Cavell 1979, 415) inasmuch as laughter points up the moral monstrosity of the town's decree. This laughter has a deadly, emancipatory purpose about it. Ellison means to identify this purpose when he refers, somewhat cryptically, perhaps, to "the *unnatural* and corrupting blackness of Negro laughter."

Ellison says that since he was in school he has always felt that "American society contained a built-in joke, and we were aware even if James wasn't—or did not choose to admit—that that joke was in many ways centered in our condition" (G, 139). This is as much as to say that when one's culture turns one into a symbol it is a matter of survival that one be forever on the alert, as Thoreau had advised. This habit made good observers of the social scene out of Ellison and his fellow students at Tuskegee. Earlier, while still under the tutelage of Mrs. Breaux in Oklahoma City, Ellison and his friends gladly learned European folk dances "as an *artistic* challenge" and "ignored" "those who thought we were stepping out of the role assigned Negroes and were expressing a desire to become white." Ellison "knew that dancing such dances would no more alter our racial identity or social status than would our singing of Bach chorales" (G, 136). The bitter joke, in other words, was on all those who were trapped by the very racism they were either fighting against or explicitly endorsing. Ellison was not only *not* trying to be white when he was learning European folk dances; his act of learning them was a constant reminder of who he truly was and was not. The artistic challenge, then, sharpened his eye for social observation and heightened his interest in comedy. "Verbal comedy was a way [at Tuskegee] of confronting social ambiguity" (G,

138). Comedy "gave expression to our secret sense of the way things really were" (G, 139). He learned early that if there is an American style, it is "that of the vernacular," by which he means "a dynamic *process* in which the most refined styles from the past are continually merged with the play-it-by-eye-and-by-ear improvisations which we invent in our efforts to control our environment and entertain ourselves" (G, 139).

It should be clear from the foregoing that the peril interesting to Ellison affects blacks and whites not equally (a whiggish interpretation) but symbiotically, or, better, dialectically. At stake is not some autonomous dark ghost held hostage to white fantasy. Autonomy itself— the disciplined life of freedom—is what has been withheld and even threatened with extinction. As Melville had shown in *Benito Cereno* (1856), the line between fantasy and reality in interracial experience, though never perfectly indelible, is completely erased in the predemocratic world of lordship and bondage. The decisive move comes, according to Melville, when the Afro-American revolts against this condition. Breaking out of it not only radically alters the circumstances of his own existence; it profoundly disturbs the whole. Or, as Ellison remarks in an essay called "Change the Joke and Slip the Yoke" (1958): "out of the counterfeiting of the black American identity there arises a profound doubt in the white man's mind as to the authenticity of his own image of *himself*" (S, 68; emphasis added).

The "counterfeiting of the black American identity" occurs at the hands of both blacks and whites, and is fully under the control of neither (or both, for that matter). The self-doubt arising in the white man's mind has a twin whose home is in the black man's experience, as all of Ellison's work shows. The self-doubt in the white American's mind may be seen as the price he must pay for continuing to engender the ghostly black Everyman. Cavell's analysis of the problems of "other minds" helps explain the nature of this self-doubt. Cavell argues that to withhold, or hedge, our concepts of psychological states from a given creature, on the ground that our criteria [for identifying them] cannot reach to the inner life of the creature, is specifically to withhold the source of my idea that living beings are things that feel; it is to withhold myself, to reject my response to anything as a living being; to blank so much as my idea of anything *having a body*. To describe *this* condition as one in which I do not know (am not certain) of the existence of other minds, is empty. There is now nothing there, of the right kind, to be known. There is nothing to read from that body, nothing the body is *of*; it does not go beyond itself, it expresses nothing; it does not so much as behave. There is no body left to manifest consciousness (or unconsciousness). It is not dead, but inanimate; it hides nothing, but is absolutely at my disposal; if it were empty it would be quite hollow, but in fact it is quite dense, though less uniform than stone. It was already at best an automaton. It does not matter to me now whether there turn out to be wheels and springs inside, or stuffing, or some subtler or messier mechanism; or rather, whether it matters depends upon my curiosity in such matters. The most *anything* inside could do (e.g., something we choose to call "nerves" or "muscles") is to *run* or *work* the thing, move it around. My feeling is: What this "body" lacks is *privacy*. (Cavell 1979, 83–84)

The black American of white fantasy is denied *privacy* in just this Cavellean sense. The denial in turn generates the publicly functioning *no-body*, the phantom automaton, that is so eloquently identified in Ellison's writings.

Similarly, the self-doubt in the black American's mind—recall Ellison's remark that "in our society it is not unusual for a Negro to experience a sensation that he does not exist in the real world at all"—lacerates the spirit but also provokes the search for personal identity (Cavellean privacy) and public art (Ellisonian symbolism). The drama that unfolds in Ellison's jokes coerces some hearers into positions from which they mistake the illusion for the reality, as happens to inept observers of F. D. R. Jones or to the white townspeople who had set up laughing barrels. Other hearers, along with the jokester himself, of course, occupy strategically superior positions, from which they covertly acknowledge the manipulative power of names and naming and recognize a ghost as a ghost—that is, as the preternatural and thing-like figuration of white psyches. Black "thinghood" is in this way simultaneously posited and dissolved in Ellison's jokes.

The significance I see in Ellison's analysis of the counterfeiting process, whose monstrous figments populate the hall of mirrors of American race relations, turns on the fact that the fantasy of a vanishing humanity, mentioned at the outset of this chapter, has *already* come true for some Americans. This is a political fact, not a literary hypothesis. No dystopian future can be more soul-blind, no more deprived of the riches of Cavellean privacy, than is the present actuality of public yet invisible Americans. It is this disembodied symbol which Ellison snatches from its prefabricated niche in the mechanism of prejudice and enlivens for his own purposes as the most prominent living legatee of the tradition that begins with Emerson.

With Ellison, the republic of letters founded by Emerson and Whitman may be down to one of its last citizens. If so, his life in, and through, literature will stand as a monument to self-invention and moral clarity. Moved by the observation, when a young man, that "my *people* seemed to appear . . . only in the less meaningful writing," Ellison set about making "some sort of closer identification with the tradition of American literature, if only by way of finding out why I was *not* there—or better, by way of finding how I could use that very powerful literary tradition . . . as a means of clarifying the peculiar and particular experience out of which I came" (G, 40–41).

EPILOGUE

Your problem is not your life as it is
in America, not that your hands, as you
tell me, are tied to do something. It is
that you were born to an island of greed
and grace where you have this sense
of yourself as apart from others. It is
not your right to feel powerless. Better
people than you were powerless.
You have not returned to your country,
but to a life you never left.

CAROLYN FORCHÉ, "Return" (1980)

The tradition of infinitude and privacy since Emerson, like Emerson's work itself, teaches us to picture human experience without history, freedom without politics, authority without community. American "social amnesia," to recall Russell Jacoby's term for an important trait in American social character, is grounded in this tradition. According to Jacoby, the habit of repressing, or forgetting, the past articulates itself everyday as resignation in the face of established social institutions as if they were immutable. The political diffidence accompanying this mentality reaches into the American nineteenth century, as I have tried to suggest. A century and a half of mistaking private pictures for American worlds ironically threatens the institutionalized rights of individuals by fulfilling itself in the "subjectivity that surfaces everywhere," in Jacoby's apt phrase, from the earliest T-groups to the latest versions of what Marcuse once called the "grisly science of human relations," and all fashionable points on the psychological compass in between (Jacoby 1975, 17). It is far from obvious that the widely capitalized human subject today is a democrat—actually, potentially, or formerly.

What school do we attend in order to learn how to give up the Emersonian habit of picturing without historicizing? This question needs to be asked, I believe, by all those who suspect that democracy in America is not something that can be remembered, inasmuch as there is little convincing evidence that it has ever existed. Obviously not everyone shares this suspicion, and definitions of democracy are legion. I have indicated at the outset of this book the basis of my own skepticism: namely, that the genres of intellectual work called academic disciplines, each with its distinctive modes of inquiry, canons of evidence, and styles of interpretation, have always seemed to me to be narrow in scope, sometimes mutually exclusive in the results they yield, and often given to begging their own leading questions. This is a belief of mine, not a claim of this book. It gets into my discussion of American worlds since Emerson, however, when I object at the outset to the conversion of democracy as the preeminent question of our time into an inert historical datum, thence into an historical *fait accompli*, as frequently happens in literary and political histories. The democratization of the American past returns like the repressed to impoverish public life in the present. This dynamic itself has a history, and in this book I have attempted to trace its literary-philosophical side. Underlying my discussion is the assumption that it is at least worth trying again to think through—and the ambiguity of that expression is intended—familiar materials that have perhaps become too familiar.

Speculation that democracy has at best a mutilated pre-history and perhaps only an idealized past should not be confused with nihilism toward the American present. Margaret Atwood's *The Handmaid's Tale* alerts whatever may remain of the bourgeois reading public to the political danger residing in any such confusion. *The Handmaid's Tale* erects a totalitarian American world set in the near future in which the severest imaginable despotism is legitimized through the systematic abolition of all distinctions between the Natural and the Artificial, the stock-in-trade of the rational imagination since Vico. The Gileadean revolution, which takes place prior to the opening of the narrative, produced a gendered caste system consistent with this anti-intellectualism. The social program of the new order has as its chief aim the eradication of love from human relationships. The Gileadeans complete the bourgeois subjugation of women, whose common lot now is to serve the theocracy as "two-legged wombs . . . sacred vessels, ambulatory chalices" (Atwood 1986, 136).

We've given them more than we've taken away, said the Commander. Think of the trouble they had before. Don't you remember the singles' bars, the indignity of high school dates? The meat market. Don't you remember the terrible gap between the ones who could get a man easily and the ones who couldn't? Some of them were desperate, they starved themselves thin or pumped their breasts full of silicone, had their noses cut off. Think of the human misery.

He waved a hand at his stacks of old magazines. They were always complaining. Problems this, problems that. Remember the ads in the Personal columns, *Bright attractive woman, thirty-five* . . . This way they all get a man, nobody's left out. And then if they did marry, they could be left with a kid, two kids, the husband might just get fed up and take off, disappear, they'd have to go on welfare. Or else he'd stay around and beat them up. Or if they had a job, the children in daycare or left with some brutal ignorant woman, and they'd have to pay for that themselves, out of their wretched little paychecks. Money was the only measure of worth, for everyone, they got no respect as mothers. This way they're protected, they can fulfill their biological destinies in peace. With full moral support and encouragement. Now, tell me. You're an intelligent person, I like to hear what you think. What did we overlook?

Love, I said.

Love? said the Commander. What kind of love?

Falling in love, I said. The Commander looked at me with his candid boy's eyes.

Oh yes, he said. I've read the magazines, that's what they were pushing, wasn't it? But look at the stats, my dear. Was it really worth it, *falling in love?* Arranged marriages have always worked out just as well, if not better.

Love, said Aunt Lydia with distaste. Don't let me catch you at it.

No mooning and June-ing around here, girls. Wagging her finger at us. *Love* is not the point.

Those years were just an anomaly, historically speaking, the Commander said. Just a fluke. All we've done is return things to Nature's norm. (Atwood 1986, 219–20)

Gileadean historical consciousness thus depicts the present moment of late bourgeois civilization merely as a brief, wild deviation from Nature's so-called norm, defined by Atwood with meticulous concreteness as ascetic unfreedom. At the end of *The Handmaid's Tale* Atwood's denuded narrator becomes an enemy of the state. Under arrest, she anticipates nothing, neither certain punishment and death nor possible liberation. Nor is she ambivalent. The future, like the present, simply "can't be helped" (Atwood 1986, 295). There is nothing in this world that is not natural—by decree.

It is with no regret at all that I admit to reaching an unoriginal conclusion. For I see these studies of the sentiment of American rationality as confirming and historically illustrating an argument advanced by

Charles Douglas Lummis in the pages of *Democracy* in 1982. The "only real education system for democracy," Lummis writes in this essay entitled "The Radicalism of Democracy," "is democracy." Whereas the constitutional tradition guaranteed the rights of individuals, promised "domestic peace," and sought to inculcate "political virtue," it did so at the expense of conceiving of the people as *"means . . . to* [these] *end*[*s*]" (Lummis 1982, 15). Essential to this means–ends calculus, with which American literary-philosophical history ambiguously resonates, is a truncated capacity to recognize the excluded Other as human. Whether sponsored by the constitutional tradition of political thought and practice or by the modern market in alliance with the bureaucratic state, the means–ends calculus retards the democratic imagination and negates its vision. As means, the people enjoy the status of private citizens, the self-contradiction of which was analyzed by Tocqueville. "It is still possible to cut oneself off from the fate of one's fellow human beings," Lummis observes, "but what we know now is that the cutting, as it were, must go on within one's own nervous system. What we cut off is not other people, but one of our own sense organs, that special organ that gives us the capacity, when we see the faces and hear the voices of others, to recognize them as human beings like ourselves" (Lummis 1982, 16). The multitudes of private talking pictures that say otherwise are belied by the plurality of American worlds. This plurality appears to everyone, to all races and to women as well as to men; but it matters only to democrats for whom the experience of democracy represents the only chance of averting the final reification of the automatonity that flourishes when recognition fails.

NOTES

INTRODUCTION. Emerson and After

1. For a sample of recent challenges to the practice of treating democracy as a more or less neutral datum in American experience, see, in addition to the article by Pitkin and Shumer, those by Dickson (1981), Goodwyn (1981), Lasch (1981), and Lummis (1982).

2. *Philosophy and the Mirror of Nature* (Princeton: Princeton University Press, 1979); cf. C. B. Macpherson, *The Political Theory of Possessive Individualism: Hobbes to Locke* (London: Oxford University Press, 1962).

3. Three informative analyses of professional literary studies are: Eagleton (1983, 17–53), Parker (1967), and Gerber (1967).

4. "Consider for example the proceedings that we call 'games.' I mean board-games, card-games, ball-games, Olympic games, and so on. What is common to them all?—Don't say: 'There *must* be something common, or they would not be called "games"'—but *look and see* whether there is anything common to all.—For if you look at them you will not see something that is common to *all*, but similarities, relationships, and a whole series of them at that. To re-peat: don't think, but look!" (Wittgenstein 1978, sec. 66).

5. I learned of Blackstone's premise from Patricia Parker's paper, "Property and Proper Names in the Discourse of the Enlightenment," Conference on Property and Rhetoric, Northwestern University, 27 June 1986.

CHAPTER 1. "The Infinitude of the Private Man": Emerson's Ideas of Nature, Culture, and Politics

1. *Emerson's "Nature"—Origin, Growth, Meaning*, ed. Merton M. Sealts, Jr., and Alfred R. Ferguson (New York: Dodd, Mead, 1969), 34. Page numbers

of all subsequent references to *Nature* (abbreviated *N*) follow this edition and appear within parentheses in the text.

2. A critique intriguingly similar to Emerson's—and to Horkheimer and Adorno's—is that of Maurice Merleau-Ponty: "Analytical reflection puts forward, instead of the absolute existence of the object, the thought of an absolute object, and, through trying to dominate the object and think of it from no point of view, it destroys the object's internal structure." *Phenomenology of Perception*, trans. Colin Smith (London: Routledge, 1962), 204. An analysis of the ego-world relation in Emerson from which I have benefited is Herbert Schneider's (Simon and Parsons 1969, 215–28).

3. Power is natural, Emerson maintains in "Power" (*Works* 6:69). Traditionally, power is artificial. See Sheldon Wolin (1960) and Hannah Arendt (1958, 199ff.).

4. On the unpredictability and fragility of politics, and especially of political action, see Arendt (1958). What Michael Rogin calls "the romance of nature" figures hugely in American politics and political theory, not only in American literature. See Rogin (1977, 5–6).

5. George Fredrickson chides the early Emerson for his alleged lack of social responsibility on the slavery issue and praises the older Emerson for coming around at last and repudiating his youthful doctrines of anti-social individualism (Fredrickson 1968, ch. 1).

CHAPTER 2. "Come Forth, Sweet Democratic Despots of the West!": Whitman's *Democratic Vistas*

1. Walt Whitman, *Prose Works 1892*, ed. Floyd Stovall (New York: New York University Press, 1964), 2:409. Page numbers of all subsequent references to *Democratic Vistas* (abbreviated *DV*) follow this definitive edition and appear within parentheses in the text.

CHAPTER 3. Was William James a Political Philosopher? "Vicious Intellectualism" Seen in a Political Light

1. William James, *The Writings of William James*, ed. John J. McDermott (New York: Modern Library, 1968), 723, 519. All subsequent references to James's

works follow this edition (abbreviated *W*), with page numbers enclosed in parentheses in the text.

2. For an example, see Harris (1884).

CHAPTER 4. Literary "Ideas" in "An Age of True Pyrrhonism": Examples of R. P. Blackmur and Robinson Jeffers

1. Clark Griffith overlooks this feature of Emersonianism in his otherwise useful literary typology of " 'Emersonianism' and 'Poeism' " (Griffith 1961).

2. The best book on Jeffers, Arthur Coffin, *Robinson Jeffers: Poet of Inhumanism* (Madison: University of Wisconsin Press, 1971), is true to this pattern and neglects the early years.

3. This poem first appeared in *The Cardinal* 1 (November 1905), a supplement to the student newspaper of the University of Southern California. It was reprinted in *The Southern California Daily Trojan*, 25 April 1940:2, the source for this discussion.

4. R. P. Blackmur, *A Primer of Ignorance*, ed. Joseph Frank (New York: Harcourt, Brace and World, 1967), 16. I use the following abbreviations for Blackmur's works; page numbers appear within parentheses in the text.

D   *The Double Agent: Essays in Craft and Elucidation*
E   *The Expense of Greatness*
L   *The Lion and the Honeycomb: Essays in Solicitude and Critique*
P   *A Primer of Ignorance*

5. Unlike the so-called post-Modernist generation that came on the literary-philosophical scene in the years following Blackmur's departure in the early 1960s, Blackmur neither proclaimed nor bemoaned "the demise of the subject," which, as Richard Wolin has said, has become a dangerous cliché of contemporary thought (Wolin 1984–85, 29). What Blackmur did was to describe the conditions under which subjectivity assumes its various purposes and objectifications in literary art.

CHAPTER 5. Shadows of Democracy

1. Joseph Heller, *Catch-22* (New York: Dell, 1962), 91. Subsequent references to *Catch-22* appear in parentheses in the text, abbreviated as *C-22*.

2. To develop and illustrate this generalization would take another book. For the distinction between knowing *that* and knowing *who*, I am indebted to Cavell (1979, ch. 3).

3. This conclusion of Ellison's echoes the main thesis of Winthrop Jordan's *White Over Black: American Attitudes Toward the Negro, 1550–1812* (Chapel Hill: University of North Carolina Press, 1968).

4. For an extensive account of Du Bois's lifelong struggle over the meaning of race, see Anthony Appiah (1985).

5. Ralph Ellison, *Shadow and Act* (New York: New American Library, 1964), 258. I use the following abbreviations for Ellison's works; page numbers appear within parentheses in the text.

    S   *Shadow and Act*
    G   *Going to the Territory*

WORKS CITED

Adams, Henry
1973   *The Education of Henry Adams.* Ed. Ernst Samuels. Boston:
            Houghton Mifflin.
Alberts, S. S.
1933   *A Bibliography for the Study of Robinson Jeffers.* New York: Ran-
            dom House.
Allen, Gay Wilson
1955   *The Solitary Singer: A Critical Biography of Walt Whitman.* New
            York: Grove Press.
Appiah, Anthony
1985   "The Uncompleted Argument: Du Bois and the Illusion of
            Race." *Critical Inquiry* 12:21–37.
Arendt, Hannah
1958   *The Human Condition.* Chicago: University of Chicago Press.
1968   *Between Past and Future: Eight Exercises in Political Thought.* Rev.
            ed. New York: Viking.
1978   *The Life of the Mind.* 2 vols. New York: Harcourt Brace
            Jovanovich.
Arvin, Newton
1967   *American Pantheon.* Ed. Daniel Aaron and Sylvan Schendler.
            New York: Delta.
Atwood, Margaret
1986   *The Handmaid's Tale.* Boston: Houghton Mifflin.
Auerbach, Erich
1953   *Mimesis: The Representation of Reality in Western Literature.* Trans.
            Willard R. Trask. Princeton: Princeton University Press.

Austin, J. L.

1961   *Philosophical Papers.* Ed. J. O. Urmson and G. J. Warnock. Oxford: Clarendon.

1962   *How To Do Things with Words.* 2nd ed. Ed. J. O. Urmson and Marina Sbisa. Cambridge: Harvard University Press.

Barbour, James, and Thomas Quirk, eds.

1986   *Romanticism: Critical Essays in American Literature.* New York: Garland.

Beer, Thomas

1954   *The Mauve Decade: American Life at the End of the Nineteenth Century.* Intro. Frank Freidel. New York, 1926. Rpt. New York: Vintage.

Bennett, Melba Berry

1966   *The Stone Mason of Tor House: The Life and Work of Robinson Jeffers.* Los Angeles: The Ward Ritchie Press.

Bercovitch, Sacvan

1976   "How the Puritans Won the American Revolution." *Massachusetts Review* 17:597–630.

Bernstein, Richard

1971   *Praxis and Action: Contemporary Philosophies of Human Activity.* Philadelphia: University of Pennsylvania Press.

1978   *The Restructuring of Social and Political Theory.* Philadelphia: University of Pennsylvania Press.

1983   *Beyond Objectivism and Relativism: Science, Hermeneutics, and Praxis.* Philadelphia: University of Pennsylvania Press.

Blackmur, R. P.

1939   "Henry and Brooks Adams: Parallels to Two Generations." *Southern Review* 5:308–34.

1955   *The Lion and the Honeycomb: Essays in Solicitude and Critique.* New York: Harcourt, Brace and World.

1958   *The Expense of Greatness.* 1940. Gloucester, Mass.: Peter Smith.

1962   *The Double Agent: Essays in Craft and Elucidation.* 1935. Gloucester, Mass.: Peter Smith.

1963   "Henry James." *Literary History of the United States: History.* 3rd
            ed. Ed. Robert E. Spiller et al. New York: Macmillan.
1967   *A Primer of Ignorance.* Ed. Joseph Frank. New York: Harcourt,
            Brace and World.
1986   *Selected Essays of R. P. Blackmur.* Ed. Denis Donoghue. New
            York: Ecco.
Boyers, Robert
1980   *R. P. Blackmur, Poet-Critic: Toward a View of Poetic Objects.* Co-
            lumbia: University of Missouri Press.
Cavell, Stanley
1979   *The Claim of Reason: Wittgenstein, Skepticism, Morality, and Trag-
            edy.* Oxford: Oxford University Press.
1981   *The Senses of Walden.* Enl. ed. San Francisco: North Point.
1986   "Hope Against Hope." *The American Poetry Review* (January-
            February), 9–13.
Coffin, Arthur B.
1971   *Robinson Jeffers: Poet of Inhumanism.* Madison: University of Wis-
            consin Press.
Cruse, Harold
1967   *The Crisis of the Negro Intellectual.* New York: William Morrow.
Dewey, John
1958   *Art as Experience.* 1934. New York: Capricorn Books.
1966   *Democracy and Education: An Introduction to the Philosophy of Edu-
            cation.* 1916. New York: The Free Press.
Dickson, David
1981   "Limiting Democracy: Technocrats and the Liberal State." *De-
            mocracy* 1:61–79.
Donoghue, Denis
1977   Introduction. *Poems of R. P. Blackmur.* By R. P. Blackmur. Prince-
            ton: Princeton University Press.
Eagleton, Terry
1983   *Literary Theory: An Introduction.* Minneapolis: University of Min-
            nesota Press.

Eliot, George
1956   *Middlemarch*. 1871–72. Ed. Gordon S. Haight. Boston: Houghton
                Mifflin.
Ellison, Ralph
1964   *Shadow and Act*. New York: New American Library.
1986   *Going to the Territory*. New York: Random House.
Emerson, Ralph Waldo
1904   *The Complete Works of Ralph Waldo Emerson*. Ed. Edward Waldo
                Emerson. 12 vols. Boston: Houghton Mifflin.
1950   *Ralph Waldo Emerson: Selected Prose and Poetry*. Ed. Reginald L.
                Cook. New York: Holt, Rinehart and Winston.
1957   *Selections from Ralph Waldo Emerson: An Organic Anthology*. Ed.
                Stephen E. Whicher. Boston: Houghton Mifflin.
1960–82   *The Journals and Miscellaneous Notebooks of Ralph Waldo Emerson*.
                16 vols. Ed. William H.Gilman et al. Cambridge: Harvard Uni-
                versity Press.
1972   *The Early Lectures of Ralph Waldo Emerson*. 3 vols. Ed. Robert E.
                Spiller and Wallace E. Williams. Cambridge: Harvard University
                Press.
Fitzgerald, F. Scott
1925   *The Great Gatsby*. New York: Scribner's.
Forché, Carolyn
1981   *The Country Between Us*. New York: Harper and Row.
Ford, Marcus Peter
1982   *William James's Philosophy: A New Perspective*. Amherst: Univer-
                sity of Massachusetts Press.
Foucault, Michel
1977   *Language, Counter-Memory, Practice: Selected Essays and Interviews*.
                Trans. Donald F. Bouchard and Sherry Simon. Ed. Donald F.
                Bouchard. Ithaca: Cornell University Press.
1979   *Discipline and Punish: The Birth of the Prison*. Trans. Alan Sheri-
                dan. New York: Vintage.
Franklin, John Hope
1965   *Three Negro Classics*. New York: Avon.

Fraser, Russell

1981 *A Mingled Yarn: The Life of R. P. Blackmur.* New York: Harcourt Brace Jovanovich.

Fredrickson, George M.

1968 *The Inner Civil War: Northern Intellectuals and the Crisis of the Union.* 1965. New York: Harper and Row.

1971 *The Black Image in the White Mind: The Debate on Afro-American Character and Destiny.* New York: Harper and Row.

Gerber, John C.

1967 "Literature—Our Untamable Discipline." *College English* 28:351–58.

Goodman, Nelson

1978 *Ways of Worldmaking.* Indianapolis: Hackett, 1978.

Goodwyn, Lawrence

1981 "Organizing Democracy: The Limits of Theory and Practice." *Democracy* 1:41–60.

Graebner, Norman A., ed.

1968 *Manifest Destiny.* Indianapolis: Bobbs-Merrill.

Griffith, Clark

1961 " 'Emersonianism' and 'Poeism': Some Versions of the Romantic Sensibility." *Modern Language Quarterly* 22:125–34.

Gunnell, John G.

1986 *Between Philosophy and Politics: The Alienation of Political Theory.* Amherst: University of Massachusetts Press.

Gutman, Herbert G.

1976 *Work, Culture and Society in Industrializing America: Essays in American Working-Class and Social History.* New York: Vintage.

Hansen, Marcus Lee

1961 *The Atlantic Migration, 1607–1860: A History of the Continuing Settlement of the United States.* 1904. Ed. Arthur M. Schlesinger. New York: Harper and Row.

Harris, W. T.

1884 "The Dialectical Unity in Emerson's Prose." *Journal of Speculative Philosophy* 18:195–202.

Hartz, Louis

1955   *The Liberal Tradition in America: An Interpretation of American Po-
            litical Thought Since the Revolution.* New York: Harcourt, Brace
            and World.

Hawthorne, Nathaniel

1962   *The Scarlet Letter, A Romance.* 1850. Ed. Larzer Ziff. Indianapo-
            lis: Bobbs-Merrill.

1977   *The Portable Hawthorne.* Ed. Malcolm Cowley. Rev. ed. New
            York: Penguin.

Heidegger, Martin

1977   *The Question Concerning Technology and Other Essays.* Trans. and
            intro. William Lovitt. New York: Harper and Row.

Heller, Joseph

1962   *Catch-22.* New York: Dell.

Horkheimer, Max

1974   *Eclipse of Reason.* New York: Seabury.

Horkheimer, Max, and Theodor W. Adorno

1972   *Dialectic of Enlightenment.* Trans. John V. Cumming. New York:
            Herder and Herder.

Howe, Irving

1986   *The American Newness: Culture and Politics in the Age of Emerson.*
            Cambridge: Harvard University Press.

Huggins, Nathan Irvin

1971   *Harlem Renaissance.* New York: Oxford University Press.

Jacobson, Norman

1963   "Political Science and Political Education." *American Political Sci-
            ence Review* 17:561–69.

Jacoby, Russell

1975   *Social Amnesia: A Critique of Conformist Psychology From Adler to
            Laing.* Boston: Beacon.

James, Henry

1964   *The Ambassadors.* 1908. Ed. S. P. Rosenbaum. New York:
            Norton.

1966   *Hawthorne.* 1879. Intro. Quentin Anderson. New York: Collier.

1984   *Henry James: Literary Criticism, Essays on Literature, American Writers, English Writers.* Ed. Leon Edel. New York: Literary Classics of the United States.

James, William

1968   *The Writings of William James: A Comprehensive Edition.* Ed. John J. McDermott. New York: Modern Library.

Jay, Martin

1973   *The Dialectical Imagination: A History of the Frankfurt School and the Institute of Social Research, 1923–1950.* Boston: Little, Brown.

1984–85   "Hierarchy and the Humanities: The Radical Implications of a Conservative Idea." *Telos* 62:131–44.

Jeffers, Robinson

1912   *Flagons and Apples.* Los Angeles: n.p.

1938   *The Selected Poetry of Robinson Jeffers.* New York: Random House.

1940   "The Steadfast Sky." *The Cardinal* 1 (November 1905). Rpt. in *The Southern California Daily Trojan,* 25 April 1940: 2.

1948   *The Double Axe and Other Poems.* New York: Random House.

Jordan, Winthrop

1968   *White Over Black: American Attitudes Toward the Negro, 1550–1812.* Chapel Hill: University of North Carolina Press.

Kaplan, Harold

1972   *Democratic Humanism and American Literature.* Chicago: University of Chicago Press.

Kaufmann, Walter

1966a   *Hegel: A Reinterpretation.* Garden City: Anchor.

1966b   *Hegel: Texts and Commentary.* Garden City: Anchor.

Kazin, Alfred

1984   *An American Procession.* New York: Alfred A. Knopf.

Kovel, Joel

1971   *White Racism: A Psychohistory.* New York: Vintage.

Langer, Suzanne K.

1957   *Problems of Art: Ten Philosophical Lectures.* New York: Scribner's.

Lasch, Christopher

1978   *The Culture of Narcissism: American Life in An Age of Diminishing
            Expectations.* New York: Norton.

1981   "Democracy and 'The Crisis of Confidence.' " *Democracy* 1:25–
            40.

Locke, John

1963   *Two Treatises of Government.* 1690. Ed. Peter Laslett. New York:
            Mentor.

Lummis, Charles Douglas

1982   "The Radicalism of Democracy." *Democracy* 2:9–16.

McDermott, John J.

1976   *The Culture of Experience: Philosophical Essays in the American
            Grain.* New York: New York University Press.

1986   *Streams of Experience: Reflections on the History and Philosophy
            of American Culture.* Amherst: University of Massachusetts
            Press.

Macpherson, C. B.

1962   *The Political Theory of Possessive Individualism: Hobbes to Locke.*
            London: Oxford University Press.

McWilliams, Wilson Carey

1973   *The Idea of Fraternity in America.* Berkeley: University of Califor-
            nia Press.

Marcuse, Herbert

1960   *Reason and Revolution: Hegel and the Rise of Social Theory.* 2nd ed.
            Boston: Beacon.

1968   *Negations: Essays in Critical Theory.* Trans. Jeremy J. Shapiro.
            Boston: Beacon.

1972   *Studies in Critical Philosophy.* Trans. Joris De Bres. Boston:
            Beacon.

Marx, Leo

1985   "Huck at 100." *The Nation* (August 31):150–52.

May, Henry F.

1959   *The End of American Innocence: A Study of the First Years of
            Our Own Time, 1912–1917.* Chicago: University of Chicago
            Press.

Mead, Sidney E.
1963   *The Lively Experiment: The Shaping of Christianity in America.*
          New York: Harper and Row.
Melville, Herman
1964   *Moby-Dick.* 1851. Ed. Charles Feidelson, Jr. Indianapolis: Bobbs-
          Merrill.
1964   *Pierre; or, The Ambiguities.* 1852. Foreword Lawrence Thomp-
          son. New York: Signet.
Merleau-Ponty, Maurice
1962   *Phenomenology of Perception.* Trans. Colin Smith. London: Rout-
          ledge and Kegan Paul.
Miller, Perry
1956   *The Raven and the Whale: The War of Words and Wits in the Era of
          Poe and Melville.* New York: Harcourt, Brace and World.
Monroe, Harriet
1926   "Power and Pomp." *Poetry* 27:160–64.
Newman, Charles
1985   *The Post-Modern Aura: The Act of Fiction in an Age of Inflation.*
          Evanston: Northwestern University Press.
Noble, David F.
1977   *America By Design: Science, Technology, and the Rise of Corporate
          Capitalism.* Oxford: Oxford University Press.
Parker, Patricia
1986   "Property and Proper Names in the Discourse of the Enlighten-
          ment." Conference on Property and Rhetoric. Northwestern
          University. Evanston, Ill., 27 June.
Parker, William Riley
1967   "Where Do English Departments Come From?" *College English*
          28:339–51.
Peirce, Charles Sanders
1955   *Philosophical Writings of Peirce.* Ed. Justus Buchler. New York:
          Dover.
Persons, Stow
1973   *The Decline of American Gentility.* New York: Columbia Univer-
          sity Press.

Pitkin, Hanna Fenichel, and Sara M. Shumer
1982   "On Participation." *Democracy* 2:43–54.
Poirier, Richard
1966   *A World Elsewhere: The Place of Style in American Literature.* New York: Oxford University Press.
Quine, Willard Van Orman
1980   *From a Logical Point of View: Nine Logico-Philosophical Essays.* 2nd ed. Cambridge: Harvard University Press.
Rahv, Philip
1969   *Literature and the Sixth Sense.* New York: Houghton Mifflin.
Rogin, Michael
1977   "Nature as Politics and Nature as Romance." *Political Theory* 5:5–30.
Rorty, Richard
1979   *Philosophy and the Mirror of Nature.* Princeton: Princeton University Press.
1982   *Consequences of Pragmatism (Essays: 1972–1980).* Minneapolis: University of Minnesota Press.
Sealts, Merton M., Jr., and Alfred R. Ferguson, eds.
1969   *Emerson's "Nature"—Origin, Growth, Meaning.* New York: Dodd, Mead.
Simon, Myron, and Thornton H. Parsons, eds.
1969   *Transcendentalism and Its Legacy.* Ann Arbor: University of Michigan Press.
Slater, Joseph, ed.
1964   *The Correspondence of Emerson and Carlyle.* New York: Columbia University Press.
Thompson, E. P.
1963   *The Making of the English Working Class.* New York: Vintage.
Thompson, Kirk
1969   "Constitutional Theory and Political Action." *Journal of Politics* 31:655–81.
Thoreau, Henry David
1966   *Walden and Civil Disobedience.* Ed. Owen Thomas. New York: Norton.

Tocqueville, Alexis de

1945   *Democracy in America.* 1835. Trans. Henry Reeve et al. Ed. Phil-
            lips Bradley. 2 vols. New York: Vintage.

Trilling, Lionel

1950   *The Liberal Imagination: Essays on Literature and Society.* Garden
            City: Doubleday.

Wellek, René

1943   "Emerson and German Philosophy." *New England Quarterly*
            16:41–62.

Wellek, René, and Austin Warren

1956   *Theory of Literature.* 3rd ed. New York: Harcourt, Brace and
            World.

Whicher, Stephen E.

1953   *Freedom and Fate: An Inner Life of Ralph Waldo Emerson.* Philadel-
            phia: University of Pennsylvania Press.

Whitman, Walt

1964   *Prose Works 1892.* Ed. Floyd Stovall. 2 vols. New York: New
            York University Press.

Williams, Raymond

1966   *Culture and Society: 1780–1950.* New York, 1958. Rpt. New
            York: Harper and Row.

Williams, William Carlos

1956   *In the American Grain.* 1925. Rpt. New York: New Directions.

Wilson, Edmund

1962   *Classics and Commercials: A Literary Chronicle of the Forties.* New
            York: Vintage.

Wittgenstein, Ludwig

1974   *Tractatus Logico-Philosophicus.* 1921. Trans. D. F. Pears and B. F.
            McGuinness. Intro. Bertrand Russell. London: Routledge and
            Kegan Paul.

1978   *Philosophical Investigations.* 1953. Trans. G. E. M. Anscombe.
            Oxford: Blackwell.

Wolin, Richard

1984–85   "Modernism Vs. Postmodernism." *Telos* 62:9–29.

Wolin, Sheldon

1960   *Politics and Vision: Continuity and Innovation in Western Political Thought*. Boston: Little, Brown.

Zabel, Morton D.

1934   "A Prophet in His Wilderness." *New Republic* 77:229–30.

Ziff, Larzer

1981   *Literary Democracy: The Declaration of Cultural Independence in America*. New York: Viking.

INDEX

LIBRARY OF DAVIDSON COLLEGE

Books on regular loan may be checked out for **two weeks**. Books must be presented at the Circulation Desk in order to be renewed.

A fine is charged after date due.

Special books are subject to special regulations at the discretion of the library staff.